D1708484

THE DRAMATIC IMAGINATION OF
W. B. YEATS

Andrew Parkin

THE DRAMATIC IMAGINATION OF W. B. YEATS

Gill and Macmillan . Dublin

Barnes & Noble Books . New York
(a division of Harper & Row Publishers, Inc.)

First published 1978 by
Gill and Macmillan Ltd
15/17 Eden Quay
Dublin 1
with associated companies in
London, New York, Delhi, Hong Kong, Johannesburg,
Lagos, Melbourne, Singapore, Tokyo

© Andrew Parkin 1978

7171 0899 6

Published in the U.S.A. 1978 by
Harper & Row Publishers, Inc.
Barnes & Noble Import Division

Library of Congress Cataloging in Publication Data

Parkin, Andrew
    The dramatic imagination of W. B. Yeats

        Bibliography: 8pp.
        Includes index.
    1. Yeats, William Butler, 1865–1939
    Criticism and interpretation. I. Title.
    PR5907.P28   821'.8   7818432
        ISBN 0-06-495396-3

Permission has kindly been given by M. B. Yeats, Miss Anne Yeats, the
Macmillan Co. of London and Basingstoke, and the Macmillan Publishing Co.
Inc. of New York for the use of extracts from the *Variorum Edition of the
Plays of W. B. Yeats*, edited by Russell K. Alspach (Copyright © Russell K.
Alspach and Bertha Georgie Yeats 1966. Copyright © Macmillan and Co. Ltd.
1965); *Explorations* (Copyright © Mrs W. B. Yeats 1962); *Autobiography*
(Copyright 1916, 1935 by Macmillan Publishing Co. Inc., renewed 1944, 1963
by Bertha Georgie Yeats); *Variorum Edition of the Poems of W. B. Yeats*
('The Cold Heaven' Copyright 1934 by Macmillan Publishing Co. Inc., renewed
1962 by Bertha Georgie Yeats, 'Parnell's Funeral' Copyright 1912 by Macmillan
Publishing Co. Inc., renewed 1940 by Bertha Georgie Yeats, 'Fragments' Copy-
right 1933 by Macmillan Publishing Co. Inc., renewed 1961 by Bertha Georgie
Yeats.

Printed in Great Britain by Bristol Typesetting Co. Ltd,
Barton Manor, St Philips, Bristol

For Christina and Ben

Contents

Acknowledgments

I am grateful to Mr George Brandt and Mr Edward Malins for valuable encouragement and suggestions in many conversations I have had with them about Yeats. I am also indebted to Professor Geoffrey Durrant, John Wilson Foster, Lee Johnson and Grosvenor Powell, all of them colleagues at the University of British Columbia, for a variety of helpful comments while I was working on this book.

I have been fortunate, too, in having obtained grants from the Committee on Research of the University of British Columbia and from the Canada Council, who awarded me a Leave Fellowship for 1976–1977.

Parts of Chapter III appeared originally in a different form as an article, 'Dramatic Elements in the Poetry of W. B. Yeats', *Anglo-Irish Studies*, II (1976), 109–27.

ABBREVIATIONS

I refer to works frequently cited in the text by means of the following abbreviations.

A	*Autobiographies* (1955)
AV	*A Vision* (1937)
DWL	*Letters on Poetry from W. B. Yeats to Dorothy Wellesley* (1940; reissued in paperback, 1964)
E	*Explorations* (1962)
E&I	*Essays and Introductions* (1961)
L	*The Letters of W. B. Yeats*, ed. Allan Wade (1954)
LTMSB	*Literatim Transcription of the Manuscripts of 'The Speckled Bird'*, ed. William H. O'Donnell (1976)
M	*Mythologies* (1959)
MS	*Memoirs*, ed. Denis Donoghue (1972)
UPI	*Uncollected Prose by W. B. Yeats*, vol. I, ed. John P. Frayne (1970)
V. Poems	*The Variorum Edition of the Poems of W. B. Yeats*, ed. Peter Allt and Russell K. Alspach (1957)
V. Plays	*The Variorum Edition of the Plays of W. B. Yeats*, ed. Russell K. Alspach (1966)

Introduction

LIKE many others I have been startled and excited by Yeats's writing. This book arises from my pleasure in responding to the intensity of feeling conveyed by those dramatisations of the working of imagination which Yeats gives us in, for instance, 'The Cold Heaven', where a sudden, heightened perception of the 'cold and rook-delighting heaven' deranges his senses 'as though ice burned' and his imagination and emotional heart 'were driven / So wild that every casual thought of that and this / Vanished'; purged of the accidental, his mind is flooded by past intensities of unhappy love, recollected in turbulence. His moral being brings remorse; the result is extreme physical reaction, until his body is 'Riddled with light'. He wonders whether after death the ghost suffers such an experience, sent, Lear-like, 'Out naked on the roads . . . and stricken / By the injustice of the skies for punishment' (*V. Poems*, 316). Yeats crams into a poem, kept just short of a conventional sonnet, an astonishing record of his own imagination distilling the pain and regret of what seems a burnt-out life, and then pushing further, daring to imagine the experience repeated in the dark beyond the grave.

For Yeats, imagination and heart go together. What we perceive through the imagination is the product of thought and feeling, mind and blood. The cry of instinct is captured in the oracular music of that 'Hound Voice' which binds him irrationally to those who

> knew
> What hour of terror comes to test the soul,
> And in that terror's name obeyed the call,
> And understood, what none have understood,
> Those images that waken in the blood.

> (*V. Poems*, 622)

But he knows too that intense tranquillity of concentration when, wrapt in its imaginings, 'Like a long-legged fly upon the stream / His mind moves upon silence' (*V. Poems*, 617). Yeats's imagination encompasses both 'Tragedy wrought to its uttermost' and 'Gaiety transfiguring all that dread' (*V. Poems*, 565–6). In short, it is a profoundly sane imagination which delights in those Chinamen of 'Lapis Lazuli' who look at life with the bright gaze of wisdom. This abundant imaginative energy recalls that moment in 'The Tower' when he realises so keenly his unflagging powers:

> Never had I more
> Excited, passionate, fantastical
> Imagination, nor an ear and eye
> That more expected the impossible—
> (*V. Poems*, 409)

He sends 'imagination forth' like a wizard's thought to invoke and question local history, folk-lore, his own life and work. Yeats, in our mechanistic, scientific, though not very rational age, dared to let his imagination explore psychic experience and take seriously the mediumship of his young wife.

This, the greatest and perhaps most extraordinary literary imagination of our century deserves some attempt at critical delineation and discussion. What is the essential nature of Yeats's imagination? The answer given here is that it is neither epic nor even wholly lyric, but essentially dramatic.

I

A Fragment of God:
Yeats's Idea of the Imagination

IT IS my contention that Yeats's imagination was not only lyrical but at root dramatic. It is time to acknowledge too that Yeats's criticism is an impressive achievement, and to make more use of it. His critical prose, the work not of one period, but of a life-time, arose out of the polemics of the Dublin literary scene, the practicalities of creating a modern Irish literature and theatre, and the forge of his own workshop as an international writer. It is a personal record, but because that particularity was the greatness of Yeats, it is an extremely significant record.

Imagination is our way of thinking in images and symbols in order to interpret the physical and psychic environment and our life in it. One of the significant things Yeats's criticism does is to produce a variety of comments upon imagination. Indeed, the nature of imagination was for Yeats a critical touchstone, and never far from his central concern, whatever that might be, in a particular essay. He described some of the processes of his own mature imagination at its most characteristic in a little-quoted passage in 'Pages from a Diary in 1930':

> When I think of Swift, of Burke, of Coleridge, or Mallarmé, I remember that they spoke as it were sword in hand, that they played their part in a unique drama, but played it, as a politician cannot though he stand in the same ranks, with the whole soul. Once or twice I have spoken words which came from no-where, which I could not account for, which were even absurd, which have been fulfilled to the letter. I am trying to understand why certain metaphysicians whom I have spent years trying to master repel me, why those invisible beings I have learned to trust would turn me from all that is not conflict, that is not from sword in hand. Is it not like this? I cannot discover

truth by logic unless that logic serve passion, and only then if
the logic be ready to cut its own throat, tear out its own eyes
—the cry of Hafiz, 'I made a bargain with that hair before the
beginning of time', the cry of every lover. Those spiritual beings
seem always as if they would turn me from every abstraction.
I must not talk to myself about 'the truth' nor call myself
'teacher' nor another 'pupil'—these things are abstract—but
see myself set in a drama where I struggle to exalt and over-
come concrete realities perceived not with mind only but as
with the roots of my hair. The passionless reasoners are pariah
dogs and devour the dead symbols. The clarified spirits own
the truth, they have intellect; but we receive as agents, never
as owners, in reward for victory. (*E*, 301–2)

Conjunction of thought and feeling; passionate perception and
utterance; life perceived as struggle, conflict, drama; the sub-
ordination of logic and abstraction to the sensuous, histrionic,
experiential; the acceptance of a spirit world as well as the
animal world; the persuasion that the mind receives, and the
imagination works with, signals from both these worlds—such
was the imagination as he saw it. Characteristically, he did not try
to expound it in the neutral prose of the scholar. He made a
paragraph intimate, personal, turbulent, and primarily for his
own eyes. It is a record of a literary imagination, lit by memory,
sudden perception, swooping on life as from a height, soaring
with the spirit to the end of a tether weighted with sensation,
doubt, and that fierce scorn for abstraction. It is always tied to his
own humanity. For Yeats, thought is struggle, the conflict of mind
with mind, whether living or dead. The imagination is so powerful
that it persists after death and existed before birth, as part of the
eternal soul. The human life cycle is the expression of conflicting
impulses: man's soul asserts its freedom through birth, incarnation,
the putting on of flesh; it relinquishes that freedom for God's,
through death and the purgatorial dreaming-back[1] which follows
it. This is the continuous cycle of being, the ceaseless activity or
process of imagination perceiving the divine ideas and construct-
ing the world from them:

If men are born many times, as I think, that must originate in
the antinomy between human and divine freedom. Man incar-
nating, translating 'the divine ideas' into his language of the

eye, to assert his own freedom, dying into the freedom of God and then coming to birth again. So too the assertions and surrender of sexual love, all that I have described elsewhere as antithetical and primary. (*E*, 306)

So too the artistic imagination, which at its best involves the whole being, holding body and soul in unresolved but fertile and dramatic tension. The imaginative work can thus express a more complete sense of human experience than the work which is mere propaganda for a single view.

Yeats captured the process in the image of the artist as a swordsman who holds down his opposite, as if Jekyll and Hyde were at sword-play: 'we hold down as it were on the sword's point that [which] would, if undefeated, grow into the countertruth, that when our whole being lives we create alike out of our love and hate' (*E*, 307). And indeed Yeats's imaginative works bear this out, from all phases of his career. His eternal combatants are numerous: Oisin and St Patrick, Cuchulain and Conchubar, the Fool and the Blind Man, Crazy Jane and the Bishop. Conflict is the basis of consciousness and passion, as well as creativity, for passion is born of the soul's struggle against all that impedes its unity; thought, however, is the clash of minds, both living and dead. These ideas were to prove fertile for Yeats as poet and dramatist.

In his essay 'Swedenborg, Mediums, Desolate Places' (1914), Yeats contrasted the view of an after-life as 'reward and punishment' with that shared by Swedenborg and Irish folk-lore, of the after-life as a 'continuance of this life'. Yeats added that 'This earth-resembling life is the creation of the image-making power of the mind, plucked naked from the body, and mainly of the images in the memory' (*E*, 34-35). With some satisfaction he also noticed that Swedenborg anticipated the modern conclusion that we forget nothing, though we may not recall everything we have experienced. It is possible therefore that souls in this or the after-life could create by imagination and memory a solid-seeming reconstruction of experience and its setting, helped by angelic spirits:

. . . but at need angelic spirits who act upon us there as here, widening and deepening the consciousness at will, can draw forth all the past, and make us live again all our transgressions and see our victims 'as if they were present, together with the place, words, and motives'; and that suddenly, as when a scene bursts upon the 'sight' and yet continues 'for hours together', and like the transgressions, all the pleasures and pains of sensible life awaken again and again, all our passionate events rush up about us and not as seeming imagination, for imagination is now the world. (*E*, 35)

There is little doubt that Yeats himself accepted this Sweden-borgian account, for, together with the pages which follow it describing the purification, simplification and remoulding of the soul after death, it forms the basis of much speculation in *A Vision* (1925) and provides the ground rules for such plays as *The Dreaming of the Bones* (1919), *The Words Upon the Window-Pane* (1934) and *Purgatory* (1939), which all exploit the dreaming-back. The imagination at such times helps to create a situation which, in order to distinguish it from the usual percep-tion of the world, can be called a phantasmagoria. The physical world, which we perceive only passively, is created actively by the perceptions of God.[2]

Our own active creation seems to spring from division and con-flict striving for unity. The difficulties facing the creative artist Yeats recognised as enormous but manageable, if only he could maintain the discipline and abnegation involved in the fascination and pursuit of the difficult. This was especially true in an age, as it seemed to him in 1919, of the divided soul. 'Are we approach-ing,' he asked in 'A People's Theatre', 'a supreme moment of self-consciousness, the two halves of the soul separate and face to face?' (*E*, 259). Yeats, however, never whined about the difficulties of imaginative work. Rather, he plunged into the polemics neces-sary for the foundation of a modern Irish literature in English, and for the growth of an Irish theatre movement dedicated to art above politics (a very tall order in Dublin at that time), and kept working away at the arts of poetry, drama and prose. As a young reviewer he projected confidence; as a mature writer he dramatised his own conflicting emotions, but always had the courage to take his insights to unorthodox, even irrational conclusions in an age of materialism. This courage and pugnacity was born of faith in his own imagination, and, following Blake, the holiness of that imagination. In his 1901 essay 'On Popular Poetry', Yeats argued that there were a few thousand people who knew the oral folk

tradition, one great storehouse of imagination, and gained from it
true taste and the faith that imagination was the man himself 'and
that the world as imagination sees it is the durable world' (*E&I*,
12). It is through the imagination, then, that we perceive and
envisage the enduring or the eternal. The connections between the
rural tradition of folk art and oral literature and imagination were
not a matter of propaganda. Yeats argued that for our minds to be
receptive to the thoughts and visions which come from super-
natural revelation, we need time for passive meditation. Rural
peoples have that time whereas our culture of cities works against
this type of imaginative experience 'for our life of cities, which
deafens or kills the passive meditative life, and our education that
enlarges the separated, self-moving mind, have made our souls
less sensitive' (*E&I*, 41). This Yeatsian version of the primitivist
myth was doubtless in accord with his own experience (love of
Sligo; hatred of London) and that Wordsworthian boyhood he
gave to Michael in his unpublished novel *The Speckled Bird.*

Equally vivid in the Yeatsian account of imagination is the in-
voluntary nature of the faculty, its susceptibility to symbols as
instigators. In his essay 'Magic' (1901), Yeats recalled that some
symbolic numbers and a magical 'form of words' made his im-
agination work 'of itself and to bring before me vivid images that,
though never too vivid to be imagination, as I had always under-
stood it, had yet a motion of their own, a life I could not change
or shape' (*E&I*, 29). The experience Yeats went on to describe is
clearly not a matter of hallucination but of vision, impalpable yet
vivid, and, amazingly, a vision seen independently by Yeats and
his 'seeress' who both seemed to be looking through the inner eyes
of the imagination at scenes from another man's previous life.
Yeats's sceptical intellect came to the conclusion that such visions
were not necessarily the phantoms of previous lives, but rather
symbolic incidents related to the 'dominant moods and moulding
events in this life' (*E&I*, 36), just as Freud reckoned our non-
waking dreams to be. Thus the imagination is capable of project-
ing involuntary symbolic visions of our crucial, inner and often
hidden moods, visions which may be compelling enough to co-
exist in several minds. Whatever the precise mechanism, Yeats
took such visions as proof 'of the supremacy of imagination' con-
trolled not, at these times, by the self but by some external force;
proof, in fact, of 'the power of many minds to become one, over-

powering one another by spoken words and by unspoken thought till they have become a single, intense, unhesitating energy. One mind was doubtless the master, I thought, but all the minds gave a little, creating or revealing for a moment what I must call a supernatural artist' (*E&I*, 36).

Strikingly, this supernatural artist's characteristic genre is dramatic, for he evokes scenes of action which carry dominant moods before the mind's eye in the theatre of the imagination. Characteristic of the playwright is the presentation of several different consciousnesses which, the final pattern of the play reveals, are subsumed by his own dominant concerns. For Yeats the essence of the mediumistic imagination was in precisely that way dramatic and histrionic. In his 'Introduction to *The Words Upon the Window-Pane*' (1931) he summed up his many experiences investigating psychic phenomena as follows:

> I consider it certain that every voice that speaks, every form that appears, whether to the medium's eyes and ears alone or to some one or two others or to all present, whether it remains a sight or sound or affects the sense of touch, whether it is confined to the room or can make itself apparent at some distant place, whether it can or cannot alter the position of material objects, is first of all a secondary personality or dramatisation created by, in, or through the medium. (*E*, 364)

In fact, on various occasions Yeats presents human actions as being performed according to a scenario, as if the divine dramatist or director used us as his actors. Insofar as our individual imaginations are susceptible to the spell of other men's visions we are passive. Yet imagination is not only active or passive but also impersonal, as when we receive impulses from beyond our own lives and participate in the life of the great mind and memory. It is not enough, however, to realise that the supernatural artist is a dramatist, he is a dramatist who uses symbols.

Yeats had eventually come to the conclusion that symbols had the power to control imagination and to unleash its potent forces in the form of art, vision and emotions: 'I cannot now think symbols less than the greatest of all powers whether they are used consciously by the masters of magic, or half unconsciously by their successors, the poet, the musician and the artist' (*E&I*, 49). Symbols he defined as 'Whatever the passions of man have gathered about.' Every symbol is held in a collective Great Memory 'and in the hands of him who has the secret it is a worker of wonders, a caller-up of angels or of devils' (*E&I*, 50). If God were the supreme supernatural artist, it was only fitting that for Yeats He should turn out to be a symbolic dramatist. Yeats defined his belief in these things in the now notorious opening of the essay on 'Magic'. He owns to a belief in 'the practice and philosophy of what we have agreed to call magic', in the 'evocation of spirits, though I do not know what they are, in the power of creating magical illusions, in the visions of truth in the depths of the mind when the eyes are closed' and in three essential doctrines common to most magical practices from early times onward:

(1) That the borders of our mind are ever shifting, and that many minds can flow into one another, as it were, and create or reveal a single mind, a single energy.

(2) That the borders of our memories are a part of one great memory, the memory of nature herself.

(3) That this great mind and great memory can be evoked by symbols. (*E&I*, 28)

But candidly as he states his beliefs, he as frankly confesses 'I often think I would put this belief in magic from me if I could . . .' (*E&I*, 28). Yeats's speculations about our least understood powers led him to a life-long involvement in supernatural and occult experience, yet if his soul soared, his reason could not but scratch the sceptical itch. Conversely, he could not accept the world plain. One cannot resist concluding that the need to express himself in dramatic poetry and plays derived from his struggle to inhabit both real and magical worlds. None of Yeats's interests seems to have been pursued for its own sake alone; his ultimate purpose was always the creation of his own art, an art full of symbols.

It is in 'The Symbolism of Poetry' (1900) that we find Yeats's explanation of the emotional force of symbols as what T. S. Eliot later called 'objective correlatives'. Eliot deliberately used the scientific jargon so modish in his generation and subsequently; Yeats, just as deliberately, preferred a warmer animism which helped to give his theory an astonishing beauty by avoiding abstract jargon in favour of metaphor and personification:

All sounds, all colours, all forms, either because of their pre-ordained energies or because of long association, evoke indefinable and yet precise emotions, or, as I prefer to think, call down among us certain disembodied powers, whose footsteps over our hearts we call emotions. . . . Because an emotion does not exist, or does not become perceptible and active among us, till it has found its expression, in colour or in sound or in form, or in all of these, and because no two modulations or arrangements of these evoke the same emotion, poets and painters and musicians, and in a less degree because their effects are momentary, day and night and cloud and shadow, are continually making and unmaking mankind. (*E&I*, 156–7)

This essay was remarkable for more than its beautiful prose and its anticipation of Eliot's objective correlative; it provided for much of Yeats's thinking about literature a focal concept of the symbolic tendency of imagination to which his other ideas could relate. 'The Moods', 'The Autumn of the Body' and 'The Body of the Father Christian Rosencrux', all written in the nineties, related the occult to his concept of imagination. 'The Celtic Element in Literature' (1902) brought Nationalism into relationship with imagination. 'Symbolism in Painting' and the two Blake essays in *Ideas of Good and Evil*, again from the nineties, related poetry and painting to the symbolic imagination. Later, in 'Poetry and Tradition' (1907) Yeats argued an essential link between tradition and aristocracy, maintaining that the 'shaping joy' of the true artist came from a sense of tradition.

Yeats's interest in aristocracy was not mere snobbery; it was a literary necessity, for he saw the rediscovery of tradition as an essential element in the creation of a modern Irish literature in English. He foresaw, indeed, that any lasting modern literature must discover its tradition or simply be lost in the frenzy of forgotten experiments, many of which were to flail and expire in the twenties and later. The relationship between imagination and the past was a key problem, as Eliot also recognised in 'Tradition and the Individual Talent'. Yeats's essay 'Edmund Spenser' was useful, too, in distinguishing between 'that visionary air which can alone make allegory real' and the lesser kind of allegory which is merely 'thought out in a mood of edification' (*E&I*, 369). At its best, 'Allegory and, to a much greater degree, symbolism are a natural language by which the soul when entranced, or even in ordinary sleep, communes with God and with angels. They can speak of things which cannot be spoken of in any other language, but one will always, I think, feel some sense of unreality, when they are used to describe things which can be described as well in ordinary words' (*E&I*, 368). Hence the importance to Yeats of that keen sense of decorum which is one of his distinctions and strengths. Hence his insistence on symbolism and poetry for most of his plays, for they are dramas of the human soul at some point of crisis and must therefore use the language of the soul.

When we ask what was the most characteristic mode of expression for Yeats's imagination, we find that his answer is that of the classic dramatist: the sovereignty of speech governed by an unfailing sense of decorum. He followed Sainte-Beuve in the thought that style is what endures in literature. The achievement of such a style is difficult. Yeats defined it as the language a character speaks 'which is his and nobody else's' and which has 'so much of emotional subtlety that the hearer may find it hard to know whether it is the thought or the word that has moved him, or whether these could be separated at all' (*E*, 108). Many of his poems dramatised himself or some persona using this kind of speech, and he achieved it also in some of the great speeches and lyrics of his plays. Since imagination responds to the ancient and insoluble and is the voice of what is eternal in man, it needs this personal yet immortal style, and it is, inescapably in Yeats's view, religious. This is why metaphysics was central for him as a writer and a man, why Shelley's poetry was necessary to him also, for his essay 'Prometheus Unbound' concluded that Shelley 'seemed to sum up all that was metaphysical in English poetry' (*E&I*, 424) and was an even more potent influence on him than was Blake, requiring all the weight of Balzac as a counter-balance. It was in this essay that Yeats defined Shelley as a visionary though not a mystic, since his system of thought was the result of 'logic' bent on satisfying 'desire', whereas true mysticism was marked by 'a symbolical revelation received after the suspension of all desire' (*E&I*, 421–22). Yeats himself pursued and found this kind of revelation through meditation.

Yeats's imagination, contemplative and religious, though not in a specifically doctrinal sense, was even in these moods unshakeably dramatic. The connection between the metaphysical and the dramatic is made very clear in 'The Holy Mountain' (1934), that introduction to Shri Purohit Swami's translation of Bhagwān Shri Hamsa's 'Story of a Pilgrimage to Lake Mānas and of Initiation on Mount Kailās in Tibet' and its sequel, the *Criterion* piece 'The Mandukya Upanishad' (1935). The supreme reward of the mystic is revelation, which Yeats vividly described in his introduction to *The Mandukya Upanishad*, where he quite clearly and characteristically saw this ultimate reward of the human imagination as sudden revelation, the supreme drama, and the pilgrim as having participated in some eternal ritual, like a character in a Yeatsian dance-play.

The Yeatsian account of imagination was not merely theoretical, of course, but was in some respects part of a critical method founded on artistic practice. Other writers became for him figures in a great drama, their essential moment summed up in a symbolic image from their lives and works. His essential Blake he imagined worshipping 'in some chapel of the sun' while Shelley 'would have wandered, lost in a ceaseless reverie, in some chapel of the Star of infinite desire' (*E&I*, 94). He could mythologise J. M. Synge in this way as 'a drifting silent man full of hidden passion' who 'loved wild islands, because there, set out in the light of day, he saw what lay hidden in himself' (*E&I*, 330) or imagine 'Landor who lived loving and hating, ridiculous and unconquered, into extreme old age, all lost but the favour of his Muse' (*M*, 342). By such means Yeats dramatised a writer's imagination, selecting details from life and work to use the resultant images as critical touchstones or even models for attitudes he might cultivate, because they were admirable to him and tinged with spiritual heroism. If the essential imagination of others could be imaged in this way, so, too, can his own. His essential moment is set in a landscape of bare hills and stunted trees. There is a tower, a crescent moon in the sky, but we must add the sound of clashing swords. The sage or poet stands atop the tower imagining the scene, the warriors and himself in the battle; descending the winding stair he finds a swordsman who climbs to meet him. It is his anti-self.

2

A Daemonic Rage

YEATS was no great success as a schoolboy, nor did he read for a university degree. His nearest approach to 'tertiary education' was his time as an art student. Yet his powerful intelligence was recognised by his teachers and he worked seriously, though not at things which bored him. His mind therefore never became locked into a specific curriculum of orthodox learning reflecting the academic preferences and prejudices of his time. Occult interests shaped his reading in his latter school days and at the college of art. Mohini Chatterji's Dublin visit influenced him deeply enough to alter the direction of his early poetry. In 1888 he joined the Theosophists, but it was his initiation in 1890 into the secret Order of the Golden Dawn[1] which set him on the tougher path of prescribed studies he made to reach exalted rank in that society. He had, in fact, two opposing, external and framing influences: the readings from literature together with the comments and conversations about art with which his father confronted him, and his interest in Eastern religions, theosophy and occult matters.

Where the first influence was sceptical, aesthetic and gentlemanly, the second was speculative, unorthodox, elusive. The first made it impossible for Yeats to embrace any formal Christianity; the second made it impossible for him to abandon the spiritual quest. Although he loved strange thought, Yeats also felt the prevailing rationalism of intellectuals acutely enough to wrap up *A Vision* (1925; 1937), the mature statement of his mythical, systematic interpretation of man's life in the universe, in a few layers of self-irony by way of protective camouflage. He might have taken heart from Coleridge's similar difficulties:

Why need I be afraid? Say rather how dare I be ashamed of the Teutonic theosophist, Jacob Behmen? Many indeed, and gross were his delusions; and such as furnish frequent and ample occasion for the triumph of the learned over the poor ignorant *shoemaker*, who had dared think for himself. But while we remember that these delusions were such as might be anticipated from his utter want of all intellectual discipline, and from his ignorance of rational psychology, let it not be forgotten that the latter defect he had in common with the most learned theologians of his age.[2]

Yeats left few stones, however humble or unpopular with established academics, unturned in his lifelong search for evidence about the soul, the spiritual and imaginative life in literature, folk-tale, myth and legend, and among contemporary as well as ancient occultists and spiritualists. He cannot be blamed for willingness to examine recondite evidence; he would not dismiss an idea merely because it failed to be respectable. He never abandoned this mental fight, and over a life-time became a man of great, if curious, learning. His attitudes to supernatural phenomena are, in fact, more reasonable than he has often been given credit for, and more sceptical than one would expect of a man born in mid-nineteenth-century Ireland. He was cultivated rather than self-educated, and very properly he distinguished between the cultivated person and the one who merely picks up an education. Yet he would have agreed with Coleridge, and seen its application in part to himself, in this passage :

O! it requires deeper feeling, and a stronger imagination, than belong to most of those, to whom reasoning and fluent expression have been as a trade learnt in boyhood, to conceive with what *might*, with what inward *strivings* and *commotion*, the perception of a new and vital TRUTH takes possession of an uneducated man of genius. His meditations are almost inevitably employed on the eternal, or the everlasting; for 'the world is not his friend, nor the world's law.'[3]

Yeats knew intimately the passion and the turmoil of thought inside himself, and not least because he was full of contradictions. His until recently[4] unpublished autobiographical novel *The Speckled Bird* (*c.* 1896–1902) is a portrait of the emergent artist in boyhood, adolescence and early manhood. Fragmentary and unfinished, it gives a more immediate picture than the *Autobiographies* of Yeats's inner life in some of its aspects. It sketches the lineaments of a powerful and predatory imagination, swooping down on life and soaring upwards to lonely heights.

Yeats's gregarious side is vividly pictured in his boyhood association with local fishermen; his loneliness and artistic sense of separateness from the mundane reality of everyday life embodied in the symbolic title Yeats thought he had taken from the Book of Isaiah, but which in fact refers to Jeremiah 12:9. The artist's lot is to be isolated and disliked by his fellows. But this does not necessarily mean that he is remote from life. Michael Hearne, the hero of the book, remembers his father telling him:

> . . . Everything
> that leads the thoughts away from the
> few main occupations of men in all
> ages, is a waste of life, whether it is
> metaphysics, pleasure, politics, scholarship or
> anything else.
>   (*LTMSB*, 27)

The permanent concerns of human life provide the material of the poetry which endures. The kind of imagination which responds to the few permanent human themes rather than to what might be called the urban journalist's view of life is in part a rural imagination. Yeats, no less than Wordsworth, stresses the effect of landscape and place, as well as the talk of artists, in the formation of his hero's creative imagination. He stresses too the peasant experience at the base of 'an imagination accustomed to the stories he had heard in the cottages or from John and Peter Bruin' (*LTMSB*, 28). No less Wordsworthian is the experience of a discipline which Yeats thought of as an imaginative, or better, a spiritual one, which took Michael beyond his 'ordinary stage' into one of 'partial unconsciousness' from which it was an extremely painful struggle to return,

> . . . While
> in this state he had it seemed to him come into
> a different (CANCELLED: rela) relation to (CANCELLED:
>   earth
> and sea) the trees

and to the grass and the sky, and to living things. It was
as though he had escaped for a little while
from (CANCELLED: the associations) their merely human
association . . .

(LTMSB, 73)

The boy feels an overwhelming love for the creatures and the land,
and this emotion he recognises as the 'forerunner of vision'. The
influence, too, of books of romance such as the *Mabinogian* and
the *Morte d'Arthur* is recalled as a powerful factor in the mould-
ing of the imagination and sensibility. But the 'epiphanies' or
'spots of time' in the novel are the incidents when, as a boy,
Michael sees a holy picture and when, as a young man, he falls in
love with Margaret, the Maud Gonne figure.[5] Yeats makes much
of the way his boy's imagination delights in the details of the
religious picture, the way he thinks of it as a portion of a real
world into which he can see through the frame. Yeats presents
this incident so that we watch the boy questioning his father about
the picture, and receiving a casual little talk on the history of the
painting as a copy of a 'meister Stephan' by a family friend, and
then, in contrast, we find Michael showing the picture to an old
tinker with 'a very patched greatcoat' who tells the boy about a
man of the roads who had had a vision of the Virgin which was
like the picture.

The old man, like a figure out of mythology, like the prologue
in Yeats's last play, *The Death of Cuchulain*, speaks in the
language of myth. His words are specific, naming things which
through a sense of mystery and symbol become redolent of larger
meaning. When the boy asks him whether the whole world was
once as beautiful as the picture, he replies with a creation myth:

> That's certain for
> did not God make it [and] say it was good.
> He had a looking-glass and he looked into it
> and he saw his face in the glass and that
> was the world.

(LTMSB, 37)

The sophistication the boy picks up from his father inextricably
fuses with the rich folk imagination to which he responds so
deeply.

The old tinker reveals another fact about imagination: its heal-
ing, supportive power. He does not know the source of all his
thoughts, but he knows that they are necessary to his survival in
the cold, the wind and the rains.

It is from the tinker, too, that Michael learns of hunger as a
pre-condition of vision. The boy then begins his experiments with
visionary states of being. For Yeats, as for Michael, vision was
part of the activity of imagination and could be perhaps repeatedly
enjoyed if the right bodily conditions could be achieved and the
appropriate symbols used for meditation. Michael, through im-
agination and vision, could glimpse reality or truth. It was also
his task to remake the actual world 'nearer to the heart's desire'
(*LTMSB*, 53), to change life until it accorded with vision. But
visionary states were not always at the mind's beck and call, and
'sometimes it would / seem to him that his imagination began to
move / of himself [=itself], and that the forms it called before
him / came from their own will and not his will . . .' (*LTMSB*,
67). In one of these involuntary visions, Michael encounters his
destiny in the form of a radiant woman rising from the sea in a
cone of fire. In a low, chanting voice, she prompts him to begin
his life's work, which is to bring about through study and art a
magical revolution in opposition to the modern, urban, material-
istic world. The scene is like one of the initiation rituals Yeats
devised. The setting is like that of the early play, *The Shadowy
Waters*. The chanting anticipates his experiments with speaking
to the psaltery, while the cone of fire would become his symbol of
the 'gyre' or spiralling cone, so important to his later work as an
image of the slow unravelling of an historical epoch or of a
person's life.

Yeats presents this intense and hopeful vision so that it seems
to come to Michael as a reward for having resisted the influence
of priests. His revolution is not only against mechanistic philo-
sophy, but against institutionalised Christianity; he is returning
to a pagan world of feeling and thought. He wants to share the
thoughts and emotions of the local fishermen, '—only I want /
to think with more subtlety [?] and feel with more / delicacy than
they do. To do that is to . . . have / the wisdom of Odysseus as
distinguished from modern / wisdom' (*LTMSB*, 99).

The portrait of the artistic imagination which Yeats gives us is
one of a young man whose desire is fired by ancient books of

romance and the almost impersonal symbolic beauty of a young woman; he wishes to vanquish modern religious and non-religious thought, replacing it with an essentially rural view of wisdom and reality based on folk-lore and the best thought embodied in the great art of the past. It is an imagination on the edge of vision and trance, a religious imagination fed by nature and art. The ultimate source of imaginative ideas he finds through Shelley's poetry to be 'the souls of the dead become a part of that / ideal loveliness . . . that was some day to take us / to its heart' (*LTMSB*, 313). All the art of which his taste approves is seen as a revelation from beyond the grave, and thus has the force of Scripture or a holy book.

This puts Yeats squarely in the tradition of a Platonic and Neo-platonic view of imagination owing much to Blake, Coleridge, and Wordsworth. The supreme test of the modern imagination for Yeats is to make imagination itself sacred; hence the mystical order he forms and his experiments with symbols. Certain little clusters of symbols and the forms of prayer and ritual connected with them had become sacred to Christians in former centuries. All images and impulses from the imagination, Yeats believed, could likewise be made sacred in the modern age by shaping and ordering them 'in beauty and in peace' through association 'deliberately . . . and directly with / the history of the soul, and they must be . . . / given so coherent and intense . . . and separate / a life, that they shall seem the . . . / immortalities / and . . . perfections that they are' (*LTMSB*, 382–3). This imagination was not satisfied by symbols alone, or by the myths of the past. It desired rituals to be found for its congenial myths, like the mysteries of the ancient world. If the central purpose of Yeats's religious imagination was to remake mankind's thinking on an ancient pattern, that pattern would be expressed through ritual as well as myth, through what might be termed 'enacted myth'. Mrs Maclagan, wife of the magician with whom Michael founds a mystical order, in one scene sings a hymn in praise of Isis, moving as she sings in a dance which weaves 'old symbols . . . made / upon the temple floors by the feet of the dancers' (*LTMSB*, 167). Yeats's imagination is not only religious, thriving on symbol, but insists on giving a theatrical life to its preoccupations, foreshadowing the creation later on of the ritualistic dance-plays. The mystical adventures of the soul, recorded in myth, legend and vision, are kept strictly as ritual rather than drama, 'never enacted completely as / in / a stage play, but . . . only suggested and / symbolised / for the real adventure is eternal and spiritual' (*LTMSB*, 379). Yet the extant Greek dramas seem to Michael as fragments from a larger ritual of the holy imagination. This imagination he sees as the original fire or forge in which were shaped images akin to Plato's Ideas or Forms, existing outside time, as it were, in the mind of God. The human, temporal world and all that is in it are the shadows cast by those original images behind which gleams the divine imagination, the true and only reality. This adaptation of Plato's myth of the cave from *The Republic* appears to be the basis of Yeats's idea of Anima Mundi, the great storehouse of memories, images and emotions of an eternal life force which can touch our individual imaginations through symbols and visions.

The artist's symbolism, Yeats makes clear in his plans for one of the scenes in the novel, must be distinguished from that of the magician, Maclagan (based on MacGregor Mathers, a magician Yeats met in London). Where Maclagan's symbols are arbitrary, Michael insists on 'the introduction of such / a symbolism as will continue and make more precise the / implicit symbolism in modern art and poetry' (*LTMSB*, 143). Yeats, then, was committed to the discovery and perpetuation of a tradition of spiritual intellect which acknowledged the existence of the soul, which held that the finite world constructed by our imaginations was symbolic of a reality which was sometimes accessible to us through symbol, imagination and spiritual discipline. Like Wordsworth, Yeats describes moments in which his younger self seems blessed with special and illuminated insight: 'Suddenly a great many ideas seemed to / come to him, and the =he felt a sudden joy . . . / as if he suddenly understood every / thing . . . in the world . . .' (*LTMSB*, 297). His imagination not only perceives the mystery in this way, but characteristically seeks to embody vision and mystery in rituals using emblematic curtains, dialogue, and symbolic knights and ladies.

At the time he was working on *The Speckled Bird*, Yeats, unlike his hero Michael, had begun to dramatise his symbols and occult investigations in a play, *The Shadowy Waters* (1900). His most considerable body of work during this period was, however, the fiction collected later in *Mythologies* (1959). These stories grew out of his folkloric and, in *The Secret Rose* (1897) or *Rosa*

Alchemica (1897), his occult studies. But he was also ambitious to create stories about a powerful, distinctive personality, and in 1897 there appeared also the *Stories of Red Hanrahan*. Yeats expressed a hope that Hanrahan might even get into folk legend as if he were a real rather than a fictional person, creating a species of 'legendary realism' (*A*, 439). All this effort put into fiction (he had also published '*John Sherman*' and '*Dhoya*' under the pseudonym Ganconagh in 1891, besides collecting *Stories from Carleton* [1888]) points to a novelist in the making rather than a dramatic poet.[6] But the desire for enacted myth was an essential to Yeats's imagination. He had dramatised legend in *The Countess Kathleen* (1892), folk lore in *The Land of Heart's Desire* (1894) and was struggling to bring occult doctrine and ritual into stageworthy form with *The Shadowy Waters*, which attained its printed acting version only in 1907.

But dramatists need theatres. Yeats's theatre did not exist in London's commercial West End. He had to create an Irish theatre in Dublin, for it was in Ireland that his destiny as a writer lay; as soon as he found the little group of Irish players led by Frank and William Fay, the full reaches of Yeats's dramatic imagination could begin to be explored. By 1902 he had abandoned prose fiction for ever.

Yeats felt very strongly the sense of isolation within a community which is the lot of artists in an age when art is often complex, abstruse, difficult. He believed that in Ireland where the community was still closely knit and largely pre-industrial, a writer could reawaken an older imaginative tradition through legend and myth. Folk art he considered the record of the richest thought and feeling of former times, an 'aristocracy' of thought 'because it refuses what is passing and trivial, the merely clever and pretty, as certainly as the vulgar and insincere, and because it has gathered into itself the simplest and most unforgettable thoughts of the generations, it is the soil where all great art is rooted' (*M*, 139). It provided a long and detailed record of the human imagination. In an age when only the few understood imaginative lore, it was urgently necessary to revive that record because 'when imagination is impoverished, a principal voice—for the awakening of wise hope and durable faith, and understanding charity—can speak but in broken words, if it does not fall silent' (*M*, 139). The urgency of the need to revive the imagination through 'tribal' myth and the desire for an integrated community was a lifelong concern with Yeats. It kept him in Ireland, and it goes far to explain his political attitudes, and to explain why his dramatic imagination rested on Ireland and not, like Shaw's, on the West End theatres.

At the same time he delighted in the secret and the lonely. The narrator of *Rosa Alchemica* saw that alchemy was no mere chemistry, but a striving to transmute 'all things into some divine and imperishable substance; and this enabled me to make my little book a fanciful reverie over the transmutation of life into art, and a cry of measureless desire for a world made wholly of essences' (*M*, 267). He wanted to transform reality into vision, and stand like some reckless wizard, apart from humanity in the joy of a will powerful enough to control experience and shape all into confident beauty:

> I had gathered about me all gods because I believed in none, and experienced every pleasure because I gave myself to none, but held myself apart, individual, indissoluble, a mirror of polished steel. I looked in the triumph of this imagination at the birds of Hera, glittering in the light of the fire as though of Byzantine mosaic; and to my mind, for which symbolism was a necessity, they seemed the doorkeepers of my world, shutting out all that was not of as affluent a beauty as their own; and for a moment I thought, as I had thought in so many other moments, that it was possible to rob life of every bitterness except the bitterness of death . . . (*M*, 268–9)

This splendid vision of heroic spiritual quest is full of pride and vigour. The seer is about to leap into some eternal reality, reach some apotheosis like those mortals who become *daimons* in the Greek world, or who ride through Irish legend with the magical Sidhe or faeries. But Yeats's imagination is too honest, too contradictory, too peasant-like and too sophisticated to believe wholly in that leap into the infinite. He adds the contrary impulse:

> . . . and then a thought which had followed this thought, time after time, filled me with a passionate sorrow. All those forms: that Madonna with her brooding purity, those delighted ghostly faces under the morning light, those bronze divinities with their passionless dignity, those wild shapes rushing from despair to

B

despair, belonged to a divine world wherein I had no part; and every experience, however profound, every perception, however exquisite, would bring me the bitter dream of a limitless energy I could never know, and even in my most perfect moment I would be two selves, the one watching with heavy eyes the other's moment of content. (*M*, 269)

Yeats's prose delineates very accurately this profound conflict within his own mind, always or nearly always seeking dramatic expression or form in his poems as well as in his plays. Weary heart and weariless spirit cohabited in him, and declared themselves in passionate dialogue. Writing, in fact, never came easily to Yeats as an activity in itself. His handwriting is tortured into illegibility, letters sliding as if his pen could never keep up with his racing mind, his spelling and punctuation at best erratic. He welcomed what some writers find impossible as a method: dictation. In April 1902, he wrote to Lady Gregory, 'I am working at my novel [probably *The Speckled Bird*]—dictating to a typewriter. I dictated 2,000 words in an hour and ten minutes yesterday—and go on again tomorrow. This dictation is really a discovery' (*L*, 370). Oral composition suited him because he loved the oral tradition: as he worked on poems and plays alike, he muttered them aloud, turning again and again to the utterance of some passionate personality. The type of the writer for him was the storyteller, and all great writing had to have something of the old wives' tale about it. Yet at the same time there had to be hidden there the writer's private philosophy, the subtle, modern mind. In 1932, looking back over his lyrics, he discovered consciously what he had done perhaps unconsciously because it was so natural for his dramatic imagination:

I spend my days correcting proofs. I have just finished the first volume, all my lyric poetry, and am greatly astonished at myself. As it is all speech rather than writing, I keep saying what man is this who in the course of two or three weeks—the improvisation suggests the tune—says the same thing in so many different ways. My first denunciation of old age I made in *The Wanderings of Usheen* (end of part I) before I was twenty and the same denunciation comes in the last pages of the book. The swordsman throughout repudiates the saint, but not without vacillation. (*L*, 798)

No wonder Yeats was interested in Archibald MacLeish's[7] comment on his work from the point of view of speech and rhetoric: 'it commends me above other modern poets because my language is "public". That word, which I had not thought of myself, is a word I want' (*L*, 908–9) he wrote in a letter to Dorothy Wellesley. As early as the spring of 1899 he could write to Katherine Tynan that 'To me the dramatic is far the pleasantest poetic form' (*L*, 122). Almost forty years later, the last book he ever planned was a collection of essays 'dealing with the relations between speech and song' (*L*, 919). This was December 1938; the next month he was dead. Dramatic speech had been a lifelong discipline.

Speech depends upon a speaker, and Yeats's work is full of personae, most of them dramatic. His theory of the mask, wherein we discover what is most opposed to our true nature, bespeaks a capacity for imaginative sympathy with 'the other', akin to what Keats named the 'negative capability' of the writer. Yet at the same time, so strong is Yeats's personality, that his 'fingerprints' are unmistakable. As he confessed to Katherine Tynan, 'I see everything through the coloured glasses of my own moods' (*L*, 44). The effect he had on others was always definite, sometimes decisive, as when he sent Synge off to the Aran Islands. In some personal notes on Yeats when he was a grand old man, Lady Dorothy Wellesley recalled that 'His personality was almost overwhelming' (*DWL*, 179). She saw him as a frustrated man of action whose characteristics could be summed up as 'an excess of passion disturbed by reason' (*DWL*, 175). He loved the heroic, extravagant personality. But even here there is the duality of swordsman and sage: 'Any exhibition of excitability or violent feeling he will always welcome,' notes Lady Dorothy. 'And yet for ever he craves for philosophic "thought" ' (*DWL*, 174).

Yeats was remarkably alert to his own nature, though he preferred not to express his insights in the language of modish Freudianism. He analysed his own duality in terms of some force which a speaker battles to hold down within himself, this struggle becoming a source of power. He told his actors that the passion of the verse came from this sense of speakers holding 'down Hysterica passio' as if they were controlling some dark beast. He described this basic duality in himself through the symbolism he had made his own:

About the conflict in 'To D.W.' I did not plan it deliberately. That conflict is deep in my subconscious, perhaps in everybody's. I dream of clear water, perhaps two or three times (the moon of the poem), then come erotic dreams. Then for weeks perhaps I write poetry with sex for theme. Then comes the reversal— it came when I was young with some dream or some vision between waking and sleep with a flame in it. Then for weeks I get a symbolism like that in my Byzantium poem or in 'To D.W.' with flame for theme. All this may come from the chance that when I was a young man I was accustomed to a Kabalistic ceremony where there were two pillars, one symbolic of water and one of fire. The fire mark is △, the water mark is ▽, these are combined to make Solomon's Seal ✡. The water is sensation, peace, night, silence, indolence; the fire is passion, tension, day, music, energy. (*DWL*, 86–7)

The Star of David or, as Yeats called it, Solomon's Seal, is but a short shift away from his symbol of the interpenetrating cones or gyres his wife drew in the diagrams of *A Vision* which symbolise opposing forces and desires in the universe—the one 'subjective' or 'antithetical' in 'tincture' signifying the tendency towards individualism, self-fulfilment, lonely distinction; the other 'objective' or 'primary' in 'tincture' signifying collectiveness, self-sacrifice, subordination to the will of others—which could be discerned as conflicting types of human being, conflicting phases within the life of an individual, and conflicting epochs in the history of mankind. The duality of Yeats's imagination meant that conflict was an inescapable element in his view of everything. Moreover, even an 'objective' personality could be in conflict, because in Yeats's view, individuals of one 'tincture' might well be born into an historical epoch which was the opposite 'tincture'. They would then be out of phase and battle against the values approved by their society. Yeats saw himself as out of phase with the philosophic materialism and commercialism of his own times, and wished to bring them crashing down. His early ideas of a magical revolution faded, however, and he soon saw the ideals of the military revolution which led to the Irish Free State lost in a grubby commercialism still under the shadow of England. Characteristically, he opposed the age by imagining everything beautiful which it had lost or discarded, seeing history as a play, its development leading as inevitably as that of a Greek tragedy towards peripeteia, or the reversal of a gyre.

Long before he constructed his symbolic system in *A Vision*, Yeats was discerning the large general movement, the *Zeitgeist*: as early as 1903 he wrote to his old friend George Russell (AE) that 'The close of the last century was full of a strange desire to get out of form, to get to some kind of disembodied beauty, and now it seems to me the contrary impulse has come. I feel about me and in me an impulse to create form, to carry the realisation of beauty as far as possible' (*L*, 402). Yeats's imagination was now responding to a sense of embodied truth rather than some abstract ideal.

Dramatic form, of course, is best suited to a vision of life as conflict, action, and character in crisis. It demands multiple points of view rather than a single or partial one. Any unity it achieves is not so much a given, visible at the outset, but something which emerges from contemplation of the drama as a whole, when it is over. We are conscious of patterns of conflict, contrast and crisis developing through complexities of character relationship into a rhythm or momentum which leads to climax and resolution. Fragmentary effects build into a holistic pattern. The artist purveys truth to human experience by means of a form which organises action, and character in action—the embodiment of lived life, rather than comment on life. Comment is not so much stated as implied by contrasting actions. Dramatic form was therefore well suited for expressing a poetic imagination which, divided in itself and deeply aware of conflict, sought 'truth, not abstract truth, but a kind of vision of reality which satisfies the whole being' and which realised with Henry More 'that all our deep desires must be satisfied' and that 'the poet reveals truth by revealing those desires' (*L*, 588).

The imaginative force of great poetry does not teach by means of extrapolated formulae; according to Yeats 'it changes us' (*UP* 1:84) because it has the power to reach our deepest and entire being. Modern man, including the poets, is fragmented:

Man is like a musical instrument of many strings, of which only a few are sounded by the narrow interests of his daily life; and the others, for want of use, are continually becoming tuneless and forgotten. Heroic poetry is a phantom finger swept over all the strings, arousing from man's whole nature a song of answering harmony. It is the poetry of action, for such alone can arouse the whole nature of man. It touches all the strings—those of wonder and pity, of fear and joy. It ignores morals, but its business is not in any way to make us rules for life, but to make character. It is not, as a great English writer has said, 'a criticism of life', but rather a fire in the spirit, burning away what is mean and deepening what is shallow. (*UP* 1 : 84)

This is taken from Yeats's early essay on Sir Samuel Ferguson (9 October 1886), his first extant piece of published critical prose. At the age of twenty-one, then, Yeats, though clearly attuned to aestheticism and Pater's refining flame, goes beyond that into the poetry of action. He admires and desires heroic narrative and drama. If heroic poetry can involve the whole being of its audience, the corollary is that it demands the entire being of the poet. The poetic imagination of Yeats, even if chaotic with conflicting impulses and qualities, will seek to forge that unity. One way of doing this was to follow Dante's definition from the *Convito*, to Yeats 'the first passage of poignant autobiography in literary history' (*E*, 250). Taking Dante as the example, Yeats describes the unified being in this way:

His study was unity of being, the subordination of all parts to the whole as in a perfectly proportioned human body—his own definition of beauty— (*E*, 250)

Yeats saw himself as belonging to a type which counts Unity of Being as the most important of objectives, and he was convinced that it was possible for those like Goethe who sought it 'intellectually, critically, and through a multitude of deliberately chosen experiences' to attain only a mere combination of incompatibles, 'whereas true Unity of Being, where all the nature murmurs in response if but a single note be touched, is found emotionally, instinctively, by the rejection of all experience not of the right quality, and by the limitation of its quantity' (*A*, 354–5). Yeats had, then, to recover instinctively the unity which had been split apart by the extreme individualism of the Renaissance.

Yeats here anticipated Eliot's famous doctrine of the seventeenth-century 'Dissociation of sensibility', just as when he wrote 'poetry is any flower that brings a memory of emotion' (*E*, 251) he anticipated Eliot's 'objective correlative'.[8] So fervently did Yeats feel the necessity for this Unity of Being, that it became an obsessive thought from the age of twenty-three or four. His problem was not, however, the separation of thought and feeling, as in Eliot's 'diagnosis'. Yeats felt and thought intensely, being instinctively aware of the sensuousness of art, and even called a passage in *The Cutting of an Agate* 'The Thinking of the Body'. Instinctively, emotionally, he took as axiomatic, not as a lost condition, that we think with the body, as Donne did, whenever we respond to a work of art. Gazing at a Canaletto and a Frans Frencken (the younger), Yeats commented:

> Neither painting could move us at all, if our thought did not rush out to the edges of our flesh, and it is so with all good art . . . Art bids us touch and taste and hear and see the world, and shrinks from what Blake calls mathematic form, from every abstract thing, from all that is of the brain only, from all that is not a fountain jetting from the entire hopes, memories, and sensations of the body. (*E&I*, 292–3)

No, Yeats felt a different division than that of thought from feeling. His main concerns seemed to be separated one from another. He struggled to bring his art, politics and philosophy into unity. He thought this might be achieved by some symbolic 'mythological coherence' based on powerful tribal images which expressed some difficult ambition and were strong enough to focus the collective will:

> Nations, races, and individual men are unified by an image, or bundle of related images, symbolical or evocative of the state of mind which is, of all states of mind not impossible, the most difficult to that man, race, or nation; because only the greatest obstacle that can be contemplated without despair rouses the will to full intensity. (A, 194–5)

This is the concept of the mask applied to politics. It implies that the imaginative writer with a sense of destiny (which Yeats had in abundance) must seek out and express those masterful images of his country. Parnell had seemed one such national symbol before his fall. The Irish mythology provided in Cuchulain another. Hence the patriotic and symbolic importance for Yeats of the hero.[9] Yeats was confident that the absorbing of ancient Irish legend by the modern Irish would lead to unity of culture. 'Have not all races had their first unity from a mythology that marries them to rock and hill?' he asked, seeing a literary form emerge which he was to use in his own plays:

> We had in Ireland imaginative stories, which the uneducated classes knew and even sang, and might we not make those stories current among the educated classes, rediscovering for the work's sake what I have called 'the applied arts of literature', the association of literature, that is, with music, speech, and dance; and at last, it might be, so deepen the political passion of the nation that all, artist and poet, craftsman and day-labourer would accept a common design? (*A*, 194)

By 1926 he had, he thought, succeeded in achieving personal Unity of Being, but there was clearly no such achievement nationally. In his essay 'If I Were Four-And-Twenty' he claimed that art, politics and philosophy had become the 'discrete expression of a single conviction' (*E*, 263) that each had behind it his 'whole character'—that which was peculiar to him—and that he was now properly cultivated. He defined cultivation not in terms of scholarly bookishness or examination passing, but as shown by 'a man who brings to general converse, and business, character that informs varied interests. It is just the same with a nation—it is only a cultivated nation when it has related its main interests one to another. We are a religious nation' (*E*, 263). Yet he never saw unity of culture in Ireland, and became increasingly bitter at lost hopes. He had formulated in *A Vision* the elaborate system which, through its basic image of the twenty-eight phases of the moon, symbolised various states of the soul exhibited by twenty-six different human types and two supernatural states of being. The system expounded a view of man in relation to spirit and matter, which satisfied Yeats, accommodated his contradictory impulses, his sensuality and spirituality, his religion, his view of history and his psychology. Yet this elaborate metaphor of the ultimate Unity contained duality and conflict as a constant factor. Yeats explained this in characteristically theatrical terms by asserting that each individual not only has character (that which distinguishes him from others and permits the character conflicts we love in comedy) and personality (the universally human traits to which we all respond, and which make the tragic hero seem an archetype of ourselves) but also the mask—that anti-self which is all that is most different from what we are, and which feeds on the qualities of epochs different from our own. As he defined it in *Autobiographies:*

> My mind began drifting vaguely towards that doctrine of 'the mask' which has convinced me that every passionate man (I have nothing to do with mechanist, or philanthropist, or man whose eyes have no preference) is, as it were, linked with another age, historical or imaginary, where alone he finds images that rouse his energy. (*A*, 152)

It is not only the duality in the structure of Yeats's imagination and thinking which makes the adjective 'dramatic' so appropriate. Granted, Yeats saw conflict as the basis of all creation (*A*, 576), but drama needs more than conflict, if it is not to be mere confusion. It is also clear that Yeats's imagination dwelt on passionate human nature in action. And drama must also be the imitation of human nature in action. He saw the elements of personality in terms of drama, associating character, personality and mask with the theatre. He wished for an art, whether in a lyric or a play, which expressed human personality in crisis, at moments of passionate utterance. In *Autobiographies* we see how he feared becoming abstract to the extent of praying for an imagination 'as preoccupied with life as had been the imagination of Chaucer', finding a certain contentment only when he had learned to make abstract ideas compose themselves 'into picture and dramatisation'. He could not regard ideas as merely intellectual; informed by passion they must rest in the heart as convictions. Intellect and emotional masks are spun instinctively by those whose imagination perceives life as tragic:

> As life goes on we discover that certain thoughts sustain us in defeat, or give us victory, whether over ourselves or others, and it is these thoughts, tested by passion, that we call convictions. Among subjective men (in all those, that is, who must spin a web out of their own bowels) the victory is an intellectual daily re-creation of all that exterior fate snatches away, and so that fate's antithesis; while what I have called 'the Mask' is an emotional antithesis to all that comes out of their internal nature. We begin to live when we have conceived life as tragedy. (*A*, 189)

Yeats's imagination could turn defeats suffered at the intervention of fate into victories. And if heroism was possible in his world view, so was tragic joy. As a youth he copied Irving's Hamlet, considering it 'an image of heroic self-possession' and 'a combatant of the battle within myself' (*A*, 47). Another such image and combatant which inhabited his imagination was King Lear, figured forth in the person of Yeats's grandfather, William Pollexfen. If life was conceived as tragedy, it was tragedy peopled by heroes called from the splendid past and fused with the living; not only the Noble Prince (Hamlet and Irving) and the Old King (Lear and William Pollexfen) but also the Fatal Woman (Helen and Maud Gonne), the Faithful Wife (Emer and Mrs Yeats) and a list of others perhaps not so definitely identified with a single person: the Indian Ascetic, or Holy Man, the Sage or Wizard, the Coward, the Country Gentleman, the Spirit Medium, the Saint, the Fool, the Bardic Poet, the ragged vagrant. These are not mere ciphers. They appear in Yeats's work as obstreperous figures, springing alive out of his garrulous inner world.

Yeats's work testifies that he readily agreed with his father's view of a lyric passage—he was dissatisfied with it 'unless he felt some actual man behind its elaboration of beauty' (*A*, 65). It was his father's opinion also that 'All must be an idealisation of speech, and at some moment of passionate action or somnambulistic reverie' (*A*, 65). Yeats did not rebel against his father on this score; much of his lyric poetry is speech of one kind or another in monologue or dialogue. Yeats's histrionic imagination was alive with images of great speakers—Maud Gonne, Bernhardt, Frank Fay, William Morris reading poetry as if it were poetry, not prose, J. B. Yeats himself, and the Dublin orator, Taylor, who, speaking some political verse, gave Yeats 'a conviction of how great might be the effect of verse, spoken by a man almost rhythm-drunk, at some moment of intensity, the apex of long-mounting thought' (*A*, 99). When as a young man he read some poor patriotic verses about a dying emigrant's return to Ireland, his sympathies were at once aroused to the point of tears because, as he told his father, the verses contained 'the actual thoughts of a man at a passionate moment of life' (*A*, 102). His poetic imagination had passionate speech as much as ideas or a specific mood as its basis. Looking back over his work, he commented 'I find little but romantic convention, unconscious drama. It is so many years before one can

believe enough in what one feels even to know what the feeling
is' (*A*, 103). Despite his inability sometimes to achieve his in-
tentions, the fact remains that speech was indeed the basis of his
lyricism. The group he belonged to as a young man, The Rhymers,
held that the lyric was essentially oral; it was speech or song.
According to Yeats they attempted 'to rediscover in verse the syn-
tax of impulsive common life' (*A*, 304). In his Nobel Prize speech,
'The Bounty of Sweden', Yeats spoke as a dramatic poet, more
dramatist than lyricist, revealing, though, that he was most con-
fident of his lyrics. This was to be expected; his plays had been
totally unlike the commercial plays of the period, and were
attacked more crushingly than ever his lyric verse had been. But
Yeats's method of poetic composition, whether for lyric or drama,
was basically dramatic and histrionic, a process of soliloquy and
self-dramatisation, like the mouth in Samuel Beckett's *Not I*.

The true division in Yeats's imagination was not then between
lyric and dramatic qualities. It came rather from his deeply
religious impulses coupled to a searing intelligence, impatient and
haughty, 'The most fundamental of divisions is that between the
intellect, which can only do its work by saying continually "thou
fool", and the religious genius which makes all equal' (*A*, 467).
From this eternal conflict within him came all the contradictions
which peopled his poems and plays. His art was not so much a
celebration of disunity as a struggle during which opposing forces
were dramatised towards a precariously achieved, often ironic
balance.

This most self-conscious of artists knew the mechanism of his
own imagination very thoroughly, knew what made it thrive, and
knew what threatened it. Because he was very much a bundle of
contradictions, he feared a multiplicity of different activities, as
when in *Estrangement* he feared the loss of his lyrical faculty (*A*,
484–5), and because he felt so strongly his own destiny in Ireland's
national and political life, he recognised the dangers of fanatic
hatred to the imagination and to sexuality. Hence his dramatic
epigram satirising 'Those that hated "The Playboy of the Western
World," 1907'. Hatred dries up imagination and sexuality alike
to produce in time a 'eunuch-like tone and temper. For the last ten
or twenty years there has been a perpetual drying of the Irish mind
with the resultant dust-cloud' (*A*, 487). The destructive passion
could not possibly lead to that Unity of Being and Culture so

desirable to Yeats. Hatred, envy, jealousy, revenge could be stimulants to powerful actions and even literary works, but not indefinitely. Ultimately they starved the imagination. Despite the brief heroism of Easter, 1916, as Yeats grew older he felt increasingly a sense of the failure of his own image of Ireland and the growth of what he considered a futile imitation of English democracy and commercialism. He raged against the politics of his time; he hated the decline of his own body; he lusted after youth; he sought in culture and holiness of spirit a way of unlocking the imagination, 'For without culture or holiness, which are always the gift of a very few, a man may renounce wealth or any other external thing, but he cannot renounce hatred, envy, jealousy, revenge. Culture is the sanctity of the intellect' (*A*, 489).

The imagination is always a given. It has a basic structure, it seems, which orders sense impressions in largely similar ways in different people. It is constantly manipulating the data we feed into it, our differing experiences. Yeats, though, believed that he could alter the direction of his imagination by consciously choosing to alter its diet. His decisions were based on the scrutiny of his previous work. An example is when he points out how 'after *The Wanderings of Oisin*, I had simplified my style by filling my imagination with country stories' (*A*, 372). This leads us to a basic principle, then, of the Yeatsian imagination which he rather testily blurted out to a review editor in May 1933, 'my writings have to germinate out of each other' (*L*, 809). This was no mere chronological principle. The thoughts he has in his critical prose are linked to his current concerns as a poet, and his lyrics and plays, arising from a common method of composition, a common principle of passionate speech and an essentially dramatic imagination, are so closely linked that if his own personality refused him Yeats would use a dramatic persona to 'germinate' a lyric. As he told his lifelong friend Olivia Shakespeare in 1934:

> I have been working in bed in the morning, at first finishing that dance play, *The King of the Great Clock Tower*. There are four lyrics including the one I sent you though altogether re-written.
>
> I made up the play that I might write lyrics out of dramatic experience, all my personal experience having in some strange way come to an end. (*L*, 819)

So far in this account of Yeats's imagination, we have trusted a good deal in the teller, since Yeats was usually very clear in his understanding of his own genius and art; it is now time to trust the tale. If his imagination was essentially dramatic yet expressed itself in both lyrics and plays, it is worth examining his lyrics with that in mind.

3

More Self-Portraiture

THINKING back over his activities in the Rhymers' Club, Yeats
picked out for comment the biographical strain in the verse of
Dowson and Johnson. A letter to J. B. Yeats dated 16 February
1910 explains that 'The doctrine of the group, or rather the
majority of it, was that lyric poetry should be personal' (*L*, 548).
Yeats's own poetry never abandoned this position, but for him
'personal' implied the dramatisation of friends, ghosts, public
figures, and of his own selves. In criticising the verse of others, he
sought for dramatic qualities. His comment on John Davidson in
'The Tragic Generation' is apposite; Yeats judged that Davidson
'lacked pose and gesture, and now *no* verse of his clings to my
memory' (*A*, 318). According to Yeats, Dowson, another Rhymer,
'became a most extraordinary poet, one feels the pressure of his
life behind every line as if he were a character in a play of Shake-
speare's' (*L*, 548). In August 1913 he was again writing to his
father, distinguishing between the lyric of vision, with which
W. B. Yeats is inescapably linked in the minds of his readers, and
the lyric of self-portraiture, of natural and dramatic speech, the
kind of lyric Yeats read in the edition of Donne he received from
Professor H. J. C. Grierson. By vision Yeats meant 'the intense
realisation of a state of ecstatic emotion symbolised in a definite
imagined region' (*L*, 583). Under the influence of Donne and of
his own work for the stage, his energies and imagination also
turned increasingly to the dramatic lyric of self-portraiture which
strives for 'a speech so natural and dramatic that the hearer would
feel the presence of a man thinking and feeling' (*L*, 583). The
achievement of this dramatic quality became a lifelong concern.

Less than two years before he died, Yeats wrote 'An Intro-
duction for my Plays' (1937) in which he recalled:

Browning said that he could not write a successful play because interested not in character in action but in action in character. I had begun to get rid of everything that is not, whether in lyric or dramatic poetry, in some sense character in action; a pause in the midst of action perhaps, but action always its end and theme. (*E&I*, 530)

Historians of the lyric assert that it is difficult to define because so many different kinds of poem have accrued in the tradition, been bundled together and labelled lyrics. Our habit of calling the words to a piece of music 'the lyrics' suggests the musical origin of lyric poetry as song in the ancient world. By Renaissance times a lyric had come to mean any poem for a singer. The proliferation of printed poetry soon meant that lyrics were more often written to be read than set to music and sung. The lyric, though, tugs back towards its dramatic and theatrical origins in the songs, dances and rituals of worship. It is a relatively modern fallacy that 'lyric' and 'dramatic' are necessarily distinct, or opposing tendencies. Towards the end of the sixteenth century in Italy, the madrigal, especially in Monteverdi, became overtly dramatic; influenced by secular drama, it developed marked affinities with the *Commedia dell'Arte*.

It therefore seems best to acknowledge the close links between lyric and dramatic poetry, making the distinction, when necessary, depend upon context: the lyric poem establishes its own clearly circumscribed context in itself, and more rarely in a sequence, as in the case of some sonnets; speeches and songs in plays, however lyrical in form, feeling or performance, find their context, when their use is truly dramatic, not in themselves but in the structure, characterisation, themes or conflicts of the play in which they appear. A lyric which pre-exists the play which later uses it, if it is given the right context becomes dramatic. Lyrics are part of the poetry of performance, closely associated with an oral tradition linked with song and even dance. Thus Yeats's dramatic imagination could go far indeed to express its dramatic view of life in lyrical terms.

For Yeats the lyric, personal, expressive of aspirations, lingering on the strange and fantastic, was characteristic of the Celtic imagination. The lyric, with its moment of heightened intensity arising out of character and impulse, could sum up the poetic personality of the writer. The lyric poem of late Victorian times,

Yeats pointed out, needed but an audience of one, whereas a play needs a group audience. Nevertheless, Yeats stressed the primacy of speech, performance and rhythm for lyric poetry. Well aware of the different demands of the lyric, the long poem, and narrative in poetry, fiction and drama, he yet saw a common factor of speech in performance. He wanted a poetry written for the ear, spoken from a stage to an audience to the accompaniment of notes of music, and even imagined fiction performed in this way. Had not Dickens made monodrama from his novels? There is much modern fiction, particularly in Joyce and Virginia Woolf, which could find the right voice and perhaps the right notes. Yeats's imagination dwelt not on the silent reader, but on the performing bard and his audience: poetry was a social act. This is why he developed with Florence Farr the art of speaking to musical notes. The experiments, which met with some success as well as laughter according to contemporary newspaper reports, are described by Yeats in the essay 'Speaking to the Psaltery'. His lifelong effort to shift poetry away from what he called 'modern subjectivity' he explained in a letter to the artist Edmund Dulac in July 1937. Yeats's efforts took the form of 'insisting on construction and contemporary words and syntax. It was to force myself to this that I used to insist that all poems should be spoken (hence my plays) or sung' (*L*, 892). That he was occupied with the oral tradition of poetry to the end is clear from his collaboration with Dorothy Wellesley on the essay 'Music and Poetry' in *Broadsides* (Cuala, 1937), from the nature of his late poems and plays, and from the projected book on speech which death prevented him from writing. The reasoning and instinct Yeats followed in this matter of poetry for speech and song sprang from his desire to recover for it the imaginative unity he thought had been lost when 'speech and music fell apart at the Renaissance' (*E*, 258). Inspired by his actors and his art theatre, he sought to pull lyricism back towards its origins from the almost alchemical state it had reached in Mallarmé, where refined essences were 'separated one from another in little and intense poems' (*E&I*, 194). Mallarmé, we are often reminded, wanted the language of the tribe, but refined and refined into an idealised purity. Yeats was earthier, more accommodating, less fastidious:

> . . . we have looked for the centre of our art where the players of the time of Shakespeare and of Corneille found theirs—in

speech, whether it be the perfect mimicry of the conversation of two countrymen of the roads, or that idealised speech poets have imagined for what we think but do not say. Before men read, the ear and the tongue were subtle, and delighted one another with the little tunes that were in words; every word would have its own tune, though but one main note may have been marked enough for us to name it. They loved language, and all literature was then, whether in the mouth of minstrels, players, or singers, but the perfection of an art that everybody practised, a flower out of the stem of life. (*E*, 211–12)

If we accept what he tells us of his own method of composition, Yeats's poetry, it seems, certainly arose from his own speech rhythms and his inner voices, derived in turn from those of his family, his social class, his Ireland and, perhaps, literary and artistic conversation. There is a famous passage in *Autobiographies* in which Yeats describes his manner of composition. This description accords with that of others who heard him at work; it is an accurate account:

Every now and then, when something has stirred my imagination, I begin talking to myself. I speak in my own person and dramatise myself, very much as I have seen a mad old woman do upon the Dublin quays, and sometimes detect myself speaking and moving as if I were still young, or walking perhaps like an old man with fumbling steps. Occasionally, I write out what I have said in verse, and generally for no better reason than because I remember that I have written no verse for a long time. I do not think of my soliloquies as having different literary qualities. They stir my interest, by their appropriateness to the men I imagine myself to be, or by their accurate description of some emotional circumstance, more than by any aesthetic value. When I begin to write I have no object but to find for them some natural speech, rhythm and syntax, and to set it out in some pattern, so seeming old that it may seem all men's speech, and though the labour is very great, I seem to have used no faculty peculiar to myself, certainly no special gift. I print the poem and never hear about it again, until I find the book years after with a page dog-eared by some young man, or marked by some young girl with a violet, and when I have seen that, I am a little ashamed, as though somebody were to attribute to me a delicacy of feeling I should but do not possess. What came so easily at first, and amidst so much drama, and was written so laboriously at the last, cannot be counted among my possessions. (*A*, 532–3)

This is the poet 'plain' whom friends heard crooning and mumbling to himself as he composed. The influence of a father who had 'exalted dramatic poetry above all other kinds' (*A*, 66) is detectable in this method of writing practised by the youth who turned out plays in a style imitative of Spenser or Shelley, by the Rhymer of the nineties and by the sleeker Nobel prize-winner. Although Yeats's poetry can be divided up into 'periods', each with some new emphasis or manner, he never abandoned the idea that poetry was essentially a voice or voices, mouths articulating.

His poetry is full of dialogues between conflicting voices; narratives in which dialogue is embedded; ballads using dialogue; poems of prayer, blessing or curse; fragments in dramatic forms or choruses and lyrics taken from his own plays. The conventional dramatic monologue, which one would expect to abound in such a writer, is in fact rare—'An Irish Airman Foresees his Death' is the well-known example. Sometimes, and this has been well noted by other critics, the very placing of poems in juxtaposition to one another achieves not only continuity of thought, but dramatic effects of conflict and contrast, suspense and surprise. Of the 386 poems in the poetic canon, as reprinted in *The Variorum Edition of the Poems of W. B. Yeats* (1957) at least two-thirds are dramatic in one way or another beyond that basic sense of the poet as persona.

Of all the dramatic aspects of Yeats's poetry, perhaps the best known to the non-specialist reader is his public tone. He is supreme among the poets of our century for commanding attention in the manner of the bard. The man who wrote *The Tower* and *Easter 1916*, and addressed future generations of Irish poets in *Under Ben Bulben*, could very easily presume to offer *A Model for the Laureate*, and issue poems in the form of a prayer, a blessing or a curse. No wonder he should imagine himself after death as a bird, wonderfully crafted in gold, performing in eternity the very function of the Celtic 'Fili' or court bard as he sings to the lords and ladies 'Of what is past, or passing, or to come' (*V. Poems*, 408). Nor was the sense of mission and its public voice confined to

Yeats's mature verse. They were there from the beginning in that conflicting pair of pastoral monologues which are the twin heralds announcing *Crossways* (1889), 'The Song of the Happy Shepherd' and 'The Sad Shepherd'. Here Yeats faces the 'Grey Truth' of his own times, laments the passing of an Arcadian world, and speculates that the word might be the basis of reality: 'The wandering earth herself may be / Only a sudden flaming word' (*V. Poems*, 65). What follows is a public statement about the poetry Yeats will present. Such manifestoes in verse appear as guides to what he is doing throughout his career. 'To the Rose upon the Rood of Time' states the twin themes of *The Rose* volume, and, indeed, a good deal of his life's work: mystic knowledge and 'old Eire and the ancient ways'. The public and political voice appears again to close that same volume. 'To Ireland in the Coming Times' makes vivid a consciousness of Irish tradition in which poetic craftsmanship is in itself ineradicably political:

> Know that I would accounted be
> True brother of a company
> That sang, to sweeten Ireland's wrong,
> Ballad and story, rann and song;
> (*V. Poems*, 137)

From the early manifestoes through the curt, aphoristic renunciation of the early style in 'A Coat' and the elaborate, pivotal declaration of faith in imagination and spirit which is 'The Tower', to the last poetic testament of 'Under Ben Bulben', Yeats is acutely aware of what he is doing. In each volume poems build context for each other just as each volume relates to his other works. His lyrics strain for that larger context we associate with drama.

His poetry is at times self-consciously dramatic and theatrical in a very precise sense. In 'Parnell's Funeral' the public voice curtly offers stage directions, like a commentator setting the scene of a state funeral for his radio audience:

> Under the Great Comedian's tomb the crowd.
> A bundle of tempestuous cloud is blown
> About the sky . . .
> a brighter star shoots down;
> (*V. Poems*, 541)

By a dramatic shifting of the scene from historical into mythic times, Parnell is seen as a sacrifice, like the unfortunate child who enacts the death and resurrection of Apollo:

> A beautiful seated boy; a sacred bow;
> A woman, and an arrow on a string;
> A pierced boy, image of a star laid low.
> That woman, the Great Mother imaging,
> Cut out his heart.
>
> *(V. Poems*, 541)

The politician's funeral is made to seem a repeat performance of the mysterious scenario of an ancient and barbarous rite. And then the theatrical imagery becomes explicit in the magnificent rhetoric of the third stanza. Yeats's voice dramatises his bitterness, indignation and contempt:

> We lived like men that watch a painted stage.
> What matter for the scene, the scene once gone:
> It had not touched our lives. But popular rage,
> *Hysterica passio* dragged this quarry down.
>
> *(V. Poems*, 542)

The imagery of the ephemeral stage set (Yeats in 'The Fascination of What's Difficult' curses its use in the theatre) expresses the 'staginess', in its worst sense, the hypocrisy of Irish politics; popular feeling for previous Irish heroes seemed only a kind of play-acting, for Parnell was dragged down by the Irish themselves. The foreign English were this time not to blame. Then Yeats strikes the stage set and gives us ritual instead: the hunt for the victim, then the cannibal sacrifice:

> None shared our guilt; nor did we play a part
> Upon a painted stage when we devoured his heart.
>
> *(V. Poems*, 542)

What the poem dramatises so convincingly is the sense of collective guilt and, in the final stanza, individual responsibility, for here Yeats challenges those who hounded Parnell to make him their next victim: 'Come, fix upon me that accusing eye. / I thirst for accusation.' The public voice is now full of scorn and pride. The last stanza is like the speeches with which Yeats fought the mob from the stage of the Abbey Theatre when he defended Synge or

O'Casey. The monologue hurls out its own accusations. It leaves us with the image of the speaker torn apart by the mob, yet winning a moral victory:

> Leave nothing but the nothings that belong
> To this bare soul, let all men judge that can
> Whether it be an animal or a man.
> <div align="right">(<i>V. Poems</i>, 542)</div>

And the rhyme scores one more telling hit in the sly phrase 'that can', and this points up the contrast, too, between the mere animal and the man.

As we might expect of a poet whose imagination was dramatic, whose manner was histrionic, and who was also a playwright, theatrical imagery appears quite frequently throughout the poetry. Even exasperation with the administration and directing of the Abbey cannot rid his mind of theatre, and the poetry would be the poorer had we not 'The Proud Furies each with her torch on high', those circus animals, Malachi Stilt-Jack, all the drop-scenes which 'drop at once / Upon a hundred thousand stages', those tragic heroes and heroines who knew how to keep down *hysterica passio* and did not 'break up their lines to weep'. As Yeats explained in a letter to his friend Dorothy Wellesley:

> I have never 'produced' a play in verse without showing the actors that passion of the verse comes from the fact that the speakers are holding down violence or madness—'down Hysterica passio'. All depends on the completeness of the holding down, on the stirring of the beast underneath. (*DWL*, 86)

This is also, incidentally, a precise description of the effect of the poems in which we hear dramatised so many passionate voices.

The voices in Yeats's poems are mainly human ones, but there are also those supernatural mouthings, the sweet everlasting voices out of the legendary past, and breathless voices of spirits wrought into what seems the lyric of ideas:

> Locke sank into a swoon;
> The Garden died;
> God took the spinning-jenny
> Out of his side
> <div align="right">(<i>V. Poems</i>, 439)</div>

But the perfect little stanza is really fragmentary speech, words uttered in a trance. The second part of the poem supplies the speaker and the setting of the speech :

> Where got I that truth?
> Out of a medium's mouth,
> Out of nothing it came,
> Out of the forest loam,
> Out of dark night where lay
> The crowns of Nineveh.
>
> (*V. Poems*, 439)

Fragments of speech from friends and relatives become lines in his poems, as in 'Beautiful Lofty Things'.

In many poems, particularly the early ones, Yeats is content to use dialogue as a narrative method to dramatise story through speech. The tendency is clear in shorter narratives which followed 'The Wanderings of Oisin', such poems as 'The Grey Rock' and 'The Two Kings'. The method is brilliantly achieved in that terse poem which reads like the scenario for a Yeats play in five scenes, 'Cuchulain's Fight with the Sea' (1892). It demands performance using a narrator and six other voices. The exposition, setting and introduction of the passionate Emer are all achieved within the first eight lines. The swineherd's fear of Emer and of her antici-pated reaction to the knowledge of Cuchulain's adultery is not described but enacted directly through Emer's question :

> 'But if your master comes home triumphing
> Why must you blench and shake from foot to crown?'
>
> (*V. Poems*, 106)

The beauty of Cuchulain's young mistress, Eithne Inguba, Yeats can now evoke in all its mystery with one line of pure lyrical beauty which is yet a line of dialogue within the dramatic situation, an answer to Emer's question : 'With him is one sweet-throated like a bird' (*V. Poems*, 106). Emer ends the first 'scene' by punch-ing the unfortunate messenger for his pains. The second 'scene' is the brief dialogue between Emer and her son whom she dispatches to kill his father under *geasa* or vow never to reveal his name save at the moment of death. The break between lines 38 and 39 of the poem is enough to accomplish the scene change to the Red Branch camp where minstrels praise Cuchulain, the Irish Achilles. The

change to 'scene' four is similarly swift and achieved again
by sudden cross-cutting. The climax of the poem is the climax
of this 'scene', and it is achieved entirely through terse, dramatic
dialogue :

> 'Speak before your breath is done.'
> 'Cuchulain I, mighty Cuchulain's son.'
> 'I put you from your pain. I can no more.'
>   (*V. Poems*, 110)

Down hysterica passio. The eyes are dry, the passion is held down.
The emotional impact is thereby the stronger, the eventual surge
of tragic feeling all the greater in the final 'scene', where lyricism
and drama enforce each other in the description of the druid spell
and the grief which make Cuchulain mad :

> Then Conchubar sent that sweet-throated maid.
> And she, to win him, his grey hair caressed;
> In vain her arms, in vain her soft white breast.
> Then Conchubar, the subtlest of all men,
> Ranking his Druids round him ten by ten,
> Spake thus : 'Cuchulain will dwell there and brood
> For three days more in dreadful quietude,
> And then arise, and raving slay us all.
> Chaunt in his ear delusions magical,
> That he may fight the horses of the sea.'
>   Cuchulain stirred,
> Stared on the horses of the sea, and heard
> The cars of battle and his own name cried;
> And fought with the invulnerable tide.
>   (*V. Poems*, 110–11)

Yeats confessed in his introduction to the Oxford anthology
that his own early verse suffered from 'a facile charm, a too soft
simplicity'.[1] When he managed to avoid these defects, it was more
often than not by means of dramatic elements in the poetry, either
there originally as in 'Cuchulain's Fight with Sea' or imposed by
the later revisions of the seasoned playwright. The revision of 'A
Cradle Song' is a good example. The emendations reveal a voca-
bulary of action, solidity, and harshness. The tenderness of feeling
for the baby is increased, not diminished by the greater hardness
and definition in the poem. Poetry was for Yeats made out of the

quarrel with oneself. In the great poems which appear in *The Wild Swans at Coole* (1919) and later volumes, ideas and arguments and philosophy are often, as in Plato, developed through dialogues of conflicting voices: Shepherd and Goatherd, Hic and Ille, Hunchback and Saint, Yeats and Mrs Yeats cast as Solomon and Sheba, Crazy Jane and the Bishop, Self and Soul, Man and Echo, and those phantom characters who stalk through Yeats's prose and poetry, Robartes and Aherne.

Just as Yeats invented a new kind of lyrical one-act play in *Four Plays for Dancers* (1921), he invented a new kind of poem which dramatised his attitudes by means of conflict, dialogue or confrontation with either the dead, or contemporaries or invented personae, evoked as if by magus or medium to take their places with mythic stature in a shadow-play of ideas. I refer to these poems as 'dramatic phantasmagoria' to distinguish them from more conventional lyrics. In these poems, thought is concrete, passionate, dramatic. John Donne and the metaphysicals are in the background; but the flavour is peculiarly Yeatsian. Yeats used the word 'phantasmagoria' extremely carefully to describe the volatile, flitting shapes of symbolic phantoms making a shadow play in the imagination, 'figures in a galanty show not too strained or too extravagant to speak their very thought' (*E*, 55). The phenomena of the medium's darkened rooms, 'that phantasmagoria of which I had learnt something in London', or the contents of George Russell's visions, which Yeats thought to be not 'real' but symbolic, perhaps 'so much a part of his subconscious life that they would have vanished had he submitted them to question' (*A*, 243) could both come under this label, as could the imaginary conversations of Yeats's fellow Rhymer, Lionel Johnson. Yeats, amazed to discover that Johnson's conversations with the great and famous were all invented, though repeated in detail as if true, concluded that 'they were the phantasmagoria through which his philosophy of life found its expression' (*A*, 306), using again the label he might well have discovered in his admired Landor's *Imaginary Conversations*. According to Yeats, it is a first principle for the reading of his work that we realise 'A poet writes always of his personal life, in his finest work out of its tragedy, whatever it be, remorse, lost love, or mere loneliness; he never speaks directly as to someone at the breakfast table, there is always a phantasmagoria' (*E&I*, 509). Yeats's phantasmagoria is filled with symbolic phantoms, whether out of mythology, history or his own life and times, which people his imagination, enacting his ideas, emotions and deepest concerns. Yet in previous poetry there is nothing quite like the dramatic phantasmagoria of Yeats's maturity. In 'News for the Delphic Oracle' it offers a sort of erotic masque or series of Neo-platonic *tableaux vivants*. The images projected into the mind's eye to produce these vivid visual effects which are a constant feature of the phantasmagoria derive in this poem from paintings of the nymphs, satyrs and dolphins (school of Raphael in the Papal Apartments at Castel S Angelo) and Poussin's 'The Marriage of Peleus and Thetis' in Ireland's National Gallery.[2] The method is also used in one of Yeats's best poems, 'The Municipal Gallery Revisited'. Here picture after picture is evoked until the phantasmagoria of 'permanent or impermanent images' crowding the mind's eye dramatises the poet's private and public life so that we may 'Ireland's history in their lineaments trace'.

Sometimes the phantasmagoria can take a purer lyric form. This is the case in the Crazy Jane poems of 'Words for Music Perhaps' and the sequence 'A Woman Young and Old'; the personae evoked, the dramatic situations implied, and the sequence of images built up by the succession of lyrics now construct the dramatic phantasmagoria.

Since Wordsworth, it has become increasingly difficult for a poet to present a system of ideas in verse. It is now fashionable to assign that task to the treatise and the essay in prose. Yeats, however, managed to pack a good deal of his system into poetry by means of the dramatic phantasmagoria in his volume *The Tower*. He does it in 'The Tower' itself, and 'Meditations in Time of Civil War'. But here the phantasmagoria include a good deal of reportage.

In fact, the versified philosophy is most starkly presented in another poem where the phantasmagoria has a decidedly dramatic groundplan. 'The Phases of the Moon' (1918) is a cunningly wrought little comedy of ideas. The first seven lines are stage directions. The poet as narrator sets the scene in italicised blank verse reminiscent of the similar speeches assigned to Musicians in the plays for dancers. The locus is the bridge at the foot of Yeats's tower.

The dialogue which follows rapidly establishes a jocular complicity between Yeats's two characters Robartes and Aherne. They mock the poet for his toiling after mysterious wisdom. Aherne suggests a practical joke: Robartes should tell Yeats enough of this mysterious wisdom to make the poet realise that a lifetime's search will reveal next to nothing, and then they should go on their way. But Robartes is in no mood for this joke at first; he still smarts from the fact that Yeats had killed him off in an early story. Aherne, however, does persuade Robartes to sing a brief description of the phases of the moon, each of which symbolises a different soul-state into which we may be born in successive lives, except for phases one and fifteen, the dark and full of the moon, at which only supernatural life is possible. This account is interrupted once by the narrator who describes how Aherne laughs to think of Yeats labouring at his books within the tower. When the system which is the central idea of Yeats's *A Vision* has been described, Aherne projects another little drama within the drama:

> I'd play a part;
> He would never know me after all these years
> But take me for some drunken countryman;
> I'd stand and mutter there until he caught
> 'Hunchback and Saint and Fool,' and that they came
> Under the last three crescents of the moon
> And then I'd stagger out. He'd crack his wits
> Day after day, yet never find the meaning.
>
> (*V. Poems*, 377)

The phantasmagoria is then brought swiftly to an end by four lines of narration. It is worth looking closer at the use of the narrator. The brief interruption in the middle of the poem reminded us of the narrator's presence. Perhaps he was eavesdropping, hurriedly scribbling down the wisdom revealed by Robartes. The last four lines reinforce that impression:

> And then he laughed to think that what seemed hard
> Should be so simple—a bat rose from the hazels
> And circled round him with its squeaky cry,
> The light in the tower window was put out.
>
> (*V. Poems*, 377)

The 'he' referred to is Aherne, but it could also be Yeats himself, as if he had heard Robartes' song and noted it all down. Thus when the light goes out in the tower, we may imagine Yeats going to sleep after a hard evening of study and writing; or having his own laugh at his characters' expense, and putting out his light as soon as he has jotted down what he heard pass from Robartes. It is also the stage light blacking out at the end of this phantasmagoria, bringing its dramatic structure to a fitting conclusion. And finally, it is the signal that mysterious wisdom has been won or lost at last, for it is, after all, Yeats himself who has put into Robartes' mouth the doctrine of the phases of the moon. The ironic possibilities are rich enough to provide not only a metaphor by which to read the world and Yeats's own later works, but also the possibility that this 'wisdom' is merely the attitudinising of two Yeatsian characters. In that case, the comedy of ideas puts us, the audience, in the place of seekers after wisdom on whom Yeats has played an Ahernian jest! Belief and scepticism are held in exquisite tension. The poem has a comic ingenuity which reminds one of Flann O'Brien's *At Swim-Two-Birds*. It also demonstrates an amazing capacity to dramatise the obscure and unfamiliar. Hear how Yeats fleshes out, embodies in an epic scene, the hero's phase:

> Eleven pass, and then,
> Athene takes Achilles by the hair,
> Hector is in the dust, Nietzsche is born,
> Because the hero's crescent is the twelfth.
> (*V. Poems*, 374)

and with a graphic image suddenly illuminates the vision of possible escape from the cycle of the generations:

> Hunchback and Saint and Fool are the last crescents.
> The burning bow that once could shoot an arrow
> Out of the up and down, the wagon-wheel
> Of beauty's cruelty and wisdom's chatter—
> Out of that raving tide—is drawn betwixt
> Deformity of body and of mind.
> (*V. Poems*, 377)

This central phantasmagoria expounds in gently humorous terms images and concepts Yeats will use again and again.

Two other images, crucial for the reading of Yeats, are the holy city of Byzantium and the purgatorial dreaming-back of the souls after death. He put these concepts into one of his most exciting lyrics, 'Byzantium'. But so inherently dramatic was Yeats's imagination, and so theatrical his talent, that even this lyric has its debt to Yeats the playwright. 'Byzantium', in fact, takes its structure from the Yeatsian dance-play.

Yeats's dance-plays, first collected in *Four Plays for Dancers* (1921), have a structural pattern which he varied in later plays and which can be concisely described. The dance-play usually opens with the unfolding and folding of an emblematic cloth in a ceremonial fashion by musicians. The ceremony is repeated at the end of the play. These cloth ceremonies are accompanied by songs which are linked to the action of the play by theme and imagery. A musician then tells us of the setting for the action and introduces characters. There is usually a wayfarer or quester, a ghost or supernatural being, or a character whose status as human or supernatural is somewhat ambiguous, as in the case of the Guardian of the Well in *At the Hawk's Well*. There is a persistent strain of bird imagery (the hawk in the play just mentioned, the white bird of *The Only Jealousy of Emer*, the owl and cocks of *The Dreaming of the Bones*, the heron of *Calvary*), there is sometimes a fire ritual, and the climax of the action is always expressed through dance. The result is an elegant, subtle and theatrically intriguing form of one-act drama best described as the Yeatsian dance-play, since it is not an imitation of Japanese Noh drama, though it obviously borrows some of the conventions.

By 1929 to 1930, when Yeats was working on 'Byzantium', he had thoroughly mastered and assimilated this dramatic structure. He had made an exciting modification of it in *The Resurrection* (1927) and carefully submerged it beneath the realistic surface of *The Words Upon the Window-Pane* (1930). Clearly, it was firmly fixed in his artistic imagination. In 'Byzantium' Yeats used elements of his dance-play structure to strengthen the dramatic impact of the lyric. The cloth and its songs, of course, were dropped, for that framework was devised specifically for the stage. Thus the lyric begins with the scene-setting lines in stanza one. The fading resonance of singer and gong recalls the historical and imaginary city, but also the music of the Yeatsian dance-play. The first person narrator of the poem has evoked in his 'eye of the mind' the images of Byzantium and the floating 'image, man or shade' rather as the musicians evoke the world of the quester in the dance-plays. The poet-quester in 'Byzantium' is, like the hero of a Yeats play, ready to follow the labyrinthine path of the spirit and, again like such a hero, is uncertain, perhaps heading for defeat:

> For Hades' bobbin bound in mummy-cloth
> May unwind the winding path:

The uncertainty stressed by that strategically placed 'May' is the moment of decision, of character defined by crisis, which is always at the core of the Yeatsian dance-play. The hero's decision finds its equivalent in the poem where that determination to face vision, the non-rational, the supernatural, surges into the utterance of the first 'I' used in the poem, after the impersonal scene-setting of the opening stanza:

> I hail the superhuman;
> I call it death-in-life and life-in-death.
> (*V. Poems*, 497)

The quester has responded like a hero and a poet; he has faced the challenge, and found words to name it. All that remains to fulfil the dance-play structure is bird imagery, fire ritual and climactic dance: how beautifully crafted is the allusive imagery of stanza three, referring back to 'Sailing to Byzantium' as well as to its more recondite sources; and how dramatic is its presentation once more of conflicting choice—to crow or to scorn. The fire ritual is that of purgatory itself, where supernatural flames are the medium in which 'blood-begotten spirits' at the climax of the poem, as in the climax of a dance-play, strive for simplicity and purgation in their turbulent dance. In the last stanza of the poem, the dance image multiplies; it is as if a tumultuous throng of dancers in a sort of divine Yeats play move before us over 'Marbles of the dancing floor . . .' (*V. Poems*, 498).

'Byzantium' is a subtle, allusive, intricate lyric; it also excites us with its dramatic energy, and that spectacular dance of ghosts. It could only have been written by a poet who was also a masterly dramatist.

Yeats's dramatic imagination demanded strength of syntax, characterisation or embodiment, and vigorous enactment of meaning to achieve its true expression. It is because of this that on the whole in Yeats's poetry, at least, things do *not* fall apart, and mere anarchy is *not* loosed upon his readers. At the end of his life,

Yeats wrote to a friend that man could not know truth, but he could embody it. Men's lives are the embodiment of their truth. And Yeats's imagination, being dramatic, could not help but make his verse embody his own and others' lives.

4

Drama as Personal as Lyric

THE Abbey Theatre's rejection in 1928 of Sean O'Casey's play *The Silver Tassie* led to hard-hitting letters and a good deal of controversy. After a few years the quarrel was healed, and looking back over the incident, O'Casey remarked to David Krause:

> After the rejection there were people in Dublin who did feel bitter towards Yeats—they always had, mainly because they were jealous and afraid of him—and they tried to get me to join them and go against him. Well, I told them what they could do with their dirty game, they could stuff it where the monkey put the nut. Yeats was wrong about my play, but he made the Abbey a great theatre, he and Lady Gregory. After he died it went downhill. There was no one left to fight for it and protect it from the political and clerical yahoos who torment the artist in Ireland. They're the fellas I feel bitter about. . . .
>
> His poems are more dramatic than his plays, and his plays are really poems.[1]

There is no doubt about the dramatic force of Yeats's poetry, but O'Casey was wrong about the plays. The vast majority of them go beyond dramatic poetry and exist as intense one-act poetic dramas. If the poems are highly dramatic, the plays are highly lyrical; it is as if the principle of conflict in Yeats urged his dramatic imagination to find its mask in lyricism, while all the time gazing through religious eyes, alive with myth and ritual.

To describe the lyric elements in Yeats's plays is a straightforward task. He achieved the lyric qualities through both traditional and original songs, dances and music, and verse passages of varying lyrical intensity in both dialogue and monologue. For Yeats, lyric drama meant these musical elements together with the revelation of a character's spiritual life at a moment of poetic intensity. This could be achieved relatively quickly, and so the lyric play, like the lyric poem, had to be short, as short as was compatible with establishing character and situation enough to make the crisis significant and impressive, and with allowing Yeats to pattern his events. The dramatist in him felt the necessity for this; as he remarks in *The Trembling of the Veil,* 'I must not only describe events but those patterns into which they fall' (*A,* 330). From this point of view, the uninterrupted one-act form was ideal. This meant, of course, the rejection of the five-act drama of his Elizabethan predecessors, and fortunately that of their nineteenth-century imitators. Equally, it meant the rejection of the three-acters favoured by modern realistic dramatists. Yeats instead sought a set of conventions appropriate for modern verse drama. Quite rightly, he saw that modern manners and environments were largely inimical to poetry. T. S. Eliot's very pallid verse plays provide evidence enough of that. Poetry was always speech for Yeats, but it was an idealised, sometimes outlandish speech uttering a barbarous truth. It needed fitting conventions from the past, therefore, and from a non-realistic imagination. Yeats did the ruthlessly logical and courageous thing: he attacked the commercial and the realistic avant-garde theatres of his day. The ideal form for his experiments in a new lyric verse drama was the one-acter, not for purely formal reasons either; there were various practical considerations such as its relatively low production cost and suitability for the playwright learning his craft among actors whose talents were in general very limited, at least until the Abbey company came into its own and won international recognition.

Lady Gregory tells us in *Our Irish Theatre*[2] that Yeats in 1897 revealed that he had always longed for an Irish theatre. He was practical enough to realise that it would need a good deal of money, besides an audience, actors and writers; he was realist enough to quell certain excesses of nationalism in the London branch of the Irish National Literary Society:

> . . . on one of my visits to London I had some difficulty in preventing our council there accepting a circular that began with these words: 'Ireland, despite the dramatic genius of our people, has had no dramatists like Shakespeare, but a sub-committee of the Irish Literary Society has decided that the time has come.' (*MS.* 58)

Frank O'Connor gives a clear picture of the way Yeats's imagination was stirred by drama when he reminds us that around the beginning of our century 'anyone who became friendly with Yeats was liable to break out in one-act plays.'[3] Yeats's advice to the pseudonymous Michael Field, in a letter arguing against submission of a play, *Deirdre*, to the Irish players on the grounds that its staging requirements were too big for them, is very revealing:

> Did you ever try your hand in a one act play? They are far easier to construct than a long play. I have myself as you know been writing one act plays in prose lately. I have done this chiefly as a discipline, because logic (and stage success is entirely a matter of logic) works itself out most obviously and simply in a short action with no change of scene. If anything goes wrong one discovers it at once and either puts it right or starts on a new theme, and no bones are broken. But I suppose every playwright finds out the methods that suit him best. (*L*, 408)

Yeats was very practical when he was writing or working on committees. He had more confidence in himself, a precious commodity for any writer, when he was working on a one-acter and so confined his major effort as a dramatist to that form. At about this time, the summer of 1903, Yeats was so enthusiastic about his work as a playwright that his one wish for his own work concerned drama rather than the other genres in which he wrote. In a letter to John Quinn he mused that 'if Finvara . . . were to come into the room with all his hosts of the Sidhe behind him and offer me some gift, I know right well the gift I should ask. I would say "Let my plays be acted, sometimes by professional actors if you will, but certainly a great many times by Irish societies in Ireland and throughout the world . . ."' (*L*, 406). No doubt he was angling for an American tour to boost the fame and fortune of the company, but Yeats was also clearly aware of the power to capture the national imagination which belongs to drama as a medium.

Until recently the main critical question about Yeats the playwright was quite simply, 'Are Yeats's plays dramatic?' Most of the critics, like O'Casey, thought not. T. S. Eliot, though, praised Yeats's *Purgatory*,[4] and directed our attention to the importance of Yeats as a verse dramatist, if only for that one play. The verse drama of *entre deux guerres* soon expired, however, after those somewhat stagey post-war death throes arranged by Mr Christopher Fry. Peter Ure then encouraged readers to take Yeats seriously, though not uncritically, as a dramatist, in what remains the best book so far on the plays, *Yeats the Playwright* (1963). After that, several books on the topic appeared;[5] most were very selective, using the plays for discussion of some particular Yeatsian themes, or confining attention to a certain aspect of his art; most were in some sense apologetic in tone, withholding full critical recognition from the masterpieces in Yeats's repertoire; all were literary rather than dramatic criticism. In 1974 Reg Skene's *The Cuchulain Cycle of W. B. Yeats*, however, though still selective, refused to patronise Yeats as playwright, seeking instead to give him the true dramatic criticism the plays deserve, based on both textual analysis and performance factors, rather than merely the first of these two. The same cycle of plays had been performed at the Lyric Theatre, Belfast, in 1968, and received a splendid review from Ronald Bryden in *The Observer Review* (10 November 1968), which recommended that the English National Theatre include them in its repertoire. Robert O'Driscoll and Lorna Reynolds in *Yeats and the Theatre* (1975) claimed Yeats fully as a dramatist and man of the theatre, while more recently James W. Flannery's *W. B. Yeats and the Idea of a Theatre* (1976) gives the most detailed account in print of the Abbey Theatre and Yeats's place in its development, and Liam Miller's *The Noble Drama of W. B. Yeats* (1977) is a well illustrated account of the theatre history of Yeatsian drama. Now that dramatic theory and criticism, catching up with the practice of many modern dramatists, has to take account of conventions, structures and dramatic situations alien and opposed to those of stage realism, it is at last possible to criticise Yeats's plays according to broader definitions of drama and theatre than those used previously by many critics in our century.

The basic question for the criticism of Yeats's plays is now, 'In what context are they best examined?' The answer is quite plainly—the context which has hitherto been ignored: that of the one-act play. An adequate history of this form has not yet been written. One reason for this is probably that the genre has been in certain periods a poor relative of 'legitimate theatre' and is rarely a commercial prospect. Yet it has also achieved stardom, and Yeats, of course, was not the only writer of genius to use the form.

What he did was to invent the modern Irish tradition of the one-act play; he sustained it by constant experiment in his own work; he nurtured it by encouraging his fellow-writers to write one-act plays; he exalted it by giving the one-act theatre the best dramatic verse to be written since the seventeenth century. This last cannot be matched even by the modern French dramatists, whose contributions to the one-acter have been enormous. It is an elementary fact of theatre history that much of the new drama and experimentation at the turn of the last century emerged from small art theatres working with amateur or semi-amateur players on very limited budgets. One corollary of this was the urgent need for new plays, plays which could be written fairly quickly and produced very cheaply. The one-act play thus became something of a necessity, and therefore the mother of invention. Its single, major situation, its unity of effect, its necessarily limited cast list, made it ideal for those little ensembles, often boasting one or two actors of vision and energy, which were bent on replacing the elaborate stage effect of the commercial theatres with simplicity and intensity. In France this ferment of revolution had largely spent itself by the twenties. Sacha Guitry in *Candide* (Janvier 1925) was already nostalgic for that great period of the one-acter in the Paris of Antoine. Yeats inhabited that Paris, and so did Synge. The policies of the Irish Literary Theatre and the Abbey Theatre were partly derived from this avant-garde art theatre movement. Of some thirty plays by Yeats (not counting his version of Sophocles) as many as twenty-seven are one-acters.

Yeats used the short play to make various experiments in dramatic form crucial to his art in such works as *The Shadowy Waters, The Land of Heart's Desire, At the Hawk's Well, The Player Queen* and *The Resurrection*. He explored the life and death of the hero in his cycle of plays about the Celtic warrior-god Cuchulain. The theme of the quest for the absolute he dramatised in *The Shadowy Waters* and *At the Hawk's Well*. Related to this concern is the religious theme in *The Countess Cathleen, The Hour-Glass, Calvary, The Cat and the Moon, The Resurrection,* and *The Herne's Egg*. He widened his scope yet further with his passionate treatment of politics in *Cathleen ni Houlihan, The Dreaming of the Bones,* and *The Death of Cuchulain*. His thematic range is greater yet: he gave us masterly treatments of love in *Deirdre, The Only Jealousy of Emer, A Full Moon in March, The*

Words Upon the Window-Pane and *Purgatory*. Such is their richness and suggestiveness that they can, of course, be discussed under several headings. *Purgatory*, for instance, explores the consequences of an ill-fated love-match, but it is also an exploration of the soul's relationship to necessity and free-will, besides being a grim political statement about Ireland. Yet the central action of the play is the murder of a youth by his own father. All this Yeats could cram into a short one-act play. There is an analogy for this rich use of the miniature in Yeats's poetry. It is the sonnet 'Leda and the Swan'. We can trace the development of the after-piece and curtain-raiser towards the serious one-acter through Yeats's career: for instance, we may analyse the use of the form in its nineteenth-century guise of curtain-raiser in *The Land of Heart's Desire*, and then trace the political themes in *Cathleen ni Houlihan*, an after-piece, and in *The Dreaming of the Bones* and *The Death of Cuchulain*, a group of plays which conveniently reveals the fertility of Yeats's one-act technique.

The Land of Heart's Desire, written for Florence Farr so that her niece Dorothy Paget, a girl of eight or nine, could make her stage debut, was first performed at the Avenue Theatre on 29 March 1894, as a curtain-raiser first to John Todhunter's *A Comedy of Sighs* and then, on 21 April, to Shaw's *Arms and the Man*. As a curtain-raiser, it undermines the attitudes of its Shavian companion piece. This is its first, if accidental, departure from orthodoxy. Shaw's play undermines the romantic notions of military heroism in its young heroine in favour of reality, whereas Yeats's play undermines reality itself, his young heroine's ties with the reality of hearth, marriage and the Roman Church. Its rebellious action, which is the seduction of the Bruin household by a powerful supernatural force, the Sidhe, in the form of a beautiful child, and the subsequent failure of the priest to drive out or exorcise the demon, is structured, however, in a very orthodox way. Just as Yeats believed in strength of syntax for poetry, he aimed for strength of structure in drama. The play's *exposition*[6] is swiftly accomplished in an introduction devoted to shrewish complaints from Bridget Bruin, the mother-in-law dissatisfied with her son Shawn's lazy wife, Mary, who neglects household chores to read a hand-made book about supernatural lore written down by Shawn's grandfather. The young bride is at the centre of conventional family squabbles (the mother-in-law syndrome) but is also in conflict with orthodox religion in the form of kindly, comfortable Father Hart. The *attack*[1]—that period which culminates in the first major issue of a play, establishing the facts necessary to make effective the remaining action—is completed when Mary dutifully first puts down her story of Princess Edain who, in a trance, went to the land of the Sidhe, and then hangs a sprig of the sacred mountain ash at the door. The protective charm is immediately stolen by a strangely dressed girl who emerges from and vanishes into the wood. Mary's first magical action is immediately balanced by the first magical intrusion from outside the world of hearth, home and church. The *conflict* thus set up is swiftly *developed* and *complicated* by the intrusion of the faery child and her messengers who appear to Mary as a weird old woman to whom she gives milk, and a queer old man to whom she takes fire. It is, though, Maurteen, the father-in-law, who brings the faery child into the house. Ironically, he is motivated by Christian charity and a desire to establish a mood of happiness in the quarrelsome household. But his action also reminds us that it was his father who had thought it worthwhile to write down the heathen Celtic stories in the hand-made book. And this is the *turning point* of the play. In a few swift pages of dialogue, the child charms them all, discards Christian bread and wine for pagan milk and honey, shrieks with horror at the tortured Christ on the cross, replaces the crucifix with song and dance, and forces the play to its *crisis*, where the enchantment is revealed in sharp focus : Shawn cannot move to protect Mary, his wife; the child's kiss puts Mary into a trance; Father Hart's exorcism fails; and Mary Bruin dies—possessed by the magical Sidhe. This *climax resolves* the action with the interest of the audience at its peak. The ending comes swiftly with just three choric lines from Bridget to her son. Curtain. The structural pattern is orthodox. But the action is the call to a magical revolution. Father Hart's sententious lines, beginning 'Thus do the spirits of evil snatch their prey / Almost out of the very hand of God;' were spoken as a kind of epilogue in front of the curtain in the Abbey Theatre. His horror at the growth of evil and the decay of Christianity is strikingly articulated in the gaunt image, 'And men and women leave old paths, for pride / Comes knocking with thin knuckles on the heart' (*V. Plays*, 210). This picks up and completes the startling stage business which earlier in the play heralded the supernatural, that sudden knocking on the door by the ghostly child.

The Land of Heart's Desire has been read as a charming little piece of Celtic twilight, essentially pretty and slight. But the swelling hymn to Celtic heathendom which mockingly soars above Father Hart's last words is uncompromising. The finale rings with the triumph of the pagan, a triumph asserted not only in words but by the powerful theatrical means of a chorus of many voices, the moving bodies of dancers and the visual symbol of the white bird, suggesting Mary's soul flying with the Sidhe. In her own way, Mary is one of those wayward late nineteenth-century women who rebelled, like Ibsen's Nora, and Hedda, against the settled life of marriage. Like Stephen Daedalus she flies by the nets of religion and family. Like Little Miles, in James's *The Turn of the Screw*, she finds release through death from a battle which rages between 'good' and 'evil'. Mary is very much of her age, although Yeats set the play 'at a remote time' (*V.Plays*, 180). The play is also experimental in daring to use the curtain-raiser as a vehicle for peasant or folk verse drama, and then making that verse highly metrical in places, to render the aura of the magical. The play demands actors who can speak verse with style, and as much conviction as they would usually bring to realistic dialogue. It demands the still, statuesque acting for which the early Abbey company became famous, that stillness setting off perfectly the dances of the limber elf and the host of the Sidhe. The play begins with a realistic domestic situation very much in tune with the commercial theatre of the day, yet rapidly undermines it not only with the remote peasant setting, but also with the intrusions of the irrational. In the scene where Mary is tempted by the Sidhe and succumbs, Yeats anticipates his even more gripping treatment of the same situation in *The Only Jealousy of Emer*, where Cuchulain's spirit is tempted by the goddess Fand to live with her in the country-under-wave. He also echoes it later in the political temptations of *Cathleen ni Houlihan* and *The Dreaming of the Bones*. The simple piece of stage business in which the ghostly arm comes around the doorpost and knocks and beckons in the silvery light from the forest must deliver a theatrical shock. It must have no hint of humour. It brings mystery and fear, while it promises delight and escape. It is one of the many such symbolic pieces of stage business which Yeats used to embody irrational, supernatural powers invading the lives of human beings. *The Land of Heart's Desire* gains strength from its orthodox structure, but it performs an experiment which rejects the world and the conventions of realistic plays in the commercial theatres of its day.

The restless world of longing symbolised by the Sidhe represents Mary Bruin's private hopes and dreams. But in *Cathleen ni Houlihan* (1902), it is the world of marriage and peasant reality which embodies these private hopes. The sterner reality of nation-alist politics, represented by the poor old woman, Cathleen ni Houlihan, is now the irrational force which knocks on the door and beckons, demanding even the sacrifice of one's life. *Cathleen ni Houlihan* is *The Land of Heart's Desire* rewritten in terms of Irish politics. The sound of the mob's cheering at the opening of the play is set against the sight of Michael Gillane's grand wed-ding clothes. This juxtaposition establishes the prime conflict of forces in the play, and the noise of the mob thus serves a purpose similar to that of the supernatural songs in the previous play. The cheering for the French troops is given a context again by the use of song. The songs help to create once more the right atmosphere for a supernatural presence, the old woman who is the Shan van Vocht, or spirit of Ireland. The Yeatsian version of the Gaelic folk song, 'Donnchadh Bán', sometimes attributed to blind Raftery, is profoundly patriotic and moving. It is therefore also a clear cry of the political heart:

> I will go cry with the woman,
> For yellow-haired Donough is dead,
> With a hempen rope for a neckcloth,
> And a white cloth on his head,
> <div align="center">(<i>V. Plays</i>, 223)</div>

It is brilliantly placed in the play, amid a series of questions which receive symbolic answers that unfold the situation of Ireland as an occupied plantation, held by force of arms. The question and answer formula is a political catechism which seems a reversal of the religious one, for it is the answerer, the old woman, herself, who teaches her stern laws:

> *Peter*: What is it you would be asking for?
> *Old Woman*: If any one would give me help he must give me himself, he must give me all.
> <div align="center">(<i>V. Plays</i>, 226)</div>

Her political rhetoric is uncompromising. It increases in fervour and transcends itself again in song. Thus the dialect prose of the play is given by the 'catechism' section a greater formality which allows it to carry and convey infinite sadness, weary indignation and cold political realism as well as the patriotic fervour of the play's development and complication:

> *Old Woman*: It is a hard service they take that help me. Many that are red-cheeked now will be pale-cheeked; many that have been free to walk the hills and the bogs and the rushes will be sent to walk hard streets in far countries; many a good plan will be broken; many that have gathered money will not stay to spend it; many a child will be born and there will be no father at its christening to give it a name. They that have red cheeks will have pale cheeks for my sake, and for all that, they will think they are well paid.
>
> *(She goes out; her voice is heard outside singing.)*
> They shall be remembered for ever,
> They shall be alive for ever,
> They shall be speaking for ever,
> The people shall hear them for ever.
>
> *Bridget (to Peter)*: Look at him, Peter; he has the look of a man that has got the touch. *(Raising her voice.)*
>
> (*V. Plays*, 229)

The song marks the transition from an extremely compressed development to an extraordinarily swift crisis in which Michael takes the decision to break away from Delia, his intended, and rushes out to join the French.

The most famous of Irish curtain lines brings all the passion of patriotism to a bright focus after a play lasting only twenty minutes: 10:15 p.m. to 10:35 p.m., according to the Abbey promptbook.[8] If *The Land of Heart's Desire* had called for a magical revolution in an experimental curtain-raiser, *Cathleen ni Houlihan* called for a nationalist revolution in a perfect afterpiece. The structure is faultless, and so is the rhetoric. No Irish crowd, emerging from St Teresa's Hall in Dublin on 2 April 1902, or from a performance on any subsequent occasion before the setting up of the Irish Free State, could have failed to feel the turbulence of revolution in its heart. When Yeats later asks his famous question in 'The Man and the Echo', 'Did that play of mine send

out / Certain men the English shot?' (*V. Poems*, 632), the answer
is an unequivocal 'yes!'

The Irish rebellion of Easter 1916 may have come as something
of a surprise to Yeats, but by May 1917[9] he had started to write
The Dreaming of the Bones. Just under three months later it was
finished. This play whose central character is a gunman on the run
from the rebels' prize position, the Dublin Post Office, was cast in
his latest experimental form, the dance-play in one-act. A letter to
Lady Gregory tells her that it 'is I am afraid only too powerful,
politically' (*L*, 626). But he must have been well enough pleased
with the play, for it is one of his least revised works.

One-act plays need strong dramatic situations if they are to work
on the stage. Yeats's plays, whatever their style, are no exception.
In *The Dreaming of the Bones*, the young rebel has fled from
Dublin and is wandering the mountains of Clare by night. He
meets a stranger and a girl who lead him higher up the mountain
side to await in hiding the coracle from Aran in which he will
make his escape. The strangers tell him that where he is to hide
the ghosts of two lovers, desolate and lonely, dream back over
their lives, but can never kiss nor rest from their burden of guilt
until their crime is forgiven. For the young girl, the lovers' crime
is one of passion. For the young rebel the crime is political: the
lovers were Diarmuid and Dervorgilla, 'Who brought the Norman
in'. All necessary exposition is complete. The escape situation has
been complicated by the sub-theme of the dead lovers. The crisis
arrives after only 230 lines:

> *Young Girl*: Yes, yes, I spoke
>   Of that most miserable, most accursed pair
>   Who sold their country into slavery; and yet
>   They were not wholly miserable and accursed
>   If somebody of their race at last would say,
>   'I have forgiven them'.
> *Young Man*: Oh, never, never
>   Shall Diarmuid and Dervorgilla be forgiven.
> *Young Girl*: If some one of their race forgave at last
>   Lip would be pressed on lip.
> *Young Man*: Oh, never, never
>   Shall Diarmuid and Dervorgilla be forgiven.
>   (*V. Plays*, 773)

The moment of decision is brutal, bitter, uncompromising. We need no special knowledge of Irish history to realise that betrayal can expect no forgiveness. The sentimental might be inclined to belittle the sympathetic portrayal of the Diarmuid and Dervorgilla story as Yeats 'stealing' from Dante Paolo and Francesca, at the same time denouncing the Sinn Féiner's refusal to forgive as vindictive, rancorous propaganda. Such a reading would be grotesquely unfair. Yeats's art is eclectic. His lovers are reminiscent of those in Irish legend, in Dante's poem and in the Noh play, *Nishikigi*. The denial of charity is politically, realistically and dramatically right. Forgiveness would have denied conflict to the play, and the sense of temptation would have been weaker. His final line is 'Terrible the temptation and the place!' (*V. Plays*, 775). The gunman's ruthlessness is also in accord with a terrible reality which holds its uncompromising and murderous loyalties in Ireland to this day.

The crisis period in a good one-act play always produces a climax. Here the climax is achieved dramatically through a recognition scene, theatrically through a poignant dance. The stranger and the girl reveal their true identity as the ghosts of Diarmuid and Dervorgilla, condemned for a further purgatory without forgiveness:

> Our country, if that crime were uncommitted,
> Had been most beautiful. Why do you dance?
> Why do you gaze, and with so passionate eyes,
> One on the other; and then turn away,
> Covering your eyes, and weave it in a dance?
> Who are you? what are you? you are not natural,
> *Young Girl*: Seven hundred years our lips have never met.
> *Young Man*: Why do you look so strangely at one another,
>   So strangely and so sweetly?
> *Young Girl*: Seven hundred years.
> *Young Man*: So strangely and so sweetly. All the ruin,
>   All, all their handiwork is blown away
>   As though the mountain air had blown it away
>   Because their eyes have met. They cannot hear,
>   Being folded up and hidden in their dance.
>
> (*V. Plays*, 774–5)

This is true poetry of the theatre and dramatic verse of superb quality. The dance of ghosts who can never truly meet and never rest is a strange occasion, for it is the climax of two alien traditions fused into one. The stagecraft of the western one-act play reaches its culmination at the moment the Japanese Noh pattern reaches its climax, traditionally the dance of ghosts whose true identity is at last revealed to the wayfarer, usually a Buddhist monk. With savage and characteristic irony, Yeats has reserved the role of the man of peace for a gunman. Yeats does not merely imitate the Noh pattern but deepens the convention he needs to temper the steely one-act structure. The play cuts like a bright sword. It is sheathed by the cloth ceremonies which are his own invention. They use songs as prologue and epilogue. They add richness and depth to the play by establishing the theatrical place for the performance of this new one-act theatre of magic. They give a further dimension to the powerful, single dramatic situation by pointing up the imagery and themes of the play.

Yeats was not content to keep rigidly to the pattern fully established in *Four Plays for Dancers* (1921). Indeed, all his dance-plays are variations on the pattern he invented in *At the Hawk's Well* (1917). Yeats later dropped the cloth ceremonies, and even discarded the dance in *The Resurrection*. He was still experimenting with the form in the last play he wrote, *The Death of Cuchulain* (1939).

The cruelty of the refusal at the centre of *The Dreaming of the Bones* is surrounded by the delicate lustre of dreaming, melancholy lovers, courtly Japanese stagecraft, Yeats's refinement and poise: grit surrounded by pearl.

In *The Death of Cuchulain*, Yeats replaces the courtly frame by a savage old man who spits and curses his way through the prologue. The climactic dance is followed not by a dignified cloth ceremony, but by the raucous music and garish light of an Irish fair *circa* 1939; not by austere musicians, but ragged beggars; not by an exquisitely refined lyric, but the harsh song of a harlot. This frame is coarse, rough-grained. The jewelled miniature has been discarded. Yeats's last play is more a weather-beaten granite relic of the Celtic past.

Again the powerful one-act structure supports everything else. The exposition is deftly achieved in the opening 'messenger' speech of nine lines. The complication is a vicious lovers' quarrel between Cuchulain and his young mistress, Eithne Inguba. This sets out the sub-theme of love and hatred of Cuchulain. The revenge motif which intensifies the central dramatic situation of Cuchulain's last battle is established by the brief appearance of that crow-headed war goddess, the Morrigu, in the first section of the play. The second section, the wounded Cuchulain's encounter with the vengeful Aoife whom he had defeated and raped in a previous battle, constitutes the development of the action. The third section and the crisis of the play is the arrival of a blind man. All Yeats's sense of theatre is unleashed as the sightless, sinister beggar fumbles towards his victim. Vicious squalor takes out a blunt old knife to hack off a hero's head: 'The stage darkens . . . Music of pipe and drum' (*V. Plays*, 1061). The crisis has reached a climax of horror. It is followed by lights up on the Morrigu and seven severed heads. What words could equal such a scene? Yeats finds them: 'The dead can hear me, and to the dead I speak' (*V. Plays*, 1061). The Morrigu's soliloquy explains the presence of the heads and makes her into a figure like Death arranging his dance. Emer, Cuchulain's faithful wife, now dances to bring the action to its final climax, the release of Cuchulain's soul in the form of a few faint bird notes. The severed head has sung—at the moment of death had not Cuchulain cried out to the blind killer, 'I say it is about to sing' (*V. Plays*, 1061)?

The three episodes of the play thus coincide with the exposition, the complication and the crisis of the one-act structure. Emer's dance of love and loathing and the appearance of the crow-headed goddess give us the resolution, and suggest the affinities between the ancient mythic Noh plays of Japan and Celtic legends. The tightly packed references to previous episodes in the Cuchulain legends recall the previous plays in the cycle Yeats wrote for Ireland's greatest hero. The singing, severed head is part of the Orphic motif in Yeats's work,[10] reminding us of *A Full Moon in March*, and of that life-long preoccupation with the soul of man. The political theme is embodied in the action of the play and its relation to the frame. The old man of the prologue curses the vile modern age and aligns himself with a Homeric past. The action of the play presents that Homeric past, but it soon becomes heroic Ireland bled for money. No wonder the killer is blind. The modern age is a tawdry fairground. But in the final song the enduring symbol of the Harlot who, like William Blake, knows that sexual love is founded on spiritual hate,[11] can at least re-

member and conjure the heroic past, linking it with the site of the
surrender of the rebels of 1916, the Dublin General Post Office:

> Who thought Cuchulain till it seemed
> He stood where they had stood?
>
> No body like his body
> Has modern woman borne
> But an old man looking on life
> Imagines it in scorn.
>
> *(V. Plays,* 1063)

Yeats has put himself into the sung epilogue as the scornful old
man, just as he had appeared as the old theatre man of the pro-
logue. Both prologue and epilogue range in reference through
history. The old man looking on life can see another world war.
Suddenly the Irish Free State is dwarfed. Even Cuchulain, especi-
ally as romanticised by Oliver Sheppard, is a figure for scorn.
Yeats had become totally disillusioned with Ireland's perpetual
politics. Over thirty years earlier he remarked to Joseph Holloway,
'People who do aught for Ireland ever and always have to fight
with the waves in the end.'[12]

Yeats's one-act plays are short but by no means thin. Their rich
texture is a major achievement. It derives from his mastery of
language, which manages to give depth and weight to his dialogue.
Another factor, as we have already seen, is his device of obtaining
a lyric dimension with the use of monologues, songs and references
which reach outside his plays into lyric poetry. His poem 'The Song
of the Old Mother' is implied for instance by the situation and
specific lines in *The Land of Heart's Desire,* while Sir Walter
Scott's rousing 'Pibroch of Donhuil Du' shadows with ironic force
the Gaelic songs of *Cathleen ni Houlihan,* for the Scottish settlers
of Northern Ireland were among the strangers in Cathleen's house.
At the same time the play has its ironic extension in Yeats's later
treatment of 'I am of Ireland'. To complain that such lyricism and
literary reference is undramatic is to make a critical axiom out of
ignorance preferred, and to subscribe to a parochial definition of
drama which hobbles criticism with a single set of conventions—
those of twentieth-century realism.

The most substantial single feature which gives the one-act play
density, though, is the sub-theme. This is the element which com-

pensates for the weight and density full-length drama achieves through the sub-plots, greater numbers of character relationships, time and scope. Yeats's stage songs are particularly potent in this respect. They enrich the sub-themes of the plays and usually reach into the metaphysic which informs all his mature work.

Finally, he had a habit of including songs from the plays, and complete plays, in some of his volumes of poetry; the plays suggest relationships with the rest of his work. *The Death of Cuchulain* is not only the last play in a group of one-act Cuchulain plays, and his last political play, but it also finds an analogue with his early narrative poem of the same title. It thus stretches back into the earlier poetry as well as into the earlier plays. The few faint bird notes after Emer's dance not only recall the bird-throat imagery of the early poem, but also suggest another extension into the volume *Last Poems* and Yeats's own dream life, through 'Cuchulain Comforted', a poem in which the ghost of the great warrior appears amid a company of cowards. The bitter irony of the play thus inhabits the poem, but the singing soul, as in the play, can transform itself in a miraculous way reminiscent of the Byzantium poems, just as Yeats can transform the lowly one-acter into something lyrically rich and strange:

> Convicted cowards all, by kindred slain
>
> Or driven from home and left to die in fear!
> They sang, but had not human tunes nor words,
> Though all was done in common as before;
>
> They had changed their throats and had the throats of birds.
> (*V. Poems*, 634–5)

5

Dramatic Expression

The truth is that the Irish people are at that precise stage of
their history when imagination, shaped by many stirring
events, desires dramatic expression. (*E*, 74)

A WRITER'S remarks about the age in which he lives are often
nothing more or less than remarks about the impetus of his own
work. But certain writers, whether they swim with or against the
current, cannot help but feel its tug and undertow, its whirls and
eddies. Yeats was extremely sensitive to the currents of his age.
He sensed in their first stirrings the resurgence of drama not only
in the British Isles but in Europe which has, in fact, made drama
in terms of public entertainment, and by using the technology of
film, radio and television, the dominant genre of this century. But
the great example and stumbling-block for the young verse drama-
tist beginning work in the Victorian age was Shakespeare. Drawn
towards lyricism and verse drama, how could Yeats avoid produc-
ing pseudo-Shakespearean closet-drama in five intolerable acts?
His answer was the lyric intensity of a single act. His dramatic
imagination rejected the material values implied in stage realism
and naturalism, and disliking the translations of Ibsen's plays and
the middle-class world they dramatise, he found no solution in
that direction.

Yeats's first three published but unperformed dramatic works,
though slight, are instructive. *The Island of Statues* (1885) reveals
the twenty-year-old writer, like his nineteenth-century predecessors,
writing under the shadow of Shakespeare,[1] repeating some of his
stage devices and aping his diction. The regenerative power of
love in a pastoral setting and the bringing to life of the 'statues'
is obviously an echo of the stunningly theatrical statue scene in
Shakespeare's *The Winter's Tale*. Yeats makes the mistake of
multiplying the number of statues by five, thus paradoxically dis-

sipating the effect to the extent that farce would take over, were it not for the power of the Shakespearean pastiche put into the mouths of the waking sleepers: 'with all his ships / I saw him from sad Dido's shores depart, / Enamoured of the Waves' impetuous lips' (*V. Plays*, 1256). This youthful exuberance comes out, too, in the opening scene which introduces the love-plot by means of a rivalry in song between Naschina's swains. This rapidly becomes intentionally comic the more it continues, culminating in the excellent direction, 'They approach one another, while singing, with angry gestures' (*V. Plays*, 1227).

Although Yeats was enough in thrall to Elizabethan verse drama to use the Shakespearean device of a heroine disguised as a boy and to write a pseudo-Shakespearean diction at this time, he rejected blank verse for rhyme and, unlike Shelley, who came nearest to a successful nineteenth-century version of Shakespeare in *The Cenci*, experimented with short plays rather than five-acters. Brief exposition, an insistence on songs, and concentration on a moment of intensity linked to magical or supernatural forces were among the features of Yeats's first printed plays. The settings of *The Island of Statues* include a Yeatsian fading moon, but also have the luxuriant late-Victorian touch he was soon to reject, as in the setting for Act I, scene 3, 'Far into the distance reach shadowy ways, burdened with the faery flowers. Knee-deep amongst them stand the immovable figures of those who have failed in their quests' (*V. Plays*, 1234). Here is the shadowiness which was later to be developed into the misty sea of *The Shadowy Waters*. Here, too, is the Yeats who would find Gordon Craig a congenial theatre artist, with his clever lighting and stylised settings suggesting the far reaches of gloom-burdened vistas. The Yeatsian theatre of stillness and the stark austerity of *At the Hawk's Well* are suggested, too, by the 'statues' of those whose quest had failed.

Yeats's dramatic imagination expresses itself also through plentiful use of monologue and soliloquy, devices he employed throughout his dramatic career. But in this early play, there is too much of it, too often exploited for extended verbal scene-painting and description of the love quest, rather than for introspective characterisation or for comment on action and interaction between characters. The magical effects of song as used by Shakespeare in *The Tempest* Yeats explores too in Ariel-like songs rendered by off-stage voices suggesting disembodied spirits. The melodramatic effects of the Victorian stage are echoed, as when Yeats uses the clumsy sensationalism of an arrow winging across the stage or another shot from off-stage and falling to its target on stage with a commentary by a disembodied voice, or when we hear the 'far-off multitudinous sound of horns' (*V. Plays*, 1244) repeated at crucial points in the magical action of the play. But the beauty of stage picture, intensity of atmosphere and concern with word-music which are enduring features of Yeats's dramatic imagination can be seen in the lovely theatrical lyricism which opens Act II, scene 3 with its remarkable set. 'Flowers of manifold colour are knee-deep before a gate of brass, above which, in a citron-tinctured sky, glimmer a few stars. At intervals come mournful blasts from the horns among the flowers' (*V. Plays*, 1245), while six disembodied voices weave the delicate lyric reprinted in *Crossways* (1889) as 'The Cloak, the Boat, and the Shoes'. The theatrical effectiveness of the lyric with its surprise of the empty stage, the six voices and the faint notes of the horn, is coupled with its dramatic force: the ambivalent linking of beauty with sorrow spreads a feeling of impending doom over the rest of the play, making the love quest highly ambiguous. Naschina, the heroine, successfully brings Almintor, her lover, back to life, along with the other sleepers. She banishes the Enchantress of the island, but not before the latter has warned Naschina, 'Thou shalt outlive thine amorous happy Time, / And dead as are the lovers of old rime / Shall be the hunter-lover of thy youth' (*V. Plays*, 1253). Naschina's loveliness and the beauty of love will be inevitably linked to sorrow; so too the beauty of faery, as we discover in the 'carpe diem' song with which Yeats stresses the pathos of the banished Enchantress: 'A man has a hope for heaven, / But soul-less a faery dies' (*V. Plays*, 1255). This ambivalence is worked out, too, in the stage directions at the end of the play. The final awakening of the 'statues' allows a great upsurge of feeling. Naschina's success has ensured the completion of Almintor's quest, and the great sense of Romance and chivalry, of late-Shakespearean happiness finds expression in the declaration of the lovers as monarchs of the island, but through the lines of the awakened sleepers the sense of mortality is also strong ('She is long ages dust') and Naschina standing in the light of the 'rising moon' is seen to be 'shadowless', thus leaving us in no doubt that she is soulless, and will know in her turn the anguish the Enchantress suffers.

Yeats's next dramatic poem, *The Seeker* (1885), abandons the two-act format for two short scenes. Again, the settings are thoroughly of their age, and had it been written for the stage, totally impracticable for so short a work. Yeats again shows a taste for the theatrical possibilities of the supernatural in the astonishing device of a shepherd's flute which utters a piercing cry instead of a musical note. But now the quest theme is not so much ambiguous as frankly pessimistic. The poem dramatises the illusion and falsehood attached to the love quest of the Old Knight, and its failure. Yeats's imagination, full of Keats's 'La Belle Dame Sans Merci' has picked out the theme of cheating, mocking supernatural forces, bent on alluring to destroy. The visionary lady who seemed to promise 'joys unhuman' turns out to be the hideous witch, Infamy. The Old Knight like the Old Man in *At the Hawk's Well* has wasted his life, and all that remains for him is death. The poem is Yeatsian in its concentration on a brief crisis in which the hero sheds illusions to face defeat.

Mosada (1886) is more a play than a dramatic poem, and is again Elizabethan pastiche in its blank verse, diction and apparatus of monks, Moors and the Spanish Inquisition. It is full of Shakespearean echoes, the Moorish theme recalling *Othello*, and the ill-timed death of Mosada owing a good deal to *Romeo and Juliet*. Its three scenes which concentrate on the crisis deciding Mosada's fate add up to a one-acter which seems like the last twenty minutes of a five-act tragedy. Once more Yeats's theme is frustrated love.

In *Time and the Witch Vivien* (1889) Yeats's diction is plainer, the dramatic verse less decorative, and also less Shakespearean. The action is a simple confrontation between Vivien and Time in which Time, of course, wins. It is the germ of *The Hour-Glass*. The hour-glass, the magical dice and the chess set are stage properties which clung to Yeats's theatrical imagination, appearing later in *The Hour-Glass* itself, *Calvary* and *Deirdre*. Yeats thus tested ideas which intrigued him enough to be developed later, and in his early dramatic poems worked at short, striking scenes with monologue, verse dialogue and songs—the main building blocks of his one-act plays for the stage.

Although Yeats's first play to be staged was *The Land of Heart's Desire*, he had previously published *The Countess Kathleen* in 1892, substantially revising it[2] before and after its first performance by the Irish Literary Theatre in May 1899. During the revision process it became known as *The Countess Cathleen*, under which name I shall refer to the final version of the play. *The Countess Kathleen* was a short play in five scenes, set in six-teenth-century Ireland. Although it is based on a legend Yeats published in his anthology, *Fairy and Folk Tales of the Irish Peasantry* (1889), has characters named Teig and Shemus, scandal-ised Irish Catholics, made much of superstitious peasants and decorated the Countess's great hall 'with tapestry representing the wars and loves and huntings of the Finian and Red-branch war-riors' (*V. Plays*, 42), there is still a good deal of sententious Victorianism about the verse, as when old Oona, Kathleen's foster-mother, tells her, 'The great God / Smiling condemns the lost. Be mirthful: He / Bids youth be merry and old age be wise' (*V. Plays*, 46). Nevertheless, it is still Yeats's first play based, as he thought, though Skeffington[3] and his cohorts did not, on Irish legend. Its title page patriotically proclaims it to be 'An Irish Drama'. The conflict between the spiritual values of Kathleen and the materialistic commercialism of the devils in a play dedicated to, and to some extent begotten by, Maud Gonne—who in one production played the title role—certainly establishes one level of meaning at least as a satire of English commercialism for all that the devils appear as Middle-Eastern merchants. It also lashes the tendency of some people in Ireland to sell their souls to English commercialism. In this early version of the play, the devils who roam Ireland as merchants eager to buy souls display a bitter, brutal streak which issues in violence at the end of the first scene, giving the impression that they are melodramatic caricatures of ruthless landlords. This violence, which extends to the breaking up of stage furniture for firewood, is a feature of Yeats's dramatic imagination which he usually implies rather than brings on stage in his later plays, but it is always very near to the surface.

The disembodied voices of his earliest plays Yeats now brings on to the stage as a phantasmagoria of supernatural beings such as sobolths and tevishies in scene three just before the Countess wakes from a troubled sleep murmuring a paternoster. It is as if she has combated these forces of decay in her dreams as well as in her waking life. The phantasmagoria also prepares for the con-trasting vision of spirits at the final climax of the play, signalling Kathleen's victory over evil.

The most significant changes to survive the various revisions were, from the point of view of Yeats's dramatic imagination, firstly the attempts to make the play into four acts, and the accurate instinct which brought it back into a one-acter by the final version; secondly, and even more significant, the decision to build up the part of Kevin, a bard, into Aleel, a poet. Aleel, in love with Cathleen, in the hopeless way that Yeats was with Maud Gonne, gives the Countess a chance for a moment of inner conflict and choice before she resolves to sacrifice her soul for those of her people. Meanwhile, Aleel becomes a symbol not only of personal fulfilment in sexual love, but of the restless imagination. His first song, although making the Shakespearean equation of music and love, stresses the 'crazy' aspect of poet-lover in true Yeatsian tones, and we are left in no doubt by his exit lines that his imagination is visionary:

> For who can say what walks, or in what shape
> Some devilish creature flies in the air; but now
> Two grey horned owls hooted above our heads.
> (V. Plays, 25)

Aleel's words, like Yeats's imagination, are full of the topography of the Sligo area and the legendary Maeve with her eternal dancers, burning with a memory-quenching fire under the restless moon. The theatrical imagination which was later to put dancers on to the stage contents itself here with perfect lyrical expression of one side of the dramatic conflict—the exquisite beauty of Irish pagan feeling:

> Lift up the white knee;
> Hear what they sing,
> Those young dancers
> That in a ring
> Raved but now
> Of the hearts that broke
> Long, long ago
> For their sake.
> But the dance changes,
> Lift up the gown,
> All that sorrow
> Is trodden down.
> (V. Plays, 58–9)

Oona's response is swift, brutal, scornful. 'The empty rattle-plate!' she says, urging the Countess to lean on a 'christened arm'. Aleel will not forgive the old woman for denying her mistress 'three minutes peace of mind' (*V. Plays*, 59). He is as implacable in his defence of ancient beauty as is the young rebel in *The Dreaming of the Bones* in his refusal to be tempted by it. And so is Cathleen herself, for like that rebel, she rejects the lure of the past in favour of loyalty to an Irish present. The imaginative motif is much the same, but in his early play it is a beautiful strand woven into the Pre-Raphaelite tapestry of the action; in *The Dreaming of the Bones* it becomes a swift, stark and more implacable rejection of the feeling heart by the tight-lipped gunman. For Aleel, as for Yeats, the poet as visionary is one 'whose mind is smitten of God' so that he is part medium or vessel, part creator of vision made real. At the end of *The Countess Cathleen*, as she, like Maeve before her, lies dead, it is Aleel's pagan imagination which conjures a vision of Christian angels made real upon the stage. With a passion recalling Hamlet at the grave of Ophelia, Aleel forces an angel to reveal that Cathleen's soul has been saved, 'And Mary of the seven times wounded heart / Has kissed her lips, and the long blessed hair / Has fallen on her face; . . .' (*V. Plays*, 167).

Meanwhile, Yeats was labouring over his equally Pre-Raphaelite counter-truth, *The Shadowy Waters*, which reached its first published version as a dramatic poem in 1900, and its acting version as a verse play, much revised in the light of stage experience, in *Plays for an Irish Theatre* (1911). Yeats spent more time and energy revising *The Shadowy Waters* to make it stageworthy than he spent on any other play. He had been working on 'the poem that became fifteen years afterwards *The Shadowy Waters*' (*A*, 73–4) at least since 1883 to 1885 and that night when at Rosses Point he roused his cousin and took out a sailing boat 'for I wanted to find what sea-birds began to stir before dawn' (*A*, 73). That cold light and the birds stayed with the play to its final version. The idea of creatures part human, part bird, fascinated Yeats. Lady Gregory recalls how her diary for 1898 contained an entry about his having stayed on after tea: 'He has put a "great deal of himself" into his own play *The Shadowy Waters* and rather startled me by saying about half his characters have eagles' faces.'[4] This last turned out to be untrue by the time the play reached the versions of 1900, though much bird imagery remained. Theoretically it is clearly not a very big step from here to the use of masks, though in practice Yeats used masks only several years later and then partly under the influence of Gordon Craig.

Where Aleel was never more than an adjunct to the Countess Cathleen, Yeats's next poet-wanderer, Forgael, is the hero of *The Shadowy Waters*, masterful enough to quell a mutiny, have a king killed and, like Richard of Gloucester, woo his victim's widow. Where Aleel was ready to abandon his soul to Satan free of charge when rejected by the Countess, Forgael, equally the crazed visionary, but now significantly central to the play, is steadfast in his quest 'through the waste places of the great sea' (*V. Plays*, 318) for the love of an immortal woman, whatever the cost, whatever the delusion, whatever the despair. While the Countess had rejected Aleel, Dectora is magically bound to Forgael through the power of his miraculous Orphic harp, and at the end of the play she decides to sail with Forgael away from the experience of common humanity into the world of eternal shadows. Where the Countess found Christian salvation, Dectora seeks a pagan exile; if the Countess has felt the long, blessed hair upon her face, it is Dectora's hair which will cover Forgael's face. Instead of the vision of angels, *The Shadowy Waters* gives us the Neoplatonic vision of souls like birds[5] and an Orphic miracle as 'The harp begins to burn as with fire'. In both plays, the religious and dramatic imagination gives us spirits transcending the physical world, but bound for opposing heavens. In *The Shadowy Waters* the mundane world of the sailors, who are like herrings in a net, is replaced by an imaginative world whose net is Dectora's hair, in which Forgael is a silver fish from the running stream. The fisher of men nets Cathleen, but the world of *The Shadowy Waters* is pre- and post-Christian, closer to the worlds of Aeschylus and Maeterlinck. The French neo-classic unities of action, place and time make the one-act structure tight and austere. The off-stage killing of 'golden-armed Iollan' and Dectora's keening lament is closer to the *Agamemnon* than to *Richard III*, as is Yeats's stylised use of monologue to separate Forgael and Dectora one from the other until he unites them in magnificent lyrical dialogue which leads inexorably to the crisis, Dectora's decision to reject the ordinary world, and to her final monologue where the action finds a swift resolution and a strong ending for the one-act structure. Forgael's mood of despair, when he tells her, 'I weep because I've nothing for your eyes / But desolate waters and a battered ship' (*V. Plays*, 335), Yeats knew all too well himself through his sterile love for Maud Gonne. But the end of the play quickly dispels it to assert the power of the experience offered by the mystical imagination by which 'dreams, / That have had dreams for father, live in us' (*V. Plays*, 339). This is the mood of that Yeatsian magical revolution which was supposed to vanquish nineteenth-century materialism. It belongs to the world of the secret Order of the Golden Dawn, such schemes as the Castle of the Heroes and the Brotherhood of the Three Kings.[6]

Considered merely as a dramatic narrative poem, the work is a member of that voyage literature which so often symbolises a journey of the spirit or the self. It reaches back to the ancient epics and such works as the 'Voyage of Bran' among other Irish 'imrama' (voyages), and less remotely to Coleridge's 'The Ancient Mariner', Rimbaud's 'Le Bâteau Ivre', or even Lautréamont's 'Chants du Maldoror: Chant Deuxième, 13'. But Yeats was striving for dramatic force on the stage—though of a kind which had few enough precedents in his age. There was *Peer Gynt*. He had, too, the example of Villiers de l'Isle-Adam's *Axël*. Fortunately, he borrowed from it only sparingly; *The Shadowy Waters* in its narrative version of 1900 is a much more concise work which, though equally serious in its use of magic, avoids the tedium of lengthy exchanges on Rosicrucian matters. Yeats's Rosicrucianism developed after his acquaintance with *Axël*; it was not until around 1897 that he produced the short stories of *The Secret Rose*—'The Adoration of the Magi', 'Rosa Alchemica', 'The Tables of the Law'. The rose had been a symbol of supreme love and beauty of a spiritual kind, but after *Axël* it was invested with a more strictly Rosicrucian significance.[7] However, the basic situation which Yeats's play and Villiers' have in common, the desire of the hero for otherworldly love and his willingness to journey even beyond death and physical destruction to attain his spiritual desire, is one which Yeats had also used in 'Dhoya' (1891)—before he had seen *Axël* on the stage in Paris. This story has for hero a solitary named Dhoya who wins the love of a faery woman and lives in great happiness with her, defeating a faery warrior who tries to break this union of the mortal with the immortal. But the same idea which torments *Axël* is repeated in the story like a musical theme: 'But always everything changes, save only the fear of Change.'[8] The warrior reappears and challenges Dhoya to a game of chess with the faery woman as the victor's prize. Dhoya plays and loses, and the story ends with his frantic pursuit of the immortals as he plunges into the Western Sea, symbolic of the route to Tir na n-Og, the land of the ever-living. This story obviously has much in common with the earlier version of *The Shadowy Waters*, for both show the quest of the hero as being essentially a lone journey to whatever lies beyond death. The similarity between the story and the play demonstrates very clearly that the Irish legendary background was probably an even more potent factor in the development of the play than the French element. *The Shadowy Waters*, besides being part of the symbolist and magical revolution, was part of that theatrical revolution bent on circumventing the contemporary commercial theatre of Victorian and Edwardian London for an Irish theatre of art, beauty and folklore after the fashion of the little avant-garde theatres in Europe and England.

In 1899, near the outset of his dramatic career, in fact, Yeats saw in an inspirational moment the kind of inexpensive staging he could use for the expression of his themes:

> I want to do a little play which can be acted and half chanted and so help the return of bigger poetical plays to the stage. This is really a magical revolution, for the magical word is the chanted word. The new 'Shadowy Waters' could be acted on two big tables in a drawing room; not that this will please you who don't much like acting at all I think. (*L*, 327)

But by the time Yeats was working on the play in preparation for the Dublin performance in January, 1904, at the Molesworth Hall, he was again thinking in terms of sets and a stage rather than a coterie performance. In trying to make his dream-like play fit the conditions of the stage at his disposal, he was quick to admit and to recognise faults, and painstaking in his attempts to correct them.[9] While constant revision was doubtless irritating at times for actors, it was a proof of Yeats's artistic integrity, this shaping and release of imagination by means of the discipline of craft.

The revisions were also necessitated by a more particular dramatic need; Yeats had by 1900, as Parkinson and Bushrui point out,[10] started to explore new dramatic theories. Style, he insists in 'Samhain: 1902', must be based upon the spoken word:

> even though we have to speak our lyrics to the psaltery or the harp, for, as A.E. says, we have begun to forget that literature is but recorded speech. . . But when we go back to speech let us see that it is the idiom either of those who have rejected, or of those who have never learned, the base idioms of the news-papers. (*E*, 95)

Speech should not only be appropriate to the character but should be so spoken 'that the hearer may find it hard to know whether it is the thought or the word that has moved him, or whether these could be separated at all' (*E*, 108). Acting and gesture had to be simplified to express not a fidgety surface but something that would seem 'to flow up into the imagination from some deeper life than that of the individual soul' (*E*, 109). From the evidence of the letters, as well as the texts, the most important effect of revisions of *The Shadowy Waters* and his other theatre work was that Yeats found a new style and, indeed, a new aesthetic outlook through the lessons he learned. The play was now very different, for Yeats had put into it 'homely phrases' and 'the idiom of daily speech' and had 'characterised all the people more or less' without loss of the lyricism, as he described it in a letter to John Quinn:

> It has become a simple passionate play, or at any rate it has a simple passionate story for the common sightseer, though it keeps back something for instructed eyes[11] . . . I believe more strongly every day that the element of strength in poetic lan-guage is common idiom, just as the element of strength in poetic construction is common passion. (*L*, 462)

The 'common idiom', the new structural strength, the elemental passion, the sharpened dramatic climaxes, all remained with him for the rest of his career. He was concerned to write actable drama—whether for theatre or drawing-room performance.

After a period of extensive revision, then, Yeats with much effort ensured that Forgael embodied a fuller concept of the imagination than did Aleel, the visionary lover-poet. Forgael is an Orphic figure with all the magical power that implies. His opening words, spoken out of his sleep, seem to the crew merely part of another 'crazy dream': 'Yes; there, there; that hair that is the colour of burning' (*V. Plays*, 318). At the end of the play we realise they were a prophecy, for he speaks his final lines somewhat improbably swathed in Dectora's shining hair. Forgael's harp, symbol of his art, poetic and magical, is like Prospero's rod, and the abortive, mutinous plot to kill Forgael clearly owes something, like the setting itself, to *The Tempest*. Nor should we forget the Rosicrucian aspects of the harp.[12] The Shakespearean motif has become Yeats's property. The harp is capable of putting our individual imagination in touch with Anima Mundi. The harp symbol suggests the power of the poetic imagination, which is magical. It has the power to control people and to unite ideal lovers, since it came to Forgael by way of the 'white fool' from Aengus, god of love. As we can see from Yeats's letter to A.E. (27 August, possibly 1899; *L*, 324) the dramatist himself thought of Aengus as 'both Hermes and Dionysus' with Christ as one of his followers. Bushrui interprets Aengus and Edain as Man and Woman, Forgael and Dectora being their 'earthly shadows', recalling that Yeats, in an unsigned programme note, thought of his hero and heroine as respectively the mind and 'the living will'.[13] This anticipates some of the ideas of *Per Amica Silentia Lunae*, the theory of self and anti-self, will and mask. The struggle between the opposites is symbolised in the sea-battle; and the birds, the souls of the dead and Forgael's guides now, represent his communication with Anima Mundi.

The only mutation the harp as symbol of imagination undergoes in the numerous revisions of the play, is that whereas in earlier versions it is specified as a harp, in the acting versions it is sometimes referred to as 'a stringed instrument'. This change was merely a practical matter: temporary difficulty over the construction of such a harp and the easy availability of a psaltery as a fitting substitute. And if 'wonderful effects prepared for months beforehand, burning jewels on the harp and twinkling stars in the sky' (Yeats to Florence Farr, 6 Oct. 1905; *L*, 463) were replaced by the psaltery, the linking of Yeats's theories of verse-speaking to the imaginative, magical powers of Forgael's instrument was a pleasing compensation. But whether psaltery or bejewelled harp, the symbol is dramatically convincing in the play. It acquires power in the audience's imaginations from its physical presence on the stage; and its magic is prepared for by the dialogue. Associated with violence and calm, death and beauty, beneath the moon of change, imagination and subjectivity, its power over the actions of man is established, closely followed by mention of its power to induce magical vision of the other world. Its power increases as the play progresses. Its early context connects it with the main question of the story—is Forgael to be a privileged wanderer or a dupe of destructive forces? The next time the harp of the nine spells is mentioned, its power is boasted by Forgael and derided by Dectora. This has the effect of still keeping us in suspense as to whether Forgael is magus, madman or both, sure dramatic preparation for the sudden darkening of the stage, the faint glowing of the harp and Forgael's use of it—a very theatrical moment of tension this—to halt rebellion and charm Dectora to his spiritually 'lascivious' purpose, the seduction of her soul: 'Your soul shall give the kiss' (*V. Plays*, 328). A sophisticated touch now brings a further wonder. Just as we are beginning to settle for the idea that Forgael is not deceived by his gods, we are made to realise that his use of the harp for his own purposes does not mean that he is immune himself, for at his moment of triumph he has an unexpected and very disturbing vision of the birds which shakes his confidence. The harp has given him power, but it has also helped him to realise all the more keenly the relapse into squalid sobriety after the headiness of his dream. The harp symbol thus works in a dramatically integral and theatrically effective way to illuminate, emphasise and even control the main theme of the lure and power of the other world. It also expresses something of the underlying conflict of the theme born of doubt, and a suspicion that the immortals offer perhaps a cheating, destructive experience rather than everlasting happiness. It is highly significant for Yeats that the Rosicrucian harp should have been so clearly connected with the elements of language as well as heavenly music. This is strikingly in accord with the aesthetic theories of the nineties, in particular the idea of literature aspiring to the condition of music. Moreover, the heraldic connotations of the symbol, of maiden and dragon, although there is no evidence that Yeats envisaged a stage harp carved in such a way, do in fact link with some aspects of the play as it was before the 1900 versions. The Venus aspect of the harp woman certainly proves relevant to a major concern of the play—the quest for love.

But these further occult or ulterior meanings of the symbol would have no direct impact on most members of an audience.

They would clearly have realised above all that the harp was of course the symbol of Ireland. This is of no specific significance to the themes but a pleasing example of the link between Ireland and ancient myth from elsewhere, a bonus so far as Yeats's and his audience's nationalistic feelings were concerned.

Enough has been said to show that the harp is effective, though, on a theatrical level—it glows before our eyes—and that it is intimately part of the dramatic structure of the play, from 1900 onwards. That this is so is a result of Yeats's growing skill as a playwright. In early drafts of the play, Yeats was tempted to use mythical creatures with eagles' heads, but the reduction of such striking theatrical images to mentions only was, like the throwing overboard of much peripheral symbolism, a good move on Yeats's part, because central to his action is the ambiguous power of *human* imagination. His characters thus had to be human, if emblematic.

The text in *Plays for an Irish Theatre* shows Forgael denying that he is being led to his death, and then qualifying the denial by saying, 'What matter / If I am going to my death, for there, / Or somewhere, I shall find the love they have promised / That much is certain.'[14] We thus encounter in the acting version a more introspective Forgael, readier to admit his doubts, one who achieves his vision and rhapsody out of a more human breast than that of the demi-god he was in early drafts: Forgael's moods of exaltation and despair are perfectly in accord with the theme. The audience confronts the mystery of the inner life, its baffling mixture of bewilderment and certainty, the imagination's powerful insight and its ability to transform experience. Forgael's entire motivation is faith in this central force of the inner-life, that imaginative power the loss of which brings despair:

> I can see nothing plain; all's mystery.
> Yet sometimes there's a torch inside my head
> That makes all clear, but when the light is gone
> I have but images, analogies,
> This mystic bread, the sacramental wine,
> The red rose where the two shafts of the cross,
> Body and soul, waking and sleep, death, life,
> Whatever meaning ancient allegorists
> Have settled on, are mixed into one joy.

For what's the rose but that? miraculous cries,
Old stories about mystic marriages,
Impossible truths? But when the torch is lit
All that is impossible is certain,
I plunge in the abyss.

(V. Plays, 323)

The symbols of the speech are set in a clearly explanatory context
in conformity to the demands of an audience. The speech brings
out the mixture of blessedness and anguish which is the lot of the
visionary. When his visions possess him he is in a state of bliss and
certainty, but when they leave his human world he feels all the
pain of its inadequacy. Yet its solid, temporal reality calls all in
doubt, and plunges him into confusion. This expression of the
tension between belief and scepticism in Forgael occurs at a crucial
point in the action. It is now that the other ship is sighted. The
belief and scepticism of the audience are also being manipulated:
is the other ship a prize sent by the ever-living to protect their
disciple from the mutiny of the sailors? Is Forgael's trust after all
justified?

Forgael has a vision, while Aibric and the other sailors plunge
into the world of human conflict. But Forgael's vision does not
bring him the certainty of which his earlier speech had boasted. Its
confusion and turbulence, its broken, incomplete messages mirror
the confusion and the garbled cries coming from the contending
crews behind the sail. The reeling shadows are themselves con-
fused and unable to act ('What can we do, being shadows?') so
that Forgael tells us that he has received no message about 'that
shadowless unearthly woman / At the world's end.' Instead he
finds 'All mystery, / And I am drunken with a dizzy light' (*V.
Plays*, 325).

The next bit of action brings Forgael a step nearer to the loss
of his certainty. He is now faced by a mortal woman with the
awkwardly worldly accoutrements of a shadow, a ship full of
treasure, the title of queen, the benefits of such rank, and, most
ironic of all, a husband whom she loves dearly and with sensuous
delight as her 'golden-armed Iollan'. In reply to Forgael's testy
disappointment that she casts a shadow, she pours out her in-
dignation at the fate she has encountered and death of her loved
one. She cuts through the metaphysical vagaries of Forgael's speech

with the directness and urgency of regal authority and the calamity she suffers: 'You've nothing but wild words, / And I would know if you would give me vengeance' (*V. Plays*, 326). She, like Aibric, focuses our worldly, common-sense reactions to the play's situation. She is a living reminder of the fact that Forgael has not yet found a shadowless, immortal love. Her attempt to kill Forgael and to turn the discontent of the sailors to her own advantage shows a heroic spirit very different from the self-preoccupation of Forgael.

This of course presents another dramatic problem for Yeats. If he is not careful, his hero is going to look not only cruel like Conchubar in *Deirdre* but spiritually weak beside a woman of such mettle. Yeats's answer is instinctively right. The magical working of the harp intervenes. It shifts attention to the fascination of seeing how this courageous queen can be made to forget her newly butchered husband and love instead the mysterious Forgael. The situation is similar to the wooing of Ann in *Richard III*, though Shakespeare did not need magic to help him. The magic is not only highly theatrical, it is also a means of recalling the central question of the play as to the existence of a love to transcend the human. The cheating aspect of magic is not forgotten. The magic works, but the love it brings is very dubious. The acting versions contain a moment of self-recognition by Forgael as he realises that to have won Dectora by easy, dishonest enchantment is no answer to his problem. He confesses and repents. He even admits the probability that the cries of the birds are 'railing and reproach', even 'mockery / Because I have awakened her to love / By magic strings . . .' (*V. Plays*, 333). Yeats stresses the possibility that Forgael is the dupe of these powers so that his hero may be seen to make a difficult, maybe perilous, choice. Forgael sees his decision as irreversible, though after it is made, doubt besets him. His decision to enchant Dectora into submission has brought with it the problem of whether love can be founded on deceit. He tries to resolve the situation by taking a dual attitude. He is now prepared to accept Dectora as the woman the Ever-living have promised. At the same time, he still suspects that this may not be the case. He has an answer to this: that the feelings and means of courtship for all lovers are all a species of deceit; but whichever way Forgael interprets the clamour of the birds, it is clear that his love is now for an earthly woman and his arguments are in terms of human love. His remorse is that of a human being confronted by another he has wronged. But Dectora is now enchanted, living the dream he once inhabited. Forgael's remorse and pity for his deluded victim now issue in a moving lack of illusion, an honest, gentle and regretful dispiritedness : 'I weep because I've nothing for your eyes / But desolate waters and a battered ship' (*V. Plays*, 335).

This short episode in the play succeeds in restoring sympathy to him and is in itself an effective piece of writing for the stage. Rather cleverly, Forgael's pity for the deluded Dectora encourages an audience to share in it and also realise if Forgael himself is a victim of these delusions, as he thinks he is at this point, then he, too, deserves sympathy.

Nevertheless, there is a contradiction in the ending of the play. The emotional conviction of the closing speech, the miracle of the harp and the symbolic use of lighting which is directed to grow stronger as the sailors go out leaving only one of their torches on the stage, all conspire with Dectora's choice to urge the audience to construe the scene as showing the union of two heroic spirits who have chosen, like Axël and Sara, to scorn the temporal world in favour of their pursuit of the eternal. Unfortunately, however, we cannot quite accept this act of faith in their dreams in quite this way. The power of the moment when Forgael sees no future save 'desolate waters and a battered ship' lingers still to remind us that for Dectora at least, and probably Forgael also, there is in fact no choice involved : persons enchanted by Aengus's power have no freedom of choice.

Forgael's moment of recognition was his realisation that by casting the love spell upon her he had wronged her 'Out of all reckoning' and lost all hope of an ideal love. The imbalance and inconsistency remain despite the great improvements Yeats made in the play during its various revisions. But is this necessarily a dramatic weakness, or failure of Yeats's dramatic imagination? Both characters have an urgency and emotional pressure in their words for both are in a sense absolutely right. In love, we all think we are finding what is different, and superior to ordinary sexuality. Out of love, we have to be content with the kiss for what a kiss is worth 'And let the dream go by'. And this, as we know, can be a very bitter experience—especially when we are tied to the lover with whom we once shared the dream. It is this which Axël prevents by suicide, and which Yeats, in *The Shadowy Waters*, cannot bear to resolve. Dectora bravely cuts the rope, as if Eve suddenly had turned and defeated the serpent: 'O ancient worm, / Dragon that loved the world and held us to it, / You are broken, you are broken' (*V. Plays*, 338). When the rope of the world[15] drifts away, it is still not certain what awaits them—virtual suicide, mysterious transformation of the flesh or simply disillusion with each other. But this lack of resolution is not necessarily a fault. It is a dramatisation of the uncertainty and insecurity of human experience itself.

On another level, we might say that Forgael's visionary, prophetic and artistic imagination seeks its complement, playing Adam to Dectora's Queen Eve. Yet instead of seeking the world, they renounce it for an ark. They become body and soul transcending the world in a mystical marriage. This figment of Yeats's dramatic imagination found its expression, too, in his later, more brutal Orphic dance-play, *A Full Moon in March*.

Yeats's growing interest in the Greek model for drama can be seen in his use of the unities, his desire to translate Greek plays, and his use of the net image. His repetition of the image at various points in the play makes it a motif in the Greek manner which becomes a companion symbol to that of the harp. The golden locks of Forgael's dreams are strands making the net of vision; at the same time the Ever-living hold Forgael and Dectora in a net-like fate akin to that of the Greeks, 'For neither I nor you can break a mesh / Of the great golden net that is about us' (*V. Plays*, 329). The harp of the imagination, too, is a mesh of strings which impedes violence and turns it into poetry and song.

Ellmann finds that though *The Shadowy Waters* is too much a showcase for Yeats's symbols, 'not enough a dramatic contest', it is a play which may be defended for two reasons: 'the nobility of its ideal and the virtuosity of its experimentation'; it has the distinction of being in 'the farthest range of symbolism in dramatic poetry in English until the twentieth century'.[16]

These qualities are important for revealing what Yeats had in him to exploit if the right forms could be found to release the ideas on the stage, and the direction he would have to travel to find these dramatically effective forms. He wanted to show man's restless questing after the ideal, the eternal, perhaps the impossible; he wanted to dramatise this as conflict between man and spirits; he wanted through these means to 'make the theatre a place of intellectual excitement—a place where the mind goes to be liberated by the theatres of Greece and England and France at certain great moments of their history, and as it is liberated in Scandinavia today' (*E*, 107). This theatre would bring the shock of bizarre creatures and heroic figures from mythology to the stage, and its language would be that of passion and poetry. The personages on the stage, the scenery, the properties, the colour and lighting schemes, the acting itself, all would serve the purpose of symbolism and provide an articulation for the symbolism of the text.[17] Even though he had brought more of the human world to what had been remote and ritualistic, Yeats had not yet managed to 'arrange much complicated life into a single action' (*E*, 108). This he achieved in a play which demonstrated his growing ability and need to depict the human condition: *On Baile's Strand*.

The remote and ritualistic drama was in Yeats's opinion a valid art—and indeed these elements were to reappear in his dramatic work later. But his new and different view of the stage, gained from what he was learning about the theatre from working for a particular audience, from working with the Fays and from the influence of Synge, was to develop further. In *The King's Threshold* (1903) Yeats explored the status of art in society, or the politics of imagination. Yeats was in no doubt about the importance of art and the artist in society. This certainly helped, with his growing mastery of one-act form in the light of stage experience, to make the play his first substantial one-acter conceived from the outset expressly for the kind of stage, acting, resources and audience he could command in Dublin.

The visual symbolism of the setting is startlingly direct in its reinforcement of the theme. The palace steps of King Guaire at Gort hint at the palace front of Greek tragedy. The King stands on the top step while Seanchan, his chief poet, lies starving himself to death on the steps below. The austerity of the set is perfectly in accord with the clean structural line of the play, and, more important at the time, is suitably inexpensive for the struggling company led by Frank Fay, who created the role of Seanchan. Yeats's visual imagination was now geared to the meagre resources of his company, the Irish National Theatre Society, and to the inadequacies of the Molesworth Hall where the first production was mounted.

D

The one-act structure observes the unities of action, time and place, but Yeats's episodic plotting with its series of visitors owes something to Milton's *Samson Agonistes*[18] just as the static hero clearly recalls Shelley's *Prometheus Unbound*. The clear, unimpeded structure gives the play a compelling forward thrust, an excellent corrective and contrast to the stasis of Seanchan. This impetus creates the impression of inevitability necessary to the play and also enforces that sense, so effective here and in *Deirdre*, of the action as being the main thrust of the final act of some older five-act tragedy. Yeats's dramatic imagination characteristically plunges us not 'in medias res' but into the beginning of the end of his story. King Guaire's first speech is a piece of oratory[19] which contains characterisation of Guaire, exposition and the attack of the play. The King's view is that a seat in the council is a very 'light issue' for the chief poet; Seanchan's is that the poet's right to a seat is no small matter, for it was 'Established at the establishment of the world' (*V. Plays*, 259). The artistic imagination is akin to the imagination of the Creator. The 'establishment of the world' implies for Seanchan a society and a culture in which art rightfully has an official place at the highest level. To suppose otherwise is insulting to art and belittles its supernatural inspiration and human importance. The King's argument is that of power politics.

Yeats, in this opening segment of the play, achieved a swift, compact and convincing characterisation of Guaire as genial, devious, wily and oratorical. This speed was essential for the short play. He also introduced the basic conflict clearly and trenchantly, finally, he showed Seanchan unmoved by the King, but his Oldest Pupil ready to take up the King's cause and the temptation of his Master. Yeats had set up a classic debate about freedom of the artistic imagination intensely topical for him and other Irish writers, Joyce for instance, in the Dublin of 1903. In his notes to *Poems, 1899–1905* (1906), Yeats put the matter succinctly: 'I [*The King's Threshold*] was written when our Society was having a hard fight for the recognition of pure art in a community of which one half was buried in the practical affairs of life, and the other half in politics and a propagandist patriotism' (*V. Plays* 315). A good example of the unintelligent, blinkered sort of nationalism Yeats and others had to combat in Ireland is the article headed 'An Irish National Theatre' which appeared in

The Irish Daily Independent and Nation newspaper on Thursday, 8 October 1903. The article recalls the success of previous efforts of the Irish Literary Theatre but warns against the (unspecified) dangers of producing any foreign plays whatsoever! It attacks Synge for a disgraceful portrait of the infidelity of the Irish peasant woman in *The Shadow of the Glen*, and claims that since no Irish women are unfaithful he has clearly drawn his inspiration not from the Western Isles, but from his other haunt, gay Paris. Yeats had asked the public to forbear, pleading that their National Theatre must (the article quotes him as saying):

'. . . be so tolerant, and, if this is not too wild a hope, find an audience so tolerant that the half-dozen minds who are likely to be the dramatic imagination of Ireland for this generation, may put their own thoughts and their own characters into their work.' Sincerely we hope and believe that no such tolerance will be extended to Mr Yeats and his friends.

The same newspaper's review of the performance of *The King's Threshold* that night did not mention the ways in which the fable showed that due reverence and freedom must be given to the artist. But it did quote from a speech Yeats made when he was called for by the enthusiastic audience. Yeats had asserted the right of the company to give due value to art, whatever its nationality: 'They sought to live in the light of the masterpieces of the art of the world, and they would live in no other light.' (Applause) (*The Irish Daily Independent and Nation*, 9 Oct. 1903).

Yeats never tired of stressing the need for artistic freedom because the attitude to art and artists in Ireland was viciously constricting. As he later described the situation in 'The Bounty of Sweden': 'Every political party had the same desire to substitute for life, which never does the same thing twice, a bundle of reliable principles and assertions' (*A*, 566). His experience of Irish and European politics had taught him that:

The danger to art and literature comes today from the tyrannies and persuasions of revolutionary societies and from forms of political and religious propaganda. The persuasion has corrupted much modern English literature, and—during the twenty years that led up to national revolution—the tyranny wasted the greater part of the energy of Irish dramatists and poets. They had to remain perpetually on the watch to defend their creation, and the more natural the creation the more difficult the defence. (*A*, 580–81)

There are, however, many writers and artists of all kinds who have produced great works of art under the patronage of, or despite, the power-hungry. But to be fair to Yeats we must remember the particular conditions under which the drama struggled to emerge in Ireland—obscurantism, ignorance, prejudice and violence—all springing from a state of mind difficult to comprehend and which could, for instance, be expressed by the actors themselves as well as the mob:

> . . . now an Irish classic, 'The Rising of the Moon', could not be performed for two years because of political hostility . . . The players would not perform it because they said it was an unpatriotic act to admit that a policeman was capable of patriotism. One well-known leader of the mob wrote to me, 'How can the Dublin mob be expected to fight the police if it looks upon them as capable of patriotism?' (*A*, 566)

Yeats finished his address to the Swedes with a eulogy of their Court; it was to him an example of the kind of situation Seanchan could not win back. It is, unfortunately, an issue still relevant wherever forces of political repression seek to limit the influence of art and insult or extinguish the individuality of the artist.

Yeats started out to treat the subject in tragic terms but was diverted into attempting a comic treatment.[20] He invented a philistine old man as prologue,[21] but ended by reverting to his first instinct, cutting out the prologue and making Seanchan a grimly accusatory figure, implacably accepting death by starvation as the most effective weapon the individual can use against the might of the state. Yeats was pleased to discover that he had 'invented' the hunger-strike weapon to be used by many agitators thereafter. But he had been determined from the outset that the poet would get the best of it,[22] whether the play took the form of comedy, with the King reversing his judgment, or whether Seanchan were forced to die, as in the final version, thus gaining a moral victory. The latter ending is more in accord with the bitter realities of politics, and one can see why it would appeal to the Yeats who reprinted the play in 1922 in *Plays in Prose and Verse.*

Yeats dramatises for his audience not only the contest between artistic integrity and the lackeys of King Guaire's political establishment—comic Mayor, thundering Chamberlain, and the rest— but also the social function of art, by means of Seanchan's Socratic questioning of his Oldest Pupil. The artist's imagination enables him to retrieve 'Images of the life that was in Eden' for public contemplation. These ideal images, presumably archetypes of man's spiritual life up to and including the fall, provide models of beauty and behaviour for the generations of mankind, those 'triumphant children' (*V. Plays,* 264). A world lacking such art 'would be like a woman / That, looking on the cloven lips of a hare, / Brings forth a hare-lipped child' (*V. Plays,* 265). The old wives' tales of rural superstition saw a direct link between the workings of the mother's perceptions and imagination and the formation of her baby. By using such an analogy, Yeats successfully captures the feeling and thought process of men out of the distant past. The image works dramatically also because in the theatre we often tend to associate mental and physical qualities : heroes tend to be beautiful, while types of moral depravity are ugly or deformed. The image is important, too, because it points to something which was as true of Yeats's world as it is of ours— capitalists devoid of art were erecting slum buildings, architectural disgraces, merely for profit. It also fits in with a larger scheme in the play; it connects with the image of leprosy that denotes a sick society, and contrasts with the beauty of the dance-loving girls of the court.

If beauty is so valuable, and the lack of it so ruinous, then it follows that it must be guarded. Seanchan reminds us that the 'Images of the life that was in Eden' are like 'venerable things / God gave to men before He gave them wheat' (*V. Plays,* 265), which is what he had told the King. The references to food establish the reason for the particular form of Seanchan's protest—a lying proof that we live by more than bread—a view ironically lighted by the beggars' expectations as to the food Seanchan leaves, a touch comparable to the food-stealing beggars at the end of *On Baile's Strand.*

Seanchan's speeches give us a vivid sense of the direct effect of art on our lives. He is pointing out, as Wilde did, that life imitates art, rather than the reverse. The ideas, the emotions, the images that artistic imagination presents for our contemplation are thus of supreme importance, not mere decorative frills to amuse us after our serious business is over. The true artist therefore defends his right to create out of his own personality and imagination (in touch with Anima Mundi) rather than subjugate it to some ephemeral political authority. Politicians must not be allowed to legislate which images poets use, for only the workings of the God-given artistic imagination itself can decide. Seanchan reminds his Oldest Pupil 'At Candlemas you called this poetry / One of the fragile, mighty things of God / That die at an insult' (*V. Plays*, 265). It is this very death which the symbolic action of the play dramatises through Seanchan. Yet it is the death of a phoenix. Seanchan is equally sure that destruction and calamity lead inevitably to rebirth: 'when all falls / In ruin, poetry calls out in joy, / Being the scattering hand, the bursting pod, / The victim's joy among the holy flame, / God's laughter at the shattering of the world' (*V. Plays*, 266–7). This kind of confidence, and we see it later in 'Lapis Lazuli', belongs to the imagination which envisions history as a cycle of rebirths whose constant is the eternal soul.

The plight of Seanchan is the constant visual image of the play. From it radiate the implications of the need for the artist to have freedom and respect. Seanchan is not only on the King's threshold, but at the threshold of waking and trance, reality and vision, life and death. He is the focal point of all action, themes and movement—but he is a still centre. His movements are rare and slight until the play is nearing its climax when he is dragged along by the Monk, and then, at the crisis itself, he rises to his feet and staggers before he dies. The economy of movement sets Seanchan apart from the other characters. It contrasts with their different kinds of movement: the dignity of King and Chamberlain, the grace of the court ladies, the awkwardness of the cripples, the comic motions of the Mayor and the solemn, processional ending. Thus Seanchan's heroism is stressed. Movement isolates him and bolsters his symbolic quality.

The comic interlude of Mayor and Cripples, straight from the world of Lady Gregory, enlivens the play's mood, breaking its Classical severity of form. Yeats also experiments by using lyrical curses which 'should be spoken in a rhythmical chant, or should rise into song' (*V. Plays*, 280) and issue in a thorough drubbing for the Mayor. In some versions these very rhythmical speeches were to gain a 'musical' effect[23] from the interweaving of the conflicting voices, as is clear from stage directions 'Speaking at same time as Second Cripple and Mayor and Brian, who have begun again'[24] (*V. Plays*, 280). This is, of course, a common device in opera. Yeats's experiment here is clearly distinguishable from the usual device of having several characters speaking simultaneously because it has also the 'rondo' effect of repetition. It is part of his life-long interest in verse-speaking. The clashing of voices and the strong rhythms convey clamour and protest against authority which has betrayed an ancient trust. Again the cruelty of that authority is stressed. And again, amidst the violence and vehemence the cripples bring touches of humour with 'Until he be as rotten as an old mushroom!' or 'And a little old devil looking out of every wrinkle!' (*V. Plays*, 281).

The magical form of the verse fits the historical setting of the play and thus it is, although sudden, an outburst which the audience can quickly accept as a fitting climax to the previous feeling of the scene and a good incitement to the physical violence done to the Mayor with which the episode culminates. The verse form is also appropriate in that the magical curse fits well with the picture the beggars have of Seanchan as a semi-Druidical figure. The poet as mage was an idea which the young Yeats accepted as part of his literary environment—it is clearly in the French Symbolist as well as the Irish tradition and certainly fits Yeats's interest in magic. This choric spell is thus an indispensable part of the dramatic demonstration of the power and significance of poetry. It is almost as if Seanchan, still and brooding, has charmed the others to act out his conflict for him. The Mayor is buffeted in a piece of business reminiscent of the magical japes of Dr Faustus. The poet has a broad base of popular support among the 'losers' in this society, but the Church in the person of the Monk[25] is ranged against 'The wanton imagination of the poets' (*V. Plays*, 285).

The seemingly all-powerful opposition of the state, Yeats swiftly and economically demonstrates with one clever stroke of stagecraft: Seanchan's pupils go off to reason with the King; when they next appear it is as prisoners with halters round their necks.

The King's ruthlessness and gratuitous sadism in asking them to beg for their lives can be defeated only by courage of the highest order. Each refuses in turn to beg, urging 'Die, Seanchan, and proclaim the right of the poets' (*V. Plays*, 308). What sustains the poetic imagination when it is attacked and persecuted, and Yeats believed that nothing has been so persecuted as the intellect, is the effect its best works have on future generations, nurturing them with myth, the magnanimous virtues of the heroes 'that great race / That would be haughty, mirthful, and white-bodied, / With a high head, and open hand' (*V. Plays*, 301) and finely-wrought, seemingly spontaneous songs, such as the one Seanchan gives us before he dies, which is the description of a wonderful garden containing 'a blessed well', the infinitely self-renewing well of imagination which bubbles into song, 'And all the fowls of the air / Have gathered in the wide branches / And keep singing there' (*V. Plays*, 302). This completes the play's scheme of imagery recalling Eden and gardens of the muses. The magnanimous world of the heroes was later to be explored more fully in the experimental verse-form and stagecraft of the heroic farce *The Green Helmet*, and the well of poetry was to find its barren counterpart in the waste land of *At the Hawk's Well*. This bleaker vision is anticipated by the Youngest Pupil's comment on his master's death: 'The ancient right is gone, the new remains, / And that is death' (*V. Plays*, 310). He is ready to sacrifice his life to art in the full knowledge that it will never regain its old dignified place in society. But Seanchan's point is that the survival of poetry depends upon the integrity of the artist and his freedom, not on his 'bargaining power' with authority. As we have learnt from the activities of totalitarian propaganda machines and police methods, his 'bargaining power' is negligible unless he has absolute integrity and courage.

In Yeats it is often the tramps and beggars and the crazy who represent humanity, and in this play, the cripples feel the power of poetry even if they do not understand it and are naturally more concerned with filling their stomachs. They contrast not only physically with the Mayor, but mentally. For them Seanchan has something left of the magical power of the Druid;[26] he is linked to the poor through the folk tradition in poetry and old custom. They are suspicious and fearful of his power, but there is also respect and even admiration. There is, moreover, the recognition that he is, after all, one of them rather than a lackey of the organised state.

By bringing the women's view of Seanchan to us, when the court ladies are urged to persuade the poet to eat, Yeats can explore another side of the artist: the entertainer rather than the critic of society or government, the poet who loves dancers and the dance. The Dionysiac part of the artistic imagination is touched upon in Seanchan's blessing of the Girls who love hurley and dancing: 'Your feet delight in dancing, and your mouths / In the slow smiling that awakens love' (*V. Plays*, 294). His courtesy to the Girls contrasts with his treatment of the Princesses. There is a brief moment for the audience to feel the irony of the First Girl's line: 'The dear little Princesses are so gracious' (*V. Plays*, 295). As he takes the cup from the Princess, Seanchan holds her hand and says: 'Oh, long, soft fingers and pale finger-tips, / Well worthy to be laid in a king's hand!' (*V. Plays*, 296). The sudden lifting of the verse to courtly, elaborate compliment is pleasing; equally sudden is the shock of realisation that what started as an elaborate eulogy is really an elaborate insult, connecting the court with leprosy— the leprosy of mean-souled philistines as opposed to the Dionysiac art of the dancer: 'You've eyes of dancers; but hold out your hands, / For it may be there are none sound among you' (*V. Plays*, 296). Seanchan enforces his pointed insult not only to the Princesses but to the King and all he represents, by standing up for the first time, and then flinging the wine the Princesses gave him in their faces. He threatens to curse them and they scatter, going out 'in all directions'.

The moment is a dramatic peak, and if it is to be impressive and convincing (why should they be afraid of him?) Seanchan must be thought of as having definite *magical* power as well as noble rank. This, we have already seen, was true of the ancient 'Fili'. And Yeats now stresses the supernatural powers of Seanchan by giving him his vision of a leprous god just as the beggars enter. The First Cripple identifies Seanchan's vision with the moon, earlier linked with silver and money. The leprosy, then, suggests the contagion of a philistine society with a tamed god, which replaces the older order with its Dionysiac ethos.[27] This vision of the contagion and deformity in society has surged onto the stage in the mutilated bodies of the Cripples. The contrast between their ugliness and the beauty of the Court Ladies is a vivid piece of theatre which conveys in a flash the complicity of forces in the society opposed to Seanchan's values. The deformed human shapes are at once part of his vision of reality, and hungry, unlucky wretches deserving our compassion. Their purpose fulfilled, Yeats loses no time in getting the Cripples off stage again; they fear Seanchan's curse.

Seanchan realises his loneliness and the strength of the opposition—the whole current of the age running counter to him. It seems that he might despair as he sinks down again. It is just the right moment, dramatically, for his greatest temptation. Fedelm, his beloved, now appears.

Surprisingly, she is controlled and commanding in her manner, and expresses no pity for his condition nor, indeed, even mentions it. It is tempting to see in Fedelm yet another version of the proud and purposeful Maud Gonne. At precisely the moment when he has seemed most likely to succumb to the pressures of life, the poetic imagination soars, revealing that the present age will give way eventually to yet another, supporting the great race of heroes. Nietzsche, of course, is here and also the aristocratic magnanimity loved by Yeats and dramatised later in *The Golden Helmet*. Fedelm, however, remains on a domestic level below the prophetic ardour of Seanchan. Yeats's dramatic imagination is working in a practical and fully theatrical way at this climactic point in the play. Fedelm is aligned with the Princesses and the Church through her stage business. She, too, offers him the bread and wine we cannot help but associate with Communion. From one point of view, Fedelm thinks she is getting Seanchan to eat before his journey with her, whereas we see that she is really offering a kind of absolution before his journey to death. From another point of view, her connection with the communion image links her with the previous courtly tempters and thus assures us that like them she will fail just at the moment that she is almost sure of success. All the implications of the verse can now be held in the movement of the actor. The static figure of Seanchan makes every slight movement significant. And his movement here winds up the final tension of our suspense before releasing it: 'He takes bread from Fedelm, hesitates, and then thrusts it back into her hand' (*V. Plays*, 303). He has to face the inevitable accusation that he is not in love. This new complication tightens the dramatic tension, for Seanchan now realises that love is another of the nets he must fly by; we know that Seanchan loves Fedelm, and there is anguish in his sacrifice of her.

Seanchan's death is his ultimate lesson to King, court, pupils and audience. This is not to say that it is merely didactic; it is rather a case of imagination interpreting the experience we witness enacted before us in the theatre. Seanchan dies after giving his last brief instructions. But his vivid imagining of the carrying out of these instructions reveals his answer to death: heroic gaiety and exultation, 'some strange triumphant thought' as the Oldest Pupil calls it.

> When I and these are dead
> We should be carried to some windy hill
> To lie there with uncovered face awhile
> That mankind and that leper there may know
> Dead faces laugh.
>
> (*V. Plays*, 309–10)

The lines have a casual magnificence, 'seem a moment's thought'[28] which is then seized upon, as a telling phrase is noticed by the dying poet in this his last performance for the Court now assembled around him: 'King! King! Dead faces laugh' (*V. Plays*, 310). Here is also a far-reaching suggestiveness. The 'windy hill' evokes the landscapes of Greek tragedy as well as those of Ireland. The lines project beyond the play into the centuries. It is the experience of our common humanity which is evoked and caught in the impersonal 'mankind' and 'leper'. The King is reminded, in Seanchan's last lesson, that his power and authority must give way to death.

Before the slow processional which closes the performance, the brief resolution of the action is achieved by two perfectly balanced speeches. The Youngest Pupil is given the speech of command to the silver trumpets, whose music optimistically invokes the great race prophesied by Seanchan. The speech comes from the early, 'happy' version of the play. But it is the Oldest Pupil who is given the closing lines. And these hold the bitterness of all that Yeats found worst in the life of his times.

> Not what it leaves behind it in the light
> But what it carries with it to the dark
> Exalts the soul; nor song nor trumpet-blast

> Can call up races from the worsening world
> To mend the wrong and mar the solitude
> Of the great shade we follow to the tomb.
>
> *(V. Plays,* 312)

This most moving lack of illusion circling in our minds, we realise that Seanchan's story has been raised to the tragic level. The verbal duel between the Youngest and Oldest Pupil is in fact a dialogue between the young Yeats and the older Yeats of 1921, who rewrote the ending with the deeper knowledge of his middle age that poetry counts for very little in the real world, and that it is only a very few who follow it to the tomb.

In *The King's Threshold* Yeats had found the conflict which was to dominate his dramatic imagination for the rest of his life: the struggle between a strong hero and a guileful, ruthless ruler who defeats him, whether in the guise of Guaire, or Bricriu in *The Only Jealousy of Emer,* or Conchubar in the other plays of the Cuchulain cycle[29] and in *Deirdre.* This was the Yeatsian version of that daemonic myth he had discovered in Shakespeare and described in 'At Stratford-on-Avon' (1901) when he wrote:

> I have often had the fancy that there is some one myth for every man, which, if we but knew it, would make us understand all he did and thought. Shakespeare's myth, it may be, describes a wise man who was blind from very wisdom, and an empty man who thrust him from his place, and saw all that could be seen from very emptiness. *(E&I,* 107)

This image of paradoxical blindness Yeats puts onto the stage in the Blind Man of his one-act tragedy, *On Baile's Strand* (1904).[30] But in Yeats's play the Blind Man is the shadow of the King, Conchubar, while the Blind Man's companion, the Fool, is the shadow of Cuchulain. By mirroring his two combatants, Conchubar and Cuchulain, in this way, Yeats elaborates the one-act structure and enriches its texture on a small scale in the way the sub-plot in Elizabethan drama[31] was able to do on a grander scale. The framing of the Cuchulain tragedy by the Fool and Blind Man also paid tribute to that complicating convention favoured by many other playwrights: the play within the play. By introducing a few Singing Women into the revision of his play Yeats also hinted at the Chorus of Greek tragedy. These two devices aimed

at expressing what he named 'emotion of multitude', that reson-
ance which makes the particular story cry out for all humanity and
all ages. Poetry and imagination demand that art, if it be great,
always present a fable 'and the rich, far-wandering, many-imaged
life of the half-seen world beyond it' (*E&I*, 216). While retaining
the three unities so perfect for the one-acter's demands of tight-
ness, he was yet reacting against the austerity of French neo-
classical structure. Yeats felt confident enough as a playwright by
now to try enriching his chosen form.

If *The King's Threshold* had dramatised the seeming mastery
of the politician over the artistic imagination which, though it die
in one man, cannot be extinguished, *On Baile's Strand* dramatises
the politician, King Conchubar, mastering the warrior hero,
Cuchulain, by manipulation and magic. This struggle is more than
a conflict between a warrior and a King; it is also the quarrel
within the self which Yeats held to be the origin of poetry. To
explore this aspect of the play illuminates further Yeats's dramatic
imagination. By using the Fool and Blind Man as shadows to his
hero and villain, Yeats pointed up the eternal, archetypal nature
of the combatants, especially when in later versions of the play, he
discarded their particular names, Barach and Fintain, and under
the influence of Gordon Craig,[32] suggested the use of masks for
these characters. Apparently Yeats never used masks in *On Baile's
Strand*, though he recommends their use in the stage directions of
the later editions of the play.

If we ask why Yeats should have associated Fool and Blind Man
with Cuchulain and his story, the answer is that Yeats perceived
that in Greek and Shakespearean tragedy the hero is often accom-
panied by folly and blindness whether they are qualities in him-
self (Pentheus in *The Bacchae* or Othello) or projected into other
characters, or symbolised by mutilation. Gilbert Murray (who
with Yeats had been involved in the short-lived Masquers) devel-
oped this idea brilliantly in his Annual Shakespeare Lecture (1914)
and pointed out how Shakespeare 'made his greatest tragic hero
out of a Fool transfigured'.[33] Yeats's heroes are usually defeated,
being in some sense tragic fools—Cuchulain, Congal and Christ
of *Calvary*.

The conflict is also between two aspects of human nature
operating within a single personality: the impulsive, wild, in-
stinctive and restless side of man's nature, and the cautious,

hearth-loving, controlled part of him. Yeats had used the Fool and Blind Man aspects of human nature in rudimentary form in the figure of the Pupil or Novice of the 'Notes for a Celtic Order' compiled by him and Miss Horniman.[34] These notes provide the form of certain rituals of initiation. The staging of the rituals is mainly symmetrically patterned. A gong is advocated for use at certain moments, something which Yeats was able to use in the music for his plays on the Noh pattern; the term 'scenario' is used for the basic description of what happens in a ritual, and stage directions include the grouping of initiators in the form of a symbolic triangle (cf. the Yeatsian cone and the positioning of the three musicians in the ceremony of the unfolding and folding of the cloth in some dance-plays later); the Pupil is one who seeks knowledge and wisdom, knows something but does not know all, is human but seeks contact with the superhuman—in these ways he resembles the Fool figure; he resembles the Blind Man in that he appears in the ritual sightless, for he is brought in blindfolded and leaning on a rough staff (Typescript entitled 'The Entrance of the Wayfarer'). Virginia Moore in *The Unicorn* traced connections between Yeats's rituals and his plays. These rituals of the Celtic Order contain many of the images Yeats was to introduce into his plays—the spear and sword of Cuchulain; Forgael's boat; the bird-heads dropped from *The Shadowy Waters* but used later in *At the Hawk's Well*; hornless stag and red-eared hound used in *The Shadowy Waters*; the initiator who speaks of the death of Cuchulain, a theme which Yeats held to him until the end of his life; and the ceremony of covering the altar with a white cloth which later reappears (modified no doubt by the holding of a cloth in Kathakali dance-drama) in the plays for dancers. The rituals Yeats formulated bear not only a resemblance to his own plays, but, more surprisingly, to the form of Noh drama. The rituals, like the Noh, depict one 'character' learning a story, sometimes with the aid of a simple 'property' such as altar, or stylised boat; the story is legendary in content, as in the Noh, and it contains or implies some insight into the wisdom of the spirit. The whole procedure aims at gravity, dignity, secrecy and a mood of spiritual fulfilment. No wonder Yeats was delighted by the Noh form when he came to it later. Just as Yeats saw his drama as ritual, we may see his ritual as striving towards drama.

That Yeats, approaching forty, still unmarried and without

children, still in love with Maud Gonne, put much of his own passion into his hero is beyond doubt. Yeats altered Cuchulain's age to make it nearer to his own middle age. In *The King's Threshold* he had given full weight to the temptations of domestic love in the person of Fedelm, but Seanchan had resisted. In *On Baile's Strand*, Yeats allowed Cuchulain to realise the joys of a father-son relationship in the short-lived friendship with his as yet unknown son, before contriving, with devastating tragic irony, the slaughter of the boy by his father. One side of Yeats wanted domesticity while another side of him was afraid of it. The play externalised a conflict in the psyche. In this respect, it is significant that Cuchulain is master of both Fool and Blind Man, not just the former. And the remark which makes Cuchulain so uncomfortable that he appeals to his friends to leave instantly with him is Conchubar's shrewd, 'You are but half a king and I but half; / I need your might of hand and burning heart, / And you my wisdom' (*V. Plays*, 491).

This internal drama is linked with a certain suspicion about the power of the imagination. The supernatural forces of witchcraft and the Sidhe inhabit this play, and are shown to work directly on the imagination of both the Fool and Cuchulain. The stagecraft leaves us in no doubt that the potent magic of the oath-taking scene deceives Cuchulain, working on his perceptions and mind to divert him from harming Conchubar by sending him off to kill his own son on the first occasion and to fight insanely with the waves at the end of the play. Similarly, the Blind Man distracts the Fool by appealing to his imagination through the story he tells him of Cuchulain, much as parents might use this stratagem to distract a child from a small hurt. The Blind Man cheats the Fool by interesting him in the story of Cuchulain long enough to devour the chicken. This bird is the counterpart of Cuchulain's Son, whom Conchubar 'devours' by distracting the tragic fool, Cuchulain. The image shadows the heroic hawk imagery of the tragic scenes, rather as the beggars shadow their master, and the lowly, thieving magpie becomes an image for Conchubar at the end of the play. The imagination is in part a cheat but it, too, is cheated by our lowly dependence on the comfort of orderly society and mere bodily faculties. Political cunning can send Cuchulain mad, and it is the belly's demands which drag the Fool away from tragedy at the end.

Another way in which the play adds to our view of Yeats's dramatic imagination is through its dramatic techniques. The framing device of the play gives us a deft exposition by means of the Blind Man's telling the Fool about the situation from which the action will develop. The Blind Man's groping about the stage allows him to discover Conchubar's 'big chair' from which the High King will 'put the oath' on Cuchulain because 'he ran too wild'. The Fool asks, 'How will he do that?' (*V. Plays*, 463) and with that question, after only fifty-five lines of prose, Yeats provides the play's attack. Yeats has pulled the dramatic trigger, and rather like Falstaff and Hal,[35] Blind Man and Fool enact now in grotesque parody the binding of Cuchulain to Conchubar's service. We see the dramatic imaginations of the beggars at work before the 'real' oath-taking scene later in the play. Furthermore, the Blind Man's imagination is already turning the 'reality' of the play's action into a legend, in the manner of story-tellers of the old Irish oral tradition. He promises the Fool:

> I'll tell you a story—the Kings have story-tellers while they are waiting for their dinner—I will tell you a story with a fight in it, a story with a champion in it, and a ship and a queen's son that has his mind set on killing somebody that you and I know. (*V. Plays*, 465)

This is more than an expository device, more than a distancing tactic. Yeats is also demonstrating the way events penetrate the folk imagination to conceive legend and song, for the Fool now sings his song which thrusts magic, kings, battles and Cuchulain together in an upsurge of the wanton imagination that parallels Cuchulain's fancy which 'Runs as it were a swallow on the wind' (*V. Plays*, 489). The Blind Man leads us with all the pride and self-satisfaction of those in the know to the tragic question as to who fathered the Young Man whose quest is to kill Cuchulain. Yeats thus confronts the audience's imaginations, and the answer we supply involves us with the subsequent action, arousing our dread of the inevitability of a tragedy we nevertheless hope might be avoided. Behind it all is Yeats's sense of dramatic order, organising his legendary material into an ironic symmetry by which the Blind Man's account of the Young Man's combat on the beach anticipates the Fool's account of Cuchulain's combat on that same beach at the end of the play.

Another ironic symmetry is the Fool's dithering indecision as to whether he should ask Cuchulain who fathered Aoife's son. The Fool's indecision, absent from the first version, makes excellent comedy, keeping us teetering on the brink of a comic plot which could reverse the tragic impetus of the Cuchulain action. It also mirrors the four reversals in Cuchulain's role which Yeats plants at climactic points to form the backbone of the dramatic structure of the play. Cuchulain first refuses the oath, then accepts it; he is put on his guard by the entry of the Young Man, and then stops the other warriors from attacking; having shown how much he likes the Young Man, he accepts his challenge; finally, he purposes to kill Conchubar, and then rushes to fight the waves.

If the prose framing device shows reality being turned into a legend which the total action of the play will dramatise, that core of 'reality' which is the play's main action at its point of crisis demands the resources of poetry. For Yeats's dramatic imagination, verse is almost always the medium for his highest reality. The prose scenes of Fool and Blind Man are not simply copies of Shakespearean low-life prose scenes. They are more akin to the tough prose of *King Lear*, but, as we have seen, invite judgments not based on realism. They inhabit the realm of masks and archetypes. The verse is fast-moving, spare, bold with dramatic ironies. Yet it is capable of accommodating such different tones as the acute directness of Conchubar's 'I know you to the bone' (*V. Plays*, 483) and the bounding, histrionic energy of Cuchulain's proud account of Aoife, mocking Conchubar's and his tame women's words, shading through mockery and anger to love of 'that high, laughing, turbulent head of hers / Thrown backward . . . / Or when love ran through all the lineaments / Of her wild body' (*V. Plays*, 487) which is Maud Gonne alive in Yeats's imagination. This energetic, flexible blank verse can also swing into the rhyming couplets (discreetly introduced by half-rhymes at the beginning) that we find in the song of the three Women of the oath-taking scene. The fascinating conjunction of love and hatred, delicacy and brutality, we find in Yeats's deepening imaginative vision, he renders in dramatic song of astonishing power:

> Those wild hands that have embraced
> All his body can but shove
> At the burning wheel of love
> Till the side of hate comes up.
>
> (*V. Plays*, 497)

The extraordinary strength of the lines comes from thought and context and telling phrase. But Yeats's verbal mastery operates too at the intimate level of brilliant rhyme, that unexpected linking of love with the brutal, uncouth word 'shove'. The Yeatsian imagination is as magnanimous and abundant as his heroes; he can allow the effect a lesser writer might prize to be muffled by Cuchulain's simultaneous speech, for the binding of opposites in the rhyming song runs parallel with the binding of opposites in the stage ritual of the oath-taking ceremony. The spectacle is impressive, but as soon as Cuchulain's short prayer to those supernatural 'glittering ones' that Conchubar's magic seeks to exorcise is over, Yeats loses no time in advancing his action by the sudden knocking on the gate. It is Cuchulain's son, and the tragic trap is set. The knocking recalls *Macbeth*, just as Cuchulain's repeated 'Put up your swords' echoes *Othello*. But it is no longer a question of awkward imitation. Shakespearean intensities and the bustling pageant of his plays inhabit Yeats's imagination along with the austerity of Greek tragedy and a feeling for its grim ironies. The framework, for example, delivers its own Yeatsian subtleties. The connection between Blind Man and Conchubar introduces a subtly teasing element into the ruining of Cuchulain. The Blind Man knows who the Young Man is. By analogy, we wonder as we contemplate Cuchulain's misfortune, could it be that Conchubar had guessed all along the truth which Cuchulain so tragically fails to guess?

Yeats has absorbed devices from his great precedents so well that they do not stand out at odds with his work, but become Yeatsian effects, at one with the other effects he attains in the poetry and stagecraft of the play, all caught up in the tragic impetus towards that terrible moment of silence when Cuchulain, knowing the truth at last, makes the bench shake with his grief. When Cuchulain, like some Shakespearean hero, sees himself playing a part, he is yet culminating that very Yeatsian scheme in the play which explores the heroic world as it is made fact for the imagination of the story-teller. Nor can Cuchulain escape the characteristically Yeatsian view that the heroic world has been undermined and reduced to squalor. The 'pale windy people' of the Sidhe, Cuchulain realises, 'love to blow a smoking coal / Till it's all flame, the wars they blow aflame / Are full of glory, and heart-uplifting pride, / And not like this' (*V. Plays*, 522). At the very moment of the legendary past when the hero gave the artistic imagination matter for its songs, the filthy modern tide had already turned, and was flowing in to drown the battling hero.

Yeats understood well the nature of tragedy and its irony, which he described as 'that untroubled sympathy for men as they are, as apart from all they do and seem, which is the substance of tragic irony' (*E&I*, 106). The tragic irony at the basis of the early quarrel scene in *On Baile's Strand* is the knowledge which is revealed to us that Cuchulain, in the mysterious core of his heart, really does crave the son and heir he so violently repudiates, and will later kill.

> *Conchubar* : I know you to the bone,
> I have heard you cry, aye, in your very sleep,
> 'I have no son', and with such bitterness
> That I have gone upon my knees and prayed
> That it might be amended

Cuchulain's reply shows that he takes a cynical view of Conchubar's concern :

> *Cuchulain* : For you thought
> That I should be as biddable as others
> Had I their reason for it;
>
> (V. Plays, 483)

Even if Conchubar is inventing the incident for his own purposes, it is still significant that Cuchulain's reply does not dispute the desire expressed in his sleep, but only Conchubar's motives for praying that the desire be fulfilled. Yeats has shown us the deeps of Cuchulain's mind. On another level of irony, in taking the oath, Cuchulain is following a deep impulse within himself; yet by the very nature of the oath he has to kill the fulfilment of that impulse for son and heir. But the killing is at the same time the expression of the other impulse within him to have no heir, to remain young and passionately free. The talk of love and hate is basic to the forces at work in the relationship between Cuchulain and Aoife, and Cuchulain and his son. Cuchulain's story thus dramatises the problem of those about to live their middle age, regretting youth but having ultimately to leave it behind and face maturity and what they take to be the dull trap of security; it deals also with the connected tension between the desire for children and heirs, or natural human longings to pass on a name and family influence, and that desire for a more personal immortality through the fame earned by individual qualities—in Cuchulain's case heroic feats of arms, and in Yeats's case poetic achievement. On yet another level, the Oedipus situation appears in a son who comes to kill his father. These considerations, and above all the realisation that Cuchulain, for all his boasts, really desires a son, make the catastrophe all the more moving.

When Cuchulain fights the waves, the Fool's description of the events off the stage is masterly. It is the dramatic imagination at a high point. The prose is direct, spare, factual. The emotion comes not from histrionics on the part of the Fool, nor from emotive language. It comes out of the profound, unfathomable situation itself. Yeats with fine tact and restraint lets it speak for itself:

> *Fool*: He is going up to King Conchubar. They are all about the young man. No, no, he is standing still. There is a great wave going to break, and he is looking at it. Ah; now he is running down to the sea, but he is holding up his sword as if he were going into a fight. (*V. Plays*, 523)

As the fight with the waves begins, the Fool's excitement mounts; his absorption in what he is watching is catching. The Blind Man itches to know as well: 'What is he doing now?' he cries, and 'Where are the kings? What are the kings doing?' (*V. Plays*, 524). Adroitly Yeats has put the audience into the same position as the Blind Man. We, too, are reliant upon the eyes of the Fool. It is with a sense of enormous regret that we have to leave the vivid fight with the waves when the cunning Blind Man drags the Fool off to rob the empty houses.

Yeats's next tragedy, *Deirdre* (1906), also took up the motif of the story-teller's relation to the legendary basis of the dramatic action. The exposition is again managed by the device of a character who tells part of the protagonist's story. There is now more compression and pace, though, because the framing device has simply been dropped in favour of the Chorus of three women called the Musicians.

Deirdre has a tense, simple action achieved by Yeats's characteristic pouncing at the end of the legend, at the point of the lovers' return; all that remains is their capture and death. Yet alongside his dramatisation of legend, Yeats by means of the Musicians gives us an insight into how events become legends and are transmuted into art. The play is about love and treachery, but also about his own dramatic imagination and its predilection for folk-lore and legend.

The play opens with the First Musician excitedly telling her companions that she has found further material for songs about Deirdre and Naoise, 'I have a story right, my wanderers, / That has so mixed with fable in our songs / That all seemed fabulous' (*V. Plays*, 345). She can feel that something extraordinary will happen in Conchubar's realm, for she has just had news of Deirdre's return. Yeats builds a situation in which we can watch how a legend develops from real events and human passions taken up imaginatively by professional wandering musicians. This chorus is not only humanity, but the artistic imagination itself. The Musicians are eager to weigh the details of the story, consider its possibilities. The First Musician gives us the exposition of Deirdre's story, her girlhood, and its attack: 'She put on womanhood, and he lost peace, / And Deirdre's tale began.' She then recalls the complicating factor—Naoise—and the development through elopement. The Second Musician's response is professional, cautious, a bit jaded: 'The tale were well enough / Had it a finish' (*V. Plays*, 346). The Yeats play has now achieved all the exposition it needs. The Musicians need a dénouement for their ballad. Enter Fergus expecting a message from Conchubar. He promises the musicians good material to complete their love song. But there is a too obvious prophetic irony in his words, 'For there'll be two before the night is in, / That bargained for their love, and paid for it / All that men value' (*V. Plays*, 347). He anticipates that the exiles will return unmolested, according to his own negotiations with Conchubar. Interpreted by those who know the legend's tragic burden, however, Fergus's remark has supplied at once the attack of Yeats's play and, in sum, a tragic dénouement for the Musicians. The rest of the play can now unfold, showing how Yeats's dramatic imagination characteristically seizes a situation in the fifth act, and forces it rapidly towards the crisis;

showing, too, how Yeats's lyric imagination, thoroughly integrated dramatically through the Musicians, can find matter for their song.

The First Musician is delighted by her luck in being on the spot for the return of the lovers, but having 'no country but the roads of the world' (*V. Plays*, 348) she has the insight and quick wisdom to know that the lovers face death, and old kings are jealous.

She has the predatory nature of the artist as a snapper-up of material from the lives of other people. When she asks Deirdre if 'anything lies heavy on your heart' (*V. Plays*, 359), she is not a clumsy exposition device, but an artist seeking new material. Out of her compassion and admiration for Deirdre, she also helps her to see Conchubar's motivation, which has the added effect of letting the audience know what to expect (the inevitability of tragedy) and helping us realise that the Musician is still pondering her material. There is also a complicity between the brave, the fair, the heroic people and the artistic imagination. The Musician wishes to help Deirdre by telling her of Conchubar's preparations and love charms prepared against her return, much as Hamlet has an alliance with the players. This complicity is not mere plot mechanism; it is rather a symbol of the connections between art and life. If art finds the matter for legends in the passions of great heroes and heroines, and if Yeats's art finds its subject in these very legends, life itself, as Seanchan taught, finds its models for behaviour in legend and mythic art. While the lovers await their fateful meeting with Conchubar, they aspire to the haughty detachment long before of Lugaidh Redstripe's playing chess[36] with his wife in the face of death. Naoise consciously pursues an aristocratic code of honour, and seeks its celebration in song. He wonders if an ancient poem records the incident. Deirdre appeals to the Musicians to make art out of her own story in words which echo the search for an ending at the opening of the play. 'for naught's lacking / But a good end to the long, cloudy day.' The fading evening light in the rough forest cabin signals that the end is near amidst solitude and loneliness. While she plays, Deirdre calls for 'a music that can mix itself / Into imagination, but not break / The steady thinking that the hard game needs' (*V. Plays*, 374). Her words express imperfectly the Yeatsian view of art and life. The metaphysical element is lacking, and it is this that the Musicians supply in their next song which sees lovers as symbolic of the soul's desire, 'When love-longing is but drouth / For the things come after death' (*V. Plays*, 375). When Deirdre again questions the Musicians about how they will praise the lovers should they die, she again echoes the opening of the play, indeed its first line, as she gives them her bracelet 'To show that you have Deirdre's story right' (*V. Plays*, 377).

The Deirdre legend, the most celebrated of those sorrows of Irish story-telling, Yeats presents as true—the bracelet is the artist's specific evidence that the legend is based on an eye-witness account. This helps to make his dramatisation more immediate, and accords with his theory of an art of personality at moments of passionate crisis. The fact that Deirdre obtains the dagger with which she kills herself from the Musician serves, too, as another link helping to chain together art and life.

The Musicians have watched the preparations for the King's bed; they have watched the skulking, voyeuristic and ultimately sadistic picture of the High King in love which Yeats creates in Conchubar; they have watched the confrontation between him and the lovers, his unmasked deceit, the vengeful, horrifically stealthy murder of Naoise; his pleasure that occurs even while Deirdre pleads for Naoise's life; they have observed her second, tense 'game of chess' as she manoeuvres Conchubar to allow her to see her dead lover's corpse; and they have noted the bird imagery flitting through the play. Deirdre had rejected her own identification with the cold-blooded sea-mew. Naoise had seen what she really was in his last two speeches. He called her his eagle. This is what the Musicians' imaginations can seize on, together with her pride, for their magnificent consummation of the tragic story in the last song, a dirge worthy of Elizabethan and Jacobean tragedy, worthy of a final Greek chorus, and Yeatsian to the core:

First Musician: They are gone, they are gone. The proud may lie by the proud.
Second Musician: Though we were bidden to sing, cry nothing loud.
First Musician: They are gone, they are gone.
Second Musician: Whispering were enough.
First Musician: Into the secret wilderness of their love.
Second Musician: A high, grey cairn. What more is to be said?
First Musician: Eagles have gone into their cloudy bed.

The song is a collaboration between instrumentalist and two singers. Each singer adds a line, almost casually, effortlessly, and the song grows into art. It grows from a context of events which we, like them, have seen dramatised, and which they have distilled in their imaginations, blending it perfectly with the myth-laden topography of Ireland, that landscape of ancient cairns, abode of stone and eagles.

The play's tight one-act structure allows Yeats to concentrate on tragedy wrought to the uttermost, unhampered by Synge's realism and three-act treatment which inevitably brought too much attention to the lovers' motivation for return. Yeats's deft, economical characterisation provides two fascinating roles: a subtle villain in Conchubar, and a queenly lover, proud, beautiful and hot-blooded enough to win the audience's sympathy, essential for the tragedy, and the services of an actress of the stature of Mrs Patrick Campbell. Yeats's dramatic imagination had found the skill to make a major artistic success of a new and subtle use of the one-act play; in *Deirdre*, he dramatised Irish legend in such a way as to suggest events being lived out while the artist observes and uses these very events for the creation of song. Why, in a legendary setting, should Yeats bother to tell us the realistic detail that his Musicians are handsome women of about forty? In a writer like Yeats this could not be lack of artistic decorum, or lack of gallantry. It is merely a little clue to the fact that he himself is fortyish, and the touch confirms for us the link between the Musicians and Yeats's imagination, recreating the story and musing on his own artistic processes.

In short plays characterisation is of necessity more a swift sketch or even a given trait rather than the rounded illusion of wholeness possible, though not always achieved, in three- or five-act plays. But in *Deirdre* Yeats showed by many deft touches that when he wanted to achieve an effect of depth he could do so within the limits of his characteristic form. Because many of his short plays use 'given' or emblematic characters such as Queen, King, Fool and the like, it has sometimes been too easily assumed that Yeats's dramatic imagination did not respond to human traits. But as a man of the theatre, he knew that actors need roles, and that role set against role must make sparks fly. Cuchulain and Conchubar, Fool and Blind Man in *On Baile's Strand*, Deirdre and Conchubar, are not merely schematic opposites; sparks fly when

they are on stage together. In *Deirdre* the characters are swiftly
established, and clearly distinguished one from the other. There
is a dramatic balance between the almost stoic calm of Naoise and
the passionate restlessness of Deirdre, between the humanity and
honour of Fergus and the cold treachery of Conchubar. But within
these broad limits there is a pleasing measure of subtlety. In the
second half of the play, Fergus, Conchubar and Deirdre reveal
deeper natures than might be expected in so short a play. Fergus,
for instance, emerges at the end with a new authoritative manner,
having lived through to the other side of tragic deception to con-
template the last great irony of the play, Deirdre's suicide, which
deceives Conchubar, the slow and patient deceiver, in one swift
moment of heroism. Fergus counters Conchubar's rage at his
cheated lust with a high and noble coolness which carries instinc-
tive authority and a sense of what is fitting at this moment. His
words have the pressure of deep but restrained emotion; they
convey the sacred, taboo, and profoundly private nature of love
and of death :

> *Fergus*: King, she is dead; but lay no hand upon her.
> What's this but empty cage and tangled wire,
> Now the bird's gone? But I'll not have you touch it.
> (*V. Plays*, 388)

Fergus's lines recapitulate previous imagery in the play in a truly
Shakespearean manner. There have been throughout numerous
recurring images of prey and hunters, birds and nets, traps or
cages. Naoise is caught in a net and murdered like a hunted
animal, and the setting of the play, its hut and inner recess, with
woods outside, is imaged as a trap or cage. At the end of the play
Conchubar's bridal cage becomes the narrow grave, yet at the same
time, death is an escape, and in the final song, the lovers have
become not game birds but eagles who have soared. The opening
of the curtain to reveal the corpses is an opening of the cage, and
the bodies themselves remind one of the ancient image of the soul
as bird, body as cage. Thus the image patterns are not only verbal,
but find physical presence in the set and the actors' bodies and
roles in a truly dramatic and theatrical way. All this culminates
in, and richly surrounds, Fergus's comment on the tragic spectacle.
Simultaneously, the image of the broken cage, in conveying the
pathetic, useless frailty of a corpse, paradoxically lifts the emotion

from the poor and broken to the level of nobility and heroism, perhaps more effectively than a longer speech containing what might be considered 'noble' imagery. It is a very powerful, indelible moment, and almost any dramatist could be excused for finishing the play at this point, by merely clearing up the bodies with a conventional phrase. But Yeats achieves one last effect by making Conchubar repeat his angry but characteristically un-illusioned appraisal of the situation, and then summon a stance of haughty courage and cruelty:

> *Conchubar*: I have no need of weapons,
>   There's not a traitor that dare stop my way.
>   Howl, if you will; but I, being King, did right
>   In choosing her most fitting to be Queen,
>   And letting no boy lover take the sway.
>
> (V. Plays, 388)

The compulsion to accept the lines at their face value is *almost* irresistible, so powerful is their rhetorical use of the idea of Kingship. It is with a slight feeling of surprise that we remember Naoise has, in fact, not only taken but *held* 'the sway' for at least seven years. Yeats brilliantly ends by *demonstrating* Conchubar's duplicity and persuasive power over men. We see him facing the anger of the mob, and we realise just how Fergus could have been so deceived by him. Moreover, on looking back at Conchubar's part, we realise another subtlety of his characterisation. His kingly motives for his actions he has made public, but we glimpse a human, private aspect of his sexuality.

Yeats sketches with a few exquisitely suggestive strokes the lineaments of a sadistic lust. Conchubar's relationship with Deirdre has been from the beginning a gloatingly voyeuristic one. He has been grooming her from childhood for a royal deflowerment, visiting her daily to watch the progress of her puberty. During her period of exile with Naoise, he has schemed at the perfect plan to retrieve her. His lateness to appear betokens his enjoyment of the tension and fear they must feel. He peeps into the hut, like a hunter looking into the trap to see his catch. It is highly significant, for this voyeuristic aspect of Conchubar's lust, that Yeats chooses very carefully the moment when we first see him. He looks through the door at the lovers just when Deirdre remembers the very first time that Naoise made love to her, and

she asks him to kiss her again with 'that old vehement, bewilder-
ing kiss'. As they embrace, Conchubar appears.

Deirdre quickly senses Conchubar's sadistic sexuality and uses
it as her strongest weapon to win the chance to kill herself on
Naoise's body. She appeals to this sadism when she tells him:

> It is enough that you were master here.
> Although we are so delicately made,
> There's something brutal in us, and we are won
> By those who can shed blood. It was some woman
> That taught you how to woo. . . .

Because he is what he is, Conchubar accepts this without gain-
saying it. When Deirdre goes on to plead that she must lay out
Naoise's body, to do 'what's customary' or be haunted by her
lover's ghost, he cuts harshly across her pleas, 'You are deceiving
me' (*V. Plays*, 384). What finally makes Conchubar give way is
Deirdre's subtle assumption of a sexual role with him combined
with taunts at his lack of virility and courage. She has become in
a flash the young and potent wife of the old man, and he, true to
type, must now do as she says. His last query, which ironically hits
the truth, she brushes aside by repeating the tactic. She assumes
the part of his wife as if it is a 'fait accompli', and combines it
with another sexual taunt:

> *Deirdre*: Have me searched,
>   If you would make so little of your queen.
>   It may be that I have a knife hid here
>   Under my dress. Bid one of these dark slaves
>   To search me for it.
> *Conchubar*: Go to your farewells, Queen.
>
> (*V. Plays*, 386)

For the first time, Conchubar calls her 'Queen'. He accepts the
false dream she has given him, and so completely that his jealousy
is aroused by her willingness to submit to a 'search' by the black
warriors. This sexual taunt with its racist overtones silences his
objections. He is too busy thinking of her erotic possibilities to
protest longer. He wants to finish with the formalities. The King
is mated by a Queen's sacrifice.

These indications of Conchubar's sexual nature are a reliable
guide to the playing of the part. To put such qualities in the body

of an ageing man of fading virility, makes this a rich part for the actor; the moment of his deception by Deirdre can now be seen as a dramatic subtlety rather than an improbability, as has sometimes been supposed. It is to Yeats's great credit that he achieves his effects within so little space.

In writing Deirdre's role, Yeats believed his dramatic imagination had soared beyond the capabilities of his local actresses at the time. He may have been right, for he felt the necessity to bring in a rising London actress of Irish origin, Miss Darragh, for the successful première at the Abbey. In a letter to his father (21 July 1906), Yeats revealed that he thought Miss Darragh represented a new kind of tragedian ready to supplant Mrs Patrick Campbell's generation. Actually, Mrs Pat's performance of Deirdre in the New Theatre production of 1908 was an even greater success than Miss Darragh's interpretation. In 1921 Yeats still remembered Mrs Pat's playing of the role with great pleasure.[37]

Mrs Campbell's hold on his imagination found expression in his attempts to write about the visible and invisible sides of a person's nature, self and anti-self, in *The Player Queen* (1919). The play, in two scenes, was begun in 1908 as a tragedy, but it gave Yeats endless trouble[38] until he turned it into farce. It is a pivotal example of that complicated comic wildness in Yeats's dramatic imagination which emerged earlier in the high spirits of *The Green Helmet* (1910) and was further developed in the strange, exciting theatricality of his later metaphysical comedy *The Herne's Egg* (1938). Moreover, of these examples of the comic side of Yeats's dramatic imagination, it is *The Player Queen* which in Septimus presents another Yeatsian dramatic treatment of the poet-dramatist. The finished comedy, set in a fantastic realm in the indeterminate past, dramatises the ideas from *Per Amica Silentia Lunae*, that each person seeks an anti-self and that history is a cycle in which one age miraculously and turbulently reverses itself. Septimus, the poet-dramatist, and his troupe are to perform 'The Tragical History of Noah's Deluge' in a country where the mob is bent on deposing their shy old maid of a queen.

As the medieval play of Noah deals farcically with a divinely ordained cataclysm which brings one age to an end and begins another, so Yeats's play reveals the reversal of the historical gyre from a worn-out Christian era to a new era whose god is imaged as the Unicorn heralded by a prophet, celebrated by the poet,

Septimus, and accompanied by mob disorder. It is not difficult to discern notions and themes here which recur many times in Yeats's later works. But the manner of the play is fantastic, funny and ironic. Yeats exploits a double point of view, much as he did later in the preamble to *A Vision*. His dramatic imagination therefore gives us double interpretations of actions and characters, using appropriately enough a two-scene structure. On one level the prophet of the new age is a reincarnation of the ass on which Christ rode into Jerusalem, yet on the ironic level he is a filthy old vagrant caught up in mass hysteria who rolls in the straw and brays like a donkey. Septimus is the inspired, Dionysiac imagin-ation of the land; he is the Bard who sees past, present and future; defender of the chaste Unicorn; he is superior to popular poets, as Seanchan has been superior to the Chamberlain, and, again like Seanchan, spends much of his time lying on the stage. But he is also a drunkard, a purveyor of sounding rhetoric, a hen-pecked adulterer, absurdly superior to poets called Peter of the Purple Pelican and Happy Tom, lying incapable from drink and then packed off into exile by his own wife, the new Queen, rather than dying for art before an inflexible King. The drink and lechery recall the Rhymers, Johnson and Dowson,[39] but also suggest sexual problems, even impotence. From one point of view, Septimus is the Romantic poet, a Cyrano, a Dumas, in whose world Peter of the Purple Pelican would be a minor irritant; from another he is an impotent rhetorician, a Yeatsian Carlyle: in short, phase seven of Yeats's system at its best and at its worst.[40] The Saint Octema, invoked by the Queen as her 'patroness' is an invented figure, supposedly martyred at Antioch. To the Queen she is a holy martyr, but to those who read Yeats's description of phase eight in *A Vision*, she will seem the virginal Queen's mask: 'Here for the most part are those obscure wastrels who seem powerless to free themselves from some sensual temptation—drink, women, drugs—and who cannot in a life of crisis create any lasting thing.' Yet the saintly connection is also there, for Yeats cites Dostoievsky's *Idiot* as 'almost certainly an example' (*AV*, 118) of the phase. Nona, Septimus's mistress, is just another actress, having nothing obviously in common with Yeats's phase nine personality beyond the designation 'unnamed artist' (*AV*, 119). Decima, however, has more in common with the phase ten personality whose will Yeats describes as 'The Image-Breaker', True Mask as 'Organisation', True Creative Mind as 'Domination through emotional construction', but whose type is Parnell. Decima, as a masterful woman who forsakes play-acting for the role of monarch, and seeks to 'end ambition through the command of multitudes' may hint at phase ten. But such correspondences are suggestive touches only and cannot be closely worked out or pushed very far at all. Yeats's double vision ensures, in fact, that we cannot erect a rigid allegorical framework. Elements from his system appear in motley and the whole effect is one of baffling fun, an Ahernian jest, like the poem 'The Phases of the Moon', which juggles with mystery, humour and ideas. As stolid old Joseph Holloway noted of the first production, 'Though its purport is wrapt in mystery, its beauty won home.'[41]

This Yeatsian double vision is held firmly by the double structure which wrenches him away from his usual kind of one-acter toward the format of a two-act play. The first scene builds towards mob violence, the revelation of a miraculous beast, the Unicorn, begetting a new age on the Virgin Queen or Priestess, with Septimus as a Dionysiac bard linked to the aged prophet. The scene is framed by a comic chorus of three old men in grotesque masks. But in the ironic light of scene two the Queen actually appears as a timid little nun-manquée; the bard as an adulterer who can be unceremoniously turfed out, a Noah with scold for wife; while the new Queen takes not a Unicorn but a Prime Minister to bed and the talk of the emblematic creature becomes the theatrical fun of pantomime beasts in a dance, circus animals who are put to flight. The disintegration of a dynasty in scene one becomes merely the break-up of a marriage in scene two.

The overall effect of the play is to express a dramatic imagin-ation which parodies its own previous stage devices and symbols and boots them off-stage at the end in the form of Septimus and his troupe. Yet in devising all this, Yeats had also created a matrix in which the new theatre form he found for *At the Hawk's Well* could evolve. Embedded in *The Player Queen* are conven-tions of the new dance-plays such as the Chorus who set the scene and time at the beginning of the play, the symbolic, supernatural songs represented by Attracta's song about the mask, a guiding metaphor and concept, and the comic dance of the animals itself, which as in the dance-plays has erotic overtones attended by seeming revelation. *The Player Queen*, then, says farewell to Yeats's old stagecraft, not with a curse as in 'The Fascination of What's Difficult' but with comedy—his ounce of civet to sweeten imagination—and hints at his new drama: it marks a reversal of his theatrical gyre, a pivotal moment in the history of his dramatic imagination. If Septimus is a grotesque parody of Seanchan, he also anticipates those wild old wicked men who look through glinting eyes in Yeats's later years.

6

The Eye of the Mind

I

EMOTIONALLY, intellectually and dramatically, though not chronologically, *The Player Queen* in its finished version is the pivot between Yeats's public stage plays and his private drawing-room plays. Its development in embryo spans the barren hiatus between his theatre and its anti-self. Losing heart with the Abbey,[1] Yeats plunged into a difficult, unproductive time of disillusion which found its expression in the harsher toned poetry of *Responsibilities* (1914) and the bitter defeats dramatised in the first four dance-plays.[2] However, his delight in Japanese Noh drama helped him to invent the new dance-play form evolved under its influence. He was deeply unhappy at the time of his marriage, but his excitement at Mrs Yeats's automatic writing soon inspired him to develop and organise their metaphysical speculations into *A Vision*. The Easter Rebellion of 1916 soon gave him the sense of Ireland's ancient heroism alive again, even amid the horror of the unprecedented slaughter of the 1914–18 war. He got a creative second wind and lived on to enjoy his marriage and write much of his greatest work. No wonder that pivotal play, conceived as tragedy, was eventually born as comedy.

Before the publication of *The Player Queen* in 1922, both as a single volume and in *Plays in Prose and Verse*, where it appeared with stage plays from the Abbey period and earlier, Yeats had published the first plays of his new dramatic style in *At the Hawk's Well* (1917),[3] *Two Plays for Dancers* (1919) and *Four Plays for Dancers* (1921). He forged this style in response to new external conditions—the theatre as he now found it—and from the effect of Noh drama on his dramatic imagination. The use he made of

Noh can best be explained as the borrowing of useful conventions from an alien poetic drama to create an entirely new kind of western dance-drama which, without upsetting decorum, brilliantly extends the scope of the one-act play. He did not write Irish Noh. Anyone who has witnessed Noh in Japan can see in a flash that it is very different from a Yeatsian dance-play. Critics and audiences who see drama according to the assumptions of western realism have regularly thought Yeats's plays undramatic. Now that so much anti-realist experimentation has occurred over the last eighty-odd years and a growing number of play-goers have been exposed to various kinds of oriental drama and theatre, the realist conventions can be seen more easily as conventional alone, rather than the test of what is dramatic. A contemporary definition of drama cannot be adequate if it remains parochial. It must take into account conventions from the East as well as the West. In such a definition Yeatsian drama can take its place without any apologies.

The story of Yeats's turning to Noh drama, partly under the influence of Ezra Pound, has been well documented by Yeats himself in his 'Certain Noble plays of Japan' (1916) and the open letter to Lady Gregory, 'A People's Theatre' (1919) as well as by other writers.[4] But it is worth recalling here that Yeats's rationale for seeking an anti-theatre has much to recommend it, given the fact that he was above all a verse dramatist. He saw that even Shakespeare's poetry could arouse ironic noises in the gallery. He sat behind a bored, yawning man at a performance of *The King's Threshold* at the Court theatre. Yeats rightly concluded that in a modern theatre audience, very few people have an ear for poetry. He also knew better than to yoke verse to modern realistic conventions. He had always been careful to set his verse plays in the past, using conventions for which speech in verse seemed appropriate. The number of poetry lovers was small. That he concluded his plays would henceforth best be conceived for a drawing-room rather than a theatre, is not a sign that he knew very little about it, but rather confirmation that he was a practical man of the theatre who had no illusions any longer about the drawing power of poetry. Complicated sets would be abandoned, and cast numbers drastically reduced. Yeats's practical knowledge of play production, his realisation that Noh offered, besides workable conventions for dealing with the supernatural, a noble precedent tested in the

E

theatre over hundreds of years, together with his mastery of the one-act form, gave him all the confidence he needed to achieve in *At the Hawk's Well* the vehicle for a modern dramatic poetry created out of a sensibility akin to that of Noh dramatists whose 'emotion was self-conscious and reminiscent, always associating itself with pictures and poems' (*E&I*, 233). Noh gave to his dramatic imagination a world of men in relationship to ghosts, where the deeps of the mind before and after death found theatrical expression of astonishing beauty and poignancy. This drama celebrated the sacred places of Japan, haunts of gods and long-dead heroes and lovers, just as Yeats wished to celebrate the haunted landscape of Ireland; it achieved a stylised beauty of voice, music, gesture and movement rather than realism; it preferred chant and song to realistic speech, ritual to realistic action; it achieved its climax through dance in a fully prepared dramatic context; it used the immobile face and the eternal expressions of the finely carved mask; and it expressed a vision of human experience which opposed, because it pre-dated, that western materialism which ignored spirit in favour of body and mechanism.[5] The result was that Yeats's dramatic imagination could face up to its own temporary barrenness and then find renewed expression through an entirely novel but congenial, half-anticipated use of the one-act form. He wanted to look through the mind's eye, and by abandoning illusion for a more austere theatricality he hoped to stimulate his audience's imagination: 'Painted scenery, after all, is unnecessary to my friends and to myself, for our imagination kept living by the arts can imagine a mountain covered with thorn-trees in a drawing room without any great trouble, and we have many quarrels with even good scene-painting' (*V. Plays*, 416).

At the Hawk's Well (1916) establishes the pattern of his dance-plays. A screen stands near the wall of a room, and on the floor drum, gong, and zither await the Musicians. The first Musician enters, carrying a folded black cloth. He stands centre front facing the audience. The other Musicians enter and slowly unfold the cloth, singing as they retreat on either side of the first Musician until 'the stretched cloth and the wall make a triangle with the first Musician at the apex supporting the centre of the cloth' (*V. Plays*, 399). The Yeatsian gyre or cone has been paced out, the area becomes not just a 'stage' but a magical place, rather as the Noh stage is sacred.[6] At the same time, the mask-like make-up on the players, their stylised movement, the emblematic golden hawk on the cloth, and the songs which suddenly break the silence, all conspire to establish instantaneously the atmosphere of a remote age, the possibility of magic, the mood for poetry and imagination to be released: 'I call to the eye of the mind' sings the Musician, and we are drawn into an art that is art because it is not nature, into a world that can accommodate the supernatural. What can the mind's eye see? In two octaves balanced one against the other it sees wind-swept hill, dry well, climbing hero, a man young and old. It poses the question of the futility of life. The cloth folded, the Musicians sit by their instruments, and the audience sees that the Guardian of the Well is crouching beside a blue cloth. This girl and the well have been conjured by the cloth ceremony. Mixing song and speech the Musicians complete all the exposition we need. They establish in a couplet the theme of conflicting impulses in humanity: quest or home and hearth, action or passivity, as in *On Baile's Strand*; they give us the fact that it is night, the time of dreams and fear; they introduce the Old Man who enters through the audience. The Musicians act also as chorus, replacing the larger one used in Noh drama. Yeats has fused two Noh conventions into one with a theatrical economy perfect for a one-acter. The chorus complete their function of providing a frame for the action by repeating the cloth ceremony at the end of the play. This Yeatsian ceremony so perfect for introducing lyrical exposition and ritualised action in fact owes nothing to Japanese Noh, but is similar to a convention used in Kathakali dance-drama.

Yeats's dramatic imagination was eclectic. His cloth ceremony, and the Noh drama conventions he used, such as the central metaphor or symbol, the on-stage Musicians who accompany the action but are not characters in the play, lyrical choric comment, the dreaming-back of ghosts, the climactic dance, he blends together in a way that preserves the firm basis of western one-act structure. None of the conventions is intrinsically at odds with the one-acter, for the 'jo-ha-kyu' arrangement of the Noh is essentially a beginning, middle and end pattern.[7] The cloth ceremony and choric comment from the Musicians can rapidly establish atmosphere, setting and time, the central image and theme, introduce the main characters, and even pose the question and set the situation which gives a play its attack, as in *At the Hawk's Well*:

'why should I sleep?' the heart cries

and

> That old man climbs up hither,
> who has been watching by his well
> these fifty years.
>
> (*V. Plays*, 401)

Immediately we are asking ourselves whether the ivory-faced climber of the first song is in fact this Old Man or someone else. If the watch has lasted fifty years, is something eventually about to happen? What is the sleep of the heart?

The dialogue, therefore, can without delay proceed to the development and complication, bringing the action towards a moment of decision, of crisis, the point at which the dance might occur. The closing cloth ceremony completes the magical framework, giving us a final comment on the action, demarking it as a vision conjured in the mind's eye and, in a good production, held afterwards in the memory.

The vision in the mind's eye enacted in this first Yeatsian dance-play is one of a failed quest. A rough, suspicious, cunning Old Man awaits the bubbling waters of immortality. He is passive, for each time the well bubbles, he falls into an enchanted sleep. The other quester, Cuchulain, is a courtly, generous and impulsive young man, lover of women and man of action.

This vague parallelism and the overt contrasts between the figures make them complementary types of the visionary questor (the restless hearted man), both doomed to failure. Both have sailed, like Forgael and Dectora, across the sea to this barren land, and again the magical quester is accompanied by birds. But where Forgael's guides allured him, perhaps only to destroy him, though the outcome is left hopeful, Cuchulain is both allured and destroyed. When he rushes out to combat with Aoife, we know that the Old Man's warning of a curse was not an idle one. Cuchulain will indeed live on to kill his own son, bringing tragedy upon himself. Where Yeats allowed Forgael the possibility of finding an immortal love within the tangles of Dectora's hair, he denied Cuchulain a union with the Woman of the Sidhe, later identified as Fand in *The Only Jealousy of Emer*.

Because the dance allures Cuchulain away from the well it must in part be erotic and tempting. But it begins with fear. Just as the play dramatises the imagination's capacity for vision, so the dance choreographs the invasion and possession of a human imagination and body by a spirit, in this case the hawk god. This choreography of mediumship begins with the shivering of the Guardian. Her shuddering, her rising to strike a first pose, the shedding of her cloak to reveal the mask-like face and the stylised hawk costume amount to a 'coup de théâtre'. Her staring eyes, immobile features, shuddering body, perhaps advancing on the audience to make a transition into the hawk dance, performed effectively, can hold that audience in mingled fear, fascination and astonishment. Yeats, through the inspiration of his Japanese dancer, Michio Ito, who created the role of Guardian of the Well, had found a way of *showing* directly, rather than by narration or description, the imagination's capacity for mediumship. From the point of view of the surface action of the myth, the girl is possessed by one of the accursed dancers, a mountain witch, the Woman of the Sidhe, bent on cheating Cuchulain of immortality; from another point of view, the well is also a sexual symbol. The barren land is Yeats's own sexual landscape, his lack of a wife and 'children and dogs on the floor' (*V. Plays*, 414). On yet another level, the well is the imagination itself, and the girl a jealous muse. One part of the imagination seeks a deathless love, the other a comfortable wife: perfection of the art or of the life. Yeats shows a hero young or old, warrior or sage, defeated on all fronts. But Cuchulain has three moments of decision and in each he is bold. The Old Man tries to warn him off. Cuchulain stays. The curse begins to operate. Secondly, the Guardian begins to dance and Cuchulain decides to plant himself warily next to the well. He, too, becomes magically possessed and so misses the splashing of the water. Thirdly, he hears the clash of arms from Aoife's troops. Fully conscious again, he decides upon attack. This activates the curse, for it will result in the rape of Aoife and her terrible revenge upon him. The anguish of the Old Man who has now missed four eruptions of the waters focuses all the frustration and defeat in the play, while Cuchulain's decisive and buoyant heroism balances the pessimism to give the ending a lift up from despair. Cuchulain's rapid exit, like the swift exits of the *sh'té* (leading actor) at the end of a Noh play, seems to reinforce the buoyancy. The crushing irony is that his heroism will lead to the dire fulfilment of the curse upon him.

The imagination can give us visions of the ideal and, frighteningly, it can allow us a glimpse of an accursed future. More frightening still, it makes us vulnerable to possession by forces we can neither trust nor control.

Not surprisingly, the final song evokes not magical vision, but the merely human, familiar world: 'Come to me, human faces, / Familiar memories' (*V. Plays*, 412). There is a certain relief as well as poignant humility in the recognition of frail, foolish mortality. The heart finds its rest by choosing at last the perishable human world: 'I am content to perish; / I am but a mouthful of sweet air' (*V. Plays*, 413).

We have already seen how *The Dreaming of the Bones* (1917) maintained a firm one-act structure beneath its Noh conventions.[8] But we should briefly note that in this play Yeats dramatises yet another aspect of human imagination, its capacity to survive death, allowing the spirit to dream back over the intensities of its previous life and passionately project its dream into a situation a living person may witness. The opening song announces this theme: 'Have not old writers said / That dizzy dreams can spring / From the dry bones of the dead?' (*V. Plays*, 764). A cynic might scoff at a play, whose main character is a 1916 gunman, concerning itself with a pair of ghosts seven hundred years old. Yet this unlikely conjunction is an effective example of the esemplastic power of Yeats's dramatic imagination. The dead lovers committed treason for the sake of love, by letting the Normans into Ireland, thus starting its long history as a subject nation in modern times. It is the perfect context for the rebel's refusal to forgive. The bitterness and the implacable need for victory in Irish politics are functions of the memory of century upon century of strife. The long and painful memory is one of the constants in Irish politics. The young rebel does not have to be told the identity of the ghosts; as soon as he hears the brief details of their crime, he knows their names. The political theme of the play is entwined with the conscience-stricken imagination of the dead. In dramatising the deeps of the dead mind, Yeats shows the unfaltering obsession of the dreaming-back as a ruthless trap, a mental prison from which the spirit seeks escape. The dead lovers crave release, but imagine that release only in terms of the sexuality they enjoyed on earth: 'If some one of their race forgave at last / Lip would be pressed on lip' (*V. Plays*, 773). The living imagination of the Young

Man, in contrast, can take in a new situation although he is in danger, envisage their plight, fill him with sympathy and almost lead him to forgive. His imagination can work freely on their story, before he rejects their plea. He can look down on the Irish landscape in the dawn of a new age and imagine it as it might have been, had Diarmuid and Dervorgilla not been treasonous. The ascent of the mountain was a climb towards revelation through the activities of the imagination. Imagination can bridge the gap between the living and the dead; it can also point a vivid contrast between a lost Kingdom of Ireland that might have been beautiful as 'any old admired Italian town' (*V. Plays*, 774) and an uncertain, violent and most unlovely present. This theme was to grow in Yeats's imagination, and haunted him to the end of his life.

In *The Only Jealousy of Emer* (1919), Yeats experiments with and complicates his basic form even further. Instead of conjuring a single vision, he constructs a vision within the vision. First he sets the scene basic to the play—the poor fisherman's house in which the comatose Figure of Cuchulain on a curtained litter is watched over by his wife, Emer, and his mistress, Eithne Inguba. This vision of the heroic age includes the Ghost of Cuchulain (masked and dressed identically to the Figure) crouching immobile to one side of the playing area. Within this situation Bricriu of the Sidhe, god of discord, possesses Cuchulain's comatose Figure— his grotesque mask replaces the Cuchulain mask—and then gives Emer, as well as the audience, a second vision, that of Cuchulain's ghost being seduced by a woman of the Sidhe, Fand, in the other world. This inner vision brings the play to its crisis, Emer's moment of decision. By projecting the central vision to whip up Emer's jealousy of Fand, Bricriu has frustrated both movements of the heart: the impulse towards married love and domesticity represented by Emer is lost, and so is the quest for an ideal conjunction of the hero with immortal, represented by Fand. Cuchulain is left with the simple sexuality of Eithne Inguba. The play succeeds in projecting a moving image of Emer's tragic love and her great generosity of spirit. It also arouses sympathy for the hero when Bricriu explains how Cuchulain has lost all sense perceptions, yet still dreams in his imagination and projects his shade (the Ghost) a lonely thing, 'He crouches there not knowing where he is / Or at whose side he is crouched' (*V. Plays*, 549). The pathos of Cuchulain's and particularly Emer's plight comes out, too, when Fand asks the Ghost why it crouches with its head upon its knees. The reply reveals the Ghost locked into a dreaming-back full of remorse, as surely as the verse is locked into its rhyme scheme:

> Old memories:
> A woman in her happy youth
> Before her man had broken troth,
> Dead men and women. Memories
> Have pulled my head upon my knees.
> *(V. Plays,* 551)

Cuchulain's 'intricacies of blind remorse' are poignantly human. The bright metallic idol or statue, Fand, needs union with the human to complete her supernatural being and make her a creature of the fifteenth phase of the moon, of perfect subjectivity and beauty. Emer's choice cheats Fand of this. Yeats's later prose version of the play, *Fighting the Waves* (1929), revised for dancers, orchestra and theatre presentation, gives to Fand a final dance expressing her defeat and disappointment. But the pathos of Fand's situation is never really dramatised in either version, since she is presented as metallic, inhuman, and the emphasis properly remains on Cuchulain's remorse and his wife's bitter loss. The supernatural worlds of Yeats's plays, like the worlds we encounter in science fiction, move us insofar as they contain human passions. If Yeats has dramatised his theories that imagination can project shades, and bodies can communicate in dreams with 'more holy shades that never lived' (*V. Plays,* 549) and can receive visionary experiences, he has also in this play convincingly demonstrated that the less spectacular, more familiar qualities of imagination, insight and empathy can penetrate the supernatural, mythic action to make us feel human passion, folly and frailty. Yeats drags the audience into Emer's vision not merely as spectators of her plight, but as people who are put in the same position as Emer. Bricriu has given her a vision but in his last speech he persuades Emer by describing what he can see, though she and the audience cannot:

> Hear how the horses trample on the shore,
> Hear how they trample! She has mounted up.

Cuchulain's not beside her in the chariot.
There is still a moment left; cry out, cry out!
Renounce him, another power is at an end.
Cuchulain's foot is on the chariot step.
Cry—

(*V. Plays*, 561)

Bricriu has invaded our own imaginations. He is our eyes now as well as Emer's. We who have seen so much can feel keenly the irony of Eithne Inguba's entry. Her imagination is limited. She has not experienced vision. How little she knows of the real events, this girl who takes the world at its face value, and thinks her kiss 'brought him back to life' (*V. Plays*, 563).

Two women of great beauty, and a faery woman of almost perfect beauty, vie with each other for Cuchulain, each offering a different kind of love. They all experience suffering. A woman's beauty, speculates the opening song, is the result of the soul's toil through a variety of incarnations. It is flung onto the earth like some 'white sea-bird' out of a storm or, like Venus herself, is 'A fragile, exquisite, pale shell, / That the vast troubled waters bring / To the loud sands before day has broken.' And Cuchulain, too, has been reborn out of the waves in the play. In its final questions, the opening song echoes Blake's 'Tyger' as Japanese dramatists echoed famous poems in their Noh plays. The ultimate mystery of beauty's origins is faced. Beauty is evolved through factors encountered in the myth of the play itself: suffering, bloodshed, death, discipline, pursuit and flight; a mysterious super-sensual measurement unknown to earthly geometry; it is dragged to light out of the sea of life, and the sea of the unconscious mind, by 'bonds no man could unbind, / Being imagined within / The labyrinth of the mind' (*V. Plays*, 531).

The play has taken us into this labyrinth of the mind. Cuchulain's remorseful dream and his impulse to desert the frail shell of earthly beauty for a supernatural love have been enacted. We have seen Bricriu look into Emer's deepest wish, Cuchulain's love regained, and destroy it. Increasing beauty and the completion of being in oblivion are the strange and bitter rewards 'Of many a tragic tomb' (*V. Plays*, 563) says the final song. But the play has taken us also into the labyrinth of the mind's imaginative processes, and the final song, in commenting lyrically and therefore concisely on this, becomes as ambiguous, baffling and mysterious as imagination itself.

The Musicians advance to perform the cloth ritual, singing the while their teasing, difficult closing song. The unfolding demands that they come to the front of the stage to face the audience. The opening question of the song is thus addressed to the audience as much as to anyone else, 'Why does your heart beat thus?' The question, being framed in the indefinite second person, can refer to audience, Cuchulain, Emer, Eithne, Fand all or each. It is a universal question and an ambiguous one, asking as it does why we are moved, excited, afraid or passionate, and yet at the same time asking a more fundamental query—why we are alive, why we exist. The rest of the octave sets out as an answer to the question :

> Plain to be understood,
> I have met in a man's house
> A statue of solitude,
> Moving there and walking;
> Its strange heart beating fast
> For all our talking,
> O still that heart at last.
>   (*V. Plays*, 563)

But as an audience we cannot accept this as a direct and comprehensible answer in terms of an explanation of our restless hearts. It is more and less than that; less because it does not explain anything, more because it embodies truth rather than reducing it to a formula. What answer does it embody? It provides a memory of the central apparitions of the play, the dancing Fand, and of Cuchulain's Ghost, for both are statues of solitude in the house. This experience has made hearts pulse in agitation. Fand is a visitor from the unknown which surrounds the human world. The lines recall the impingement of the supernatural and human worlds upon each other witnessed in the play. They also comment on a spirit's 'strange heart'. Insofar as the question of the first line is addressed to Fand or the Ghost of Cuchulain, its answer must be ambiguous, for it is contained in the ambiguity of 'its strange heart beating fast / For all our talking'. The spirit is agitated in spite of the garrulous human world; it is excited by the human despite its desecrating aspects. It needs the human. But the lines also have the force of this meaning: the spirit life exists despite human attempts to talk it away, discredit it on rationalistic grounds. The song in fact recalls the confrontation of human and super-human being which the play has given us, each kind of being involving in a way the other.

We have already supposed that the audience could take the question as being posed to them. Why are we agitated or moved in some way? The song's citing of the central apparition of the play is a sufficient answer to the question. But the final line of the stanza is a plea for the heart that would turn to its rest, as in the songs of *At the Hawk's Well*. It is both a disclaimer of the passionate, heroic gestures, and a statement of part of the aesthetic purpose of the song itself—the slackening of excitement, a 'calm of mind all passion spent'.

The imagery of the play has presented a near perfect beauty in the dancing form of Fand, who is but one hour short of phase fifteen's perfection. The work of art, the artificial construction which aims at great beauty, as near perfect as possible, is suggested too by the image of idol or statue. The play itself is such a construction. The closing song can thus be taken as aesthetic commentary, having its own share of irony and bitterness. If the statue of the song may suggest a work of art, certain moments in the song could be suggestive of the connection between art and life. The refrain, for instance, could suggest that one 'reward' of human suffering is that it can be transformed into art. This is a 'bitter' reward because the art is expressive of the bitterness of the suffering that went into its creation, and bitter because in one sense art is no real reward for having suffered, for it can never eradicate suffering. In the second octave, art may be seen as a high discipline at times too rigorous for even its most dedicated devotees. Beauty of the life or of the work is a tragic choice, not merely a difficult one. In the third octave we may find that the successful creation brings its own problems—it is an exhausting process, drying the sap out of the veins. The search for the perfect expression of beauty in art may lead too near the point where it becomes in-human, unrelated to life, where the dream of the noble is no longer bound up with that of the beggarman. As the refrain reminds us, after all the suffering, discipline and dangers of creation, the artist's reward is bitter because it is so modest; all he can expect from his audience is astonishment, a more or less inarticulate shrug, a few words soon lost—a fact particularly true of the poet and unpopular dramatist. And in the theatre, the applause of past ages is lost, being more transient perhaps than the spectacle itself. There is an obviously analogous relation between the being which through many incarnations and tragic choices creates its own soul and beauty, and the artist who repeatedly creates beauty out of the broken fragments of his life. The transience of lives, of beauty, of plays and of roles is quietly stated in the final stage direction: 'When the cloth is folded again the stage is bare' (*V. Plays*, 565).

In one sense, the closing song of *At the Hawk's Well* disclaimed applause, as here the refrain describes a detached casualness. Yeats thus cuts across the older theatrical tradition of an epilogue which craves applause, for his concern is 'the theatre's anti-self'.

His concern has also been, of course, with embedding details of his nascent visionary system into the texture of the play. In the opening songs he has achieved this while producing lyrics of great beauty of form and diction. It is not quite the case, however, with the final song. This lacks the direct appeal of the opening song, and though it has the superb refrain, the startling and vivid first two octaves and the beautiful closing lines of the third octave, it is marred by the lack of sensuous solidity, the rather limp generalisation of the following: 'When beauty is complete / Your own thought will have died / And danger not be diminished;' (*V. Plays*, 565). This sounds more like a newspaper astrologer than a major writer.

To sum up the main import of the song, we could say that it warns of the suffering, the frustration and the almost inevitable defeat involved when we attempt to achieve perfection of soul, beauty, love and art. This is a bitter but fair comment on the central action of the play, the struggle to bring a reluctant Cuchulain back to life from his descent into the underworld.

The play though short is complex: that it has dramatic force and provides the opportunity for theatrical effects of great beauty in the way of music, masks, movement and costuming, cannot cogently be denied; nor can it be denied that its complexity must perplex the minds of an audience at times. But this perplexity will be part of that type of beauty which is haunting and evasive, and can be valued as a theatrical effect in itself. There is a kind of play which can be swallowed whole. But the play which demands to be savoured affords lasting sustenance. The difficulty of *The Only Jealousy of Emer* rises not out of shoddiness or artistic confusion, but from that very compression upon which much of the dramatic impact as well as the beauty of its language depends. When we listen to Yeats's dramatic verse in the theatre we hear again great and beautiful speech. Like much modern art, Yeats's theatre, compressed and difficult, never becomes irresponsibly obscure. It avoids the arbitrary, being contrived with great sophistication. Its compressions can unfold and grow like a Japanese flower.

Calvary, finished in 1920 and first printed in *Four Plays for Dancers* (1921), does not try to complicate the dance-play form any further. *The Only Jealousy of Emer* had gone far enough in that direction. Yeats rather returned to austerity and experimented with a miniature form of the play of ideas which would need some audacious dramatic design if it were not to be mere preaching of his metaphysical system. Having shown us the processes of possession, vision and dreaming-back in the human imagination, and the thoughts of Bricriu and Fand, he then took the bold step, some would call it blasphemy, of dramatising the dreaming-back of Christ's imagination. Furthermore, the dramatic structure of *Calvary*, as we shall see later, proved to be dialectic between the orthodox expectations of an audience and the heretical notions of the play's action. The attempt to dramatise even a few fragments of Christ's imagination in action is a startling hubris, but it was the next logical step for a writer whose theory of imagination included the idea that man's imagination led back to, and was, perhaps, a fragment of God.

In *Calvary* the situation of a dead Christ dreaming back over some of the events before His crucifixion demands its own characteristic construction, for after His entry, Christ remains immobile in His suffering, like Seanchan in *The King's Threshold*. As in this earlier play, Yeats used the episodic form of the medieval morality, a form singularly appropriate to his religious theme. There are, too, of course, in *Calvary* analogies with the static suffering in the Greek *Prometheus Bound*, attributed to Aeschylus. Prometheus, Satan-like, has disobeyed the father, Zeus, giving men not only fire but 'blind hopes';[9] like Christ, he has been a saviour of mankind and suffers torments. The analogies between the Christian and Greek myths, and the differences which make Prometheus seem the mask of Christ, enrich Yeats's play on a general, rather abstracted level of contemplation. The analogy can perhaps be glimpsed too in the particularity of Christ juxtaposed with the bird imagery (symbolic of the subjective gyre) in *Calvary's* songs, for Prometheus is first visited in his torment by the Daughters of Oceanos, a chorus wearing wings to give them a bird-like aspect.

It must be admitted straight away that *Calvary's* dramatic effects differ somewhat from those of Yeats's other dance plays. *At the Hawk's Well* gained in dramatic conflict from the attempts of the Old Man to send Cuchulain away from the well, from the suspense as to whether the Guardian could be defeated by the hero, from the warning and curse which Cuchulain chose to ignore. *The Only Jealousy of Emer* gained it from the rivalry of Eithne Inguba and Emer, from ironic reversals such as the unexpected appearance of Bricriu instead of Cuchulain, from the choices of Cuchulain and, centrally, of Emer, and the suspense entailed. This element of suspense and choice appeared also in *The Dreaming of the Bones*, where we wonder whether the Young Man will be betrayed, and he finds that he is led to a moment of choice. The pattern is clearly a refined version of the orthodox conception of drama. In much the same way, the unfamiliar dreaming-back employed in *The Dreaming of the Bones* and daringly used in *Calvary* to reveal the mind of Christ is a brilliantly compressed version of the sometimes clumsy retrospective exposition employed by realistic playwrights. Though he replaces his pattern of suspense and choice by one of surprising encounters in *Calvary*, Yeats retains the theatrical effects we expect in the dance-play: the cloth ceremony with its songs; stylised movement, gesture, dance, and musical effects; and the use of masks. These are powerful emotive devices in themselves, but the emotion they tend to elicit is one of aesthetic pleasure and calm. In *Calvary* this effect, however, is used with a new, ironic purpose. The smooth, polished beauty is a surface reflecting a rough turbulence which increases during the play. This contrast between the assured theatrical effects and the turbulence reaches its climax in the dance and Christ's passionate cry of despair.

The dramatic pattern in *Calvary*, different certainly from that of the other dance-plays, is nevertheless a powerfully disturbing one. It is, moreover, very appropriate for a play of theological ideas[10] in an age when God and Christianity are called in doubt as never before. The dramatic pattern of *Calvary* is a pattern of heresy—each brief episode from Christ's dreaming-back presents an unexpected heretical conflict with the broadly orthodox Christian interpretation which almost all of us have in mind. Thus Yeats has transferred his dramatic conflict to an internal position, occurring within the mind, the seat of ideas; if we are concerned with religion, either from a Christian or sceptical point of view, we are at the end of the play left disturbed, stimulated, perhaps outraged, but certainly brought to a choice of attitudes—is Christ the one true God, or is He one of the gods, or was He just a man? Yeats does not answer the question beyond implying that Christ is an objective god replacing a subjective era. Christ's own dreaming-back which ends poignantly with that last human cry from the cross reveals a bewildered rather than an omniscient god. In *The Resurrection* (1927) Yeats is more specific, presenting Christ as both man and god, and again revealing a figure who appears at the reversal of a gyre, replacing the previous god, Dionysus. This Christ is powerful, disturbing, terrifyingly silent. The Christ of *Calvary* is the victim of a series of ironies, no doubt arranged by that higher force in which free will (man's choice, God's chance) and predestination (man's chance, God's choice) become one.

The dialectical structure of *Calvary* which springs from the dramatic conflict between the orthodox Christian views of Christ and the image presented in the play, depends for its effect largely on the violence with which one reacts to these discrepancies. The advantage of assuming a thesis in the minds of the audience and putting only the antithesis in the text itself is a great gain in economy; a disadvantage is that though the thesis of Christian views could safely be assumed in certain minds, readers and audiences exist outside Ireland who would need programme notes about Christianity.

An ecclesiastical note and the dialectical structure as a whole are announced in the form of the song for the cloth: instead of having two distinct sections, as in the previous plays, it takes the form of sung stanzas from the First Musician, each followed by the refrain of the Second Musician, which has the force of a sung or chanted response or antiphon. That the hint of ecclesiastical ceremony was part of Yeats's conscious purpose in the song is confirmed by his use of archaism, unusual for him at this stage in his career, in the typescript of the play, 'The Road to [deleted]

Calvary': 'God hath not died for the white heron.'[11] The archaism was deleted and replaced by 'has'; Yeats, it seems, did not want to be too overt, preferring to hint, and at the same time avoiding the dangers of a concocted archaistic style. His usual style for these plays set in the past was, after all, a successful development from those principles he had laid down to George Moore at the time of their collaboration over *Diarmuid and Grania*: a Biblical style with archaisms and inversions left out, avoiding, in fact, all turns of phrase which immediately recall the Bible.

The first stanza of the song embodies the central, recurring, binding metaphor of the play, that the heron is the subjective aspect of Godhead. If we had not Yeats's note to the play to tell us that 'the heron, hawk, eagle and swan, are the natural symbols of subjectivity' (*V. Plays*, 789) it would be possible to deduce it from the rapt, indifferent, statuesque stillness of the lonely bird, which contrasts with the leaping of the fish. The heron as a fishing bird has strong supernatural associations also, of course, and it recalls the Woman of the Sidhe, Fand, who could take a bird's shape in *At the Hawk's Well*, and be a fisher of men with a net in the imagery of *The Only Jealousy of Emer*. The bird as fisher of men is a counterpoint, pagan in feeling, to the image of Christ. In this first stanza, the pagan or subjective god's netting of men is over. Godhead in its subjective aspect is weak and brooding, its power diminished. The implication we can assume in our own minds is that Christ is the new fisher of men. Then comes the refrain: '*Second Musician*: God has not died for the white heron' (*V. Plays*, 780). This sounds like a perfunctory statement of fact. God has died (to offer salvation) but, as Yeats pointed out in his note, He is surrounded by subjective types He cannot save, the birds, Judas, and Lazarus. As the refrain is repeated, we have time to take it in different senses. Clearly, the line is profoundly ambiguous. We can see it as meaning that God has not died *instead* of the white heron, with its implication that God in His objective aspect (Christ as Shepherd) has died, but this does not preclude God in His subjective aspect from dying in a different cycle of history. There is the further meaning that although Christ is hanging dead on the cross, the *heron* knows that God is not, in fact, dead; His influence is about to begin a new primary or objective age.

These ways of listening to the line assume that God is its subject, but the force of the negative particle suggests also that so far as the heron is concerned it is not God (but perhaps only a man) who has died; or that it is not God's death but a different mode of experience which the heron knows. The ambiguity suggests the mystery of Godhead; it makes us aware of another ambiguity, a central mystery of Christianity: its claim that God died to save mankind.

The refrain contrasts with the simpler and vividly pictorial[12] imagery of the stanzas of the song, in which the heron, weak, paralysed, dreaming, because his subjective or antithetical age is being replaced by a primary one, can only stare on his own image in the water as it appears and vanishes (like the subjective cycle) and find comfort in the thought that his cycle will come round once more as the moon travels through its phases.

The heron, like the mysterious Fisherman who appears in Yeats's poetry, encounters his own image, double or daemon, reflected in the water, and perhaps in his own mind.[13] The idea of the heron as in danger of becoming the victim of his own diet, the fish, suggests not only his weakness, but carries a parodistic link with the idea of God eaten by his worshippers, as Christ, the fisher of men, is eaten by His 'fish' at Communion. The song asserts that the subjective type has a chance to escape being totally overwhelmed or consumed by objective men, Christian 'fish'. Thus Yeats deftly uses the fish symbol of Christianity to impart a sense of the dangers and threats rather than the benevolent aspects of that religion. This is precisely what the audience do not expect of a play entitled *Calvary*. Moreover, the sense of sadness, regret and pathos in the song is centred not upon the figure of Christ, as we have come, through Christian art to expect, but upon the suffering of a weak, dreaming heron who stands as a sort of reflection of his opposite, a reflection of the Christ whom we now meet.

Christ is presented, startlingly, as a tired ghost. Our first impression of Christ as He enters, masked and carrying His cross, is that, like ordinary souls, He is rapt in a purgatorial dreaming-back. This is a brilliantly disconcerting use of the theory. We are placed astonishingly within Christ's mind to witness His thoughts as He hangs dead upon the cross.

The events of the play, even its properties, solid as they are, must be seen as mental recreations of a reality through which Christ lived. The action is a dramatisation of dreaming-back rather than a narration of it as in *The Dreaming of the Bones*. Thus

Yeats selects just the events he wishes to use from the story of Christ's life and passion, and these can be enacted upon the stage as if they were happening. Yet at the same time, because it is memory and dream we are watching, we are distanced from His suffering. The crucifixion itself, for instance, can be represented by Judas holding the cross (because he it was who betrayed Christ, and so that he is occupied while the soldiers perform their dance) while Christ stands in front of it. Yeats does not stress the agony of Christ and invite our sympathy for the man or the God, but presents it in a convention which keeps us all the time aware that we watch an image, a dramatic image, 'As though God's death were but a play' as the opening song of *The Resurrection* has it.

The dual aspect of the events as happening in Christ's memory, and yet externalised on the stage before us, is established right away by the part the First Musician plays in his narration before the dialogue begins. The Musician has been given an extra function here, that of a narrator who suddenly conjures up for us a crowd of jeerers, and voices their mockery.[14]

Our orthodox Christianity predisposes us to feel that the mockery of Christ is blasphemous, brutal, raucously vulgar; Yeats depends on these attitudes being in our minds, and then suddenly asks us to think of the mockery as a clever, delicate music. This technique of presenting an unexpected contradiction of our orthodox assumptions about Christianity is a way of showing that there is a subjective way of life contrary to the sacrifice of self which Christ asks of us; the result of this confrontation is that we question our religious assumptions; we cannot remain complacent. The song has introduced the technique; the remainder of the play is constructed from this dialectic of blasphemy in each of the episodes of Christ's dreaming-back.

Lazarus brings the miracle vividly before our eyes, but not as a great work of compassion inspiring awe and gratitude, as it is presented for example in the medieval play of *Christ's Ministry* (Glovers of Chester) where the miracle constitutes the final section. Yeats uses the sadistic imagery of a rabbit dug out of its hole by boys. Our attention is drawn from Christ to hear Lazarus's point of view, which is put most energetically. The effect is directly opposed to what we might have expected. It also contrasts with the scene in the medieval play *Christ's Ministry* (Scene 5) where Christ is the commanding figure, Lazarus having but one brief speech full of His praises. In that play Christ is, too, accompanied by a crowd in which there are two Jews who jeer at him. Moreover, Mary and Martha, sisters of Lazarus, kneel at Christ's feet after the miracle. In *Calvary* the Lazarus episode is followed by a description of Martha 'and those three Marys' falling to the ground before Christ. Although a conscious contrast with a specific play such as *Christ's Ministry* cannot be effectively proved, it is reasonable to assume that Yeats deliberately contrasted his unorthodox attitude and the more usual one towards Christ's miracle, as an ironic use of the allusiveness found in Noh drama.

After the Lazarus episode and the dispersal of His followers, Christ is overtly disconcerted, as if He is beginning to fear that there exists something outside His power. This uncertainty and self-questioning coincides with the arrival of Judas. The uncertainty becomes definite lack of omniscience, as Christ assumes that Judas doubted He was God, and Judas disillusions him:

> I have not doubted;
> I knew it from the first moment that I saw you;
> I had no need of miracles to prove it.
> (*V. Plays*, 784)

Within the framework of the play we are obliged to accept that Christ did not know in advance that Judas truly believed in His Godhead, for the whole episode is really taking place inside Christ's mind—it is His version of these events. Thus a double shock is delivered. Christ is *not* omniscient, and Judas had so much faith that he needed no miracles to convince him. The Gospels give no motive for Judas's betrayal other than that it was foreordained and that Satan entered into him (cf. John 13.27). This gives Yeats the opportunity to supply a motive suited to his own purpose in the play, and to show Christ once more confronted by something He does not first understand. Judas has to explain the motive for his betrayal:

> *Judas*: I have betrayed you
>   Because you seemed all-powerful.
> *Christ*: My Father put all men into my hands.
> *Judas*: That was the very thought that drove me wild.
> (*V. Plays*, 784)

Judas, usually our type of the wretched traitor, emerges instead as a man trying to preserve freedom of will by opposing the God whose existence he never for a moment doubts. He is presented as a type of intellectual hero, though a deformed one. He has a sinister, degraded aspect which aligns him to some extent with Yeats's Blind Man in *The Death of Cuchulain*; he is also as Helen Vendler[15] points out, the man of Phase 26, the Hunchback, betraying 'that he may call himself creator'.

Judas wears an 'old coat' and chuckles to himself over his crime. Yeats merely hints in the play at Judas's suicide as a deliberate choice of damnation and he is presented as feeling no remorse:

> I did it,
> I, Judas, and no other man, and now
> You cannot even save me.
> *(Ibid.,* 785)

This is again a shock to orthodox views of the suicide. Vendler thinks that we are meant to accept Judas as defeated and Christ as gaining the 'victory' for the time being. She argues that Judas hanged himself realising that his reaction against the primary religion was in itself an indication of its power over him.

This is not entirely satisfactory, for it does not take enough into account the dramatic effect of the Judas episode which is presented as a real encounter remembered by Christ, and not purely a theological quarrel. Judas's final words are full of confidence, cheek and unrepentant boastfulness. They sting Christ into a display of anger. But He does not manage to rid Himself of Judas, the proof that a man has been able to betray Him—Judas remains to support the cross—and Christ cannot dismiss this awkward example of defiance from His dreaming-back. The holding of the cross could have been easily dispensed with; it is, as performed by Judas, a noticeable innovation, the symbolic meaning of which should not be ignored. On the evidence of the play we are not invited to see the suicide as a recognition of God as victor. Judas himself does not realise, as we do, that the heron's subjective age is being helped round again by the betrayal. His suicide must be interpreted according to Judas as characterised in the play. It will thus be seen as a result of his desire once more to escape God's will. When he finds God's will asserted, life is unbearable for him. His suicide will be another attempt to escape, and it will damn him, putting him beyond Christ's powers of salvation. His last words boast precisely this state of unredeemable sin. The heron is not only a symbol which holds an irony for Judas, but it is also an irony against Christ who is in each episode revealed as not having a complete knowledge or power, His death being a means of salvation only for those primary natures capable of losing themselves in God, and His Godhead being one particular brand among other varieties which will occur as the conelike process of history ravels and unravels its subjective and objective phases. The total impact of the Judas episode is to reverse our traditional expectations of a wretched traitor unable to live with his crime. Christ has no final answer, cannot save him, and can only reject him. Once more a dialectical conflict with the normal view has occurred, leading us towards another opposition.

The episodes with Lazarus and Judas have shown Christ's inability to save those afflicted by human despair; these experiences culminate in the final episode which reveals that Christ cannot save even Himself from human despair. The Roman Soldiers' episode also follows the dramatic pattern of surprising conflict with the Gospels.

The physical torture of crucifixion could have been brought vividly to mind by stylised movement and mime, but Yeats avoids showing the physical suffering of Christ by merely directing that He stand with arms outstretched against the cross. He also omits the Centurion who, seeing Christ's passion, glorified God and witnessed that this was a righteous man (*Luke* 22 : 47). He presents instead only the three Roman soldiers who are neither excessively brutal nor impressed that Christ is the only God. They ask nothing of Him, not freedom nor even death, but are content to see whether chance will bring to one of them His garment. They embody what Yeats in his notes calls 'God's Chance', whereas Christ has so far realised only 'God's Choice' or Will. They therefore do not need Him; rather He needs them, for they will inflict the final ironic revelation upon Him which prevents His dying in peace. Earlier, the Third Soldier had with unwitting irony told Christ: 'Die in peace. / There's no one here but Judas and ourselves.' Throughout the episode, they display a confidence which Christ all too obviously lacks. They have accepted that

First Soldier: One day one loses and the next day wins.
Second Soldier: Whatever happens is the best, we say,
    So that it's unexpected.

(V. Plays, 786)

Their days are like the cycles of history. The god of one is not the god of others. Christ they see as a god among gods:

Third Soldier: If he were but the God of dice[16] he'd know it,
    But he is not that God.

They are, though, caught in their attitude as much as Christ is in His. They see it as their prerogative to reveal to Him the divinity of Chance by which they live, not realising the devastating effect this revelation (as symbolised by their dance) will have on Him:

First Soldier: One thing is plain,
    To know that he has nothing that we need
    Must be a comfort to him.

(V. Plays, 787)

Underlying the episode is the irony which contains the mystery of the ultimate link between God's Chance and His Choice: if we happen to think of Matthew's account, we realise that the dicing soldiers were fore-ordained (*Matt.* 27:35) themselves. But they, unlike Judas, accept their part—it is God's will yet allows for Chance. What appears as Chance and Choice in our lives is an aspect of some more extensive synthesis to which the dialectic has led—a reality containing the great wheel of life with its lunar phases and interacting cones of history. The dance acts out the conflict of opposing wills and the Chance that makes one realise the endless wheeling of opposing phases in thought, belief and action.

The dancers are a kinaesthetic image of the revelation which shows Christ that God is removed even from Him. To a Christian this cry of despair reveals that Christ is suffering that ultimate despair known to men, that He may complete His human incarnation. Now that He has experienced all human suffering He can take it upon Himself. But in the play, the words cannot be taken in this way, because of what has gone before, and the song which follows. Judas and Lazarus tried to escape God's will. Christ's suffering is different; He has passively accepted God's will or choice, when sudden confrontation with God's chance shows Him that His role is limited and Godhead can suddenly withdraw, leaving him like a fatherless child.

Christ, the play has argued, was but a god among others. His irrational turbulence attends the reversal of an age and His revelation dominates until it meets another such revelation. That is God's will or choice; His chance is that we can never forecast 'what rough beast, its hour come round at last, / Slouches towards Bethlehem to be born' (*V. Poems*, 402). The three Roman soldiers are unaware that Christ is to be the next historical God, and perhaps this indifference and unawareness are pointed up by the irony that their dice, symbols of God's chance, are carved from 'an old sheep's thigh at Ephesus' (*V. Plays*, 786). Christ is the Lamb of God, and herd animals are primary or objective like the Christian faith. The dice thus express God's chance and his choice of Christianity as the next religion. Moreover, if we ask why the soldiers dice for the garment, we realise that the cloak is not just a piece of clothing, it is suggestive of the religion that followed Him, and established itself in Rome, the centre of the Empire to which the soldiers belong. The detail stands in symmetrical balance to the flute of a heron's thigh which expresses a subjective cycle.

Yeats does not specify whether the dancers leave the stage before the cloth ceremony or not. He has therefore left us with the choice between ending the dance, having Christ speak His line while the dancers either go off or stay; or having the dance continue and freeze into a tableau as the musicians stop playing in order to perform the cloth ceremony, Christ's final line being uttered either during the dance or as it freezes. Something like the latter arrangement is better for it leaves very clearly in our minds the image of the motionless Christ, dying in despair, surrounded by the dicers. Christ Himself is no longer certain about God's choice or will, as the Great Wheel revolves around Him in the persons of the dancers. As in *The Dreaming of the Bones*, Yeats gives specific directions about some of the movements of the dance. These, as Wilson has shown,[17] are symbolic of issues raised in the play. The quarrel, as he points out, is a realistic detail. So is the throwing of dice. At the same time, they have the meaning respectively of the conflict between opposing psychological types and, indeed, between ages, and the worship of God's chance. Conflict is then transcended in the larger view of the revolving wheel of all types and ages and faiths. But there is a further aspect of the dance. Its celebration of God's chance reveals that chance to Christ and makes Him despair, as He realises that He is but one among many gods; at the same time the dance suggests worship, if unwitting, of the God in the middle of the ring. This impression, of course, is reinforced by our knowledge of the fact that Christianity flourished and Christ became a new God after His death. Figures whirling around Christ and His cross suggest worship around a totem. As we know from Frazer, whom Yeats read, there is a profound ambivalency in some religions where gods in the shape of totem animals or even other human beings can like Christ be hunted, killed and worshipped. The dance makes an appropriate climax to the movement of ideas in the play.

In *At the Hawk's Well* and *The Only Jealousy of Emer* the dances embodied the lure and temptation which brought the hero to a point of choice. In *The Dreaming of the Bones* the dance embodied the suffering of the Ghosts, the frustration and pathos which were a temptation to the Young Man. In *Calvary*, a dance play of ideas, the dance embodies an idea of metaphysical reality, which with great irony comes to Christ, usually the vehicle of revelation, with the full force of revelation. His words complete the climactic effect of the dance, for they reveal to us the fact that He has had a revelation during the dance and has been radically changed by it. Moreover, this revelation may be seen in a wider sense as a demonstration of the enlightenment which a spirit can gain from that purgatorial dreaming-back. Yeats has not, as in *The Dreaming of the Bones*, been content to narrate the dreaming-back for the purposes of pathos, but has dramatised the process itself, taking us inside the mind of Christ and showing it being *changed* by its purgatory. The play has dramatised in its own way Christ's painful brooding over what appeared to Him as a vision of evil. Some of the abstract thought which Yeats has carefully made concrete in the play may be seen in the discussion of Phase Fifteen in *A Vision*. Ideas described in his discursive prose appear in the play not as discussion, but cut down and shaped into images of events which Christ remembers.

The device of the dreaming-back allows a very rigorous selection of events in a given character's life. The concept perhaps has its origin in the psychology of old age, where the tendency to relate over and over again certain events or details from the past which have acquired some special significance very often occurs. These details seem to have established a deeply etched circuit in the brain.[18]

Christ's dreaming-back is patterned dialectically, as we have seen, but there is also a dramatic scheme of progression from climax to greater, to greatest climax in the three main episodes. This is, in its simplest form, the structure Yeats used in most of his plays, it being particularly obvious in *The King's Threshold* and *The Hour Glass*. The dreaming-back lends itself perfectly to this 'processional' structure, derived from Greek drama,[19] and so effective in the one-act play.

Despite the boldness of its experimental modification of the dance-play form to a dance of ideas embodied in images and ritualised events, *Calvary* is in some ways an unsatisfactory play. Its pattern of heresies must provide an emotional and intellectual shock as it is performed—this however depends upon the strength of one's attitudes to Christianity. Yeats also fails to suggest the symbolic richness of the Christ myth to the extent that he had managed to suggest such richness in his treatment of Cuchulain. Moreover, Yeats's new interpretation of Christ's Passion is not strong enough to overpower the older, more usual version, supported as it is by kindred myths of death and resurrection, as well as the recent residue of Christian sentiment. Finally, for all the novelty of seeing into Christ's mind, Yeats fails to show that it is full, interesting or powerful enough either to belong to Christ or to hold an audience. Yeats perhaps realised this failing, for his subsequent play about Christianity did not pursue that direction; the Christ of *The Resurrection* is a completely silent, enigmatic apparition.

II

The Words Upon the Window-Pane and *The Resurrection* were the first original plays Yeats wrote after the dance-plays.[20] Perhaps because of its use of naturalistic form, albeit for the ironic purpose of undermining naturalistic premises, *The Words Upon the Window-Pane* is often praised or at least allowed to be 'dramatic' by those otherwise unsympathetic to Yeatsian drama. Lennox Robinson gives a lucid and sharply telling appreciation of its main dramatic qualities. He affirms the swiftness and deftness of its exposition, which captures our interest and quickly individualises the persons, leading rapidly and naturally to the séance, before our attention has the slightest chance to stray. He comments also on the way the action returns to normality so that when the séance is resumed it achieves a greater intensity which builds to the terrible, moving and frightening revelation of Swift's agony when Mrs Henderson, alone after the meeting, and preparing a cup of tea, suddenly speaks again with the voice of Swift amid the silence of her homely room.

Robinson points also to the Yeatsian sense of theatre the play exhibits:

> Every dramatist must be furious with himself that he had not thought of the device of making an actress enact many characters . . . one must realise the terrific dramatic possibilities of such a conception. And every actress must long to play that medium's part—so excellently played by Miss May Craig—and be in one half-hour, Mrs Henderson, Lulu, Swift and Vanessa.[21]

The splendid and powerful device had been hinted at, but not developed as far, in Yeats's earlier plays. *The Player Queen* where the actress assumes the role of Queen, leaving her previous role as mere actress because it is not her true 'mask', presents an embryonic version of the device. But the Figure of Cuchulain which, possessed by Bricriu then reverts to the living Cuchulain in *The Only Jealousy of Emer*, is a development which has the essentials of the later device. Yeats's dramatic use of his theories of personality and of possession seems to have developed independently of Pirandello's experiments. The famous *Six Characters in Search of an Author* (1921) and *Henry IV* (1922) are anticipated by Yeats's theories of the mask and their embodiment in *The Player Queen* and *The Only Jealousy of Emer*. Yeats should be given due credit for this.

The best account of the dramatic interest and accomplishment of *The Words Upon the Window-Pane* is provided by Peter Ure,[22] and there is little to add to his account of the play, except a few comments on the use of the dreaming-back. It is enacted at one remove through the impersonations of Mrs Henderson. This is, of course, in accord with Yeats's view of the mediumistic function as essentially a dramatisation of the dead mind, a view which he put forward in the notes to the play. It also demonstrates the histrionic powers of the living human imagination through the efforts of the actress. If the actress is capable of this kind of dramatisation, so is the spirit medium, and, if we admit, even in a wild moment, the possibility of survival beyond the grave, so is the 'dead' imagination.

What the device has in common in all the plays which employ it is dramatic function of condensing into a single moment (or swift series of moments) a revelation of the essence of a human life, filtered by memory and focused by imagination to an intensity capable of projecting its own drama : the treachery and appalling frustration of Dairmuid and Dervorgilla; the passionate anguish of Swift. In *The Words Upon the Window-Pane* the dreaming-back renders not only Swift's essential suffering but also makes his personality and its condition seem a concentration of moment-ous historical forces. In the dreaming-back, Yeats imagines Swift as dominated by an 'arrogant intellect'; he despises 'the healthy rascaldom and knavery of the world' (*V. Plays*, 950) and has a dread of parenthood, not only fearing to pass on the infection he carries in his own veins, but also fearing the very fact of future generations and historical change symbolised in the white breasts of Vanessa. Her breasts, compared by her to 'the gambler's dice' in an image reminiscent of God's chance in *Calvary*, could suckle the uncertainty Swift dreads. His prayer suggests that he foresees some great disaster : 'O God, hear the prayer of Jonathan Swift, that afflicted man, and grant that he may leave to posterity nothing but his intellect that came to him from Heaven' (*V. Plays*, 951).

Through Swift Yeats was exploring not only an individual imagination, but the political imaginations of two very different ages. By showing Swift at odds with his age, Yeats was making the same point about his own imagination.

After the séance, Corbet questions Mrs Henderson about Swift, and his questions emphasise the links between Swift's personal tragedy and history :

Swift was the chief representative of the intellect of his epoch, that arrogant intellect free at last from superstition. He foresaw its collapse. He foresaw Democracy, he must have dreaded the future. Did he refuse to beget children because of that dread? Was Swift mad? Or was it the intellect itself that was mad? (*V. Plays*, 955)

If the play is about Swift, it is also about the forces of intellect
and politics in Ireland, and indeed Europe, which came to crisis
in the eighteenth century and helped to bring about 'the modern
world'. Yeats leaves us pondering Corbet's questions, which raise
the fascinating issue of the relationship of the individual person-
ality to History, and then, at the very end of the play, by question-
ing our scepticism or our superstition, he shocks us back into the
intensity of Swift's suffering, enlisting our sympathy for the
anguished spirit whatever our allegiance to the historical forces he
had loathed and feared. We remember vividly the apocryphal
Swift Mrs Henderson saw: 'His clothes were dirty, his face
covered with boils. Some disease had made one of his eyes swell
up, it stood out from his face like a hen's egg' (*V. Plays*, 955). Her
disgust, together with Corbet's quiet compassion, make us feel
more keenly the pity of it: 'His brain had gone, his friends had
deserted him. The man appointed to take care of him beat him to
keep him quiet' (*V. Plays*, 955–6). The Swift so powerfully
evoked by Yeats's play is a fierce but defeated spirit; the vision is
characteristic of Yeats's dramatic imagination, even though the
naturalistic form is so unexpected. Characteristic too, and signi-
ficant, is Yeats's passionate intelligence and nationalism, making
the defeated Swift live more powerfully in his imagination than
his previous defeated hero, the Christ of *Calvary*. He responded
intensely to the intellect, the harsh and bitter irony, the 'savage
indignation' and the nationalistic conservatism of Swift. In his
Introduction to the play he declares, 'Swift haunts me; he is always
just round the next corner' (*V. Plays*, 958). So much does he
occupy his thoughts that in the same Introduction, he proposes the
politics of Swift as a feasible idea of 'national life': 'We must, I
think, decide among these three ideas of national life: that of
Swift; that of a great Italian of his day; that of modern England'
(*V. Plays*, 957). The presentation of Swift as a tragic figure in-
dicates that Yeats was certain which idea of national life was most
admirable, but it was an idea already dead and defeated with little
likelihood of resurrection.

It is no wonder, then, given the still unsolved political troubles
in Ireland, that Yeats's imagination should be filled with images
of scorn, bitterness and defeat. After the great richness of his
volume *The Tower* (1928), his finishing the second edition of *A
Vision* and 'Byzantium', one of his best lyrics, Yeats suffered from

erratic health, as well as the loss of Lady Gregory and Coole Park in 1932, and because of these blows entered another period of barrenness. Yet he is rare among poets for the amazing power he had to keep writing good poems throughout a long career. Nor is his greatest poetry a matter of one powerful spurt. He paced himself over many laps. His lyric plays, as we have seen, gave opportunities for concentrated dramatic songs which could also stand out of their theatrical context in a collection of other lyrics, and because they were part of his world picture, could take their place without incongruity.

We have seen how the impetus of a new form and fresh conventions for dramatic poetry from Noh theatre helped to start his imagination working again after the unhappy period preceding the appearance of the dance-plays. He was able to find another aspect of personality, a new mask to express. Yeats at that time was able to review old themes through the perceptions of new conventions, dramatising, too, elements from his extraordinary 'system' or cosmic model. The barrenness of his imagination he had externalised in *At the Hawk's Well* through a portion of the Cuchulain myth. Yeats now dealt with the barrenness preceding the appearance of *A Full Moon in March* (1935) by somewhat similar means through the modern magic of a Steinach operation which apparently made him feel livelier for a short while, and the ancient magic of a ritual play.

He again wrote a play about the poetic imagination. He again turned to Irish myth in the imagery of *The King of the Great Clock Tower*. Yet he turned from that imagery in his concise rewriting of the idea which became the much better and very different play, *A Full Moon in March*. He turned from the many references to Irish myth in *The King of the Great Clock Tower* to a less specific fairy tale about an anonymous ancient Irish queen. The myth also contained Orphic elements. The basic tale is of a cruel queen who each year at the full moon in March holds her spring ritual, a dangerous song contest. She will marry the man who 'best sings his passion' (*V. Plays*, 980). The successful suitor will become King in her realm. But suitors who displease her are punished. The arbiter of taste is the Queen and her heart, the criterion the emotive power of the song. It must be able to induce 'trembling of my limbs or sudden tears' (*V. Plays*, 983).

Yeats probably derives his Orphic swineherd in *A Full Moon in March* from Shelley's 'Hellas'. Shelley has it that 'Another Orpheus sings again, / And loves, and weeps, and dies';[23] Yeats's swineherd, however, is a vile, ironic mutation, a grasping and lascivious peasant who laughs at the Queen's refinement and at death. Yet by virtue of the miracle of his singing severed head he is a poet in the line of Orpheus. He is a dramatic mask of the aged Yeats. His foul origins and rolling in the filth of swine dramatise the imagination climbing toward lyric expression from the foul rag and bone shop of the heart or the fury and the mire of human veins. He is like the lust and rage of his creator's poetic persona in the later verse. But he has lost his memory, mother of the muses. The Queen, we discover, is more muse than mistress, for her song ritual demands not praise of her but the expression of the poet's passion. She demands not compliments from a lover, but the best work. Insofar as the Queen's ritual promises marriage as a reward for the quester, the renewal of inspiration is intimately linked to an image of sexuality. Yeats had read with fascination Lawrence's *Lady Chatterly's Lover* in 1933. The union of noble lady with a lower-class lover was a motif Yeats used again with brutal force in *Purgatory*. But the union of Queen and swineherd suggests, too, a union of spirit and heart. The fact that the swineherd sings only after his head has been severed suggests both the Orphic tradition and Yeats's sense of the working of his own imagination. His ideas, he felt, sometimes inhibited his poetry. The severing of the head allows the emotional, the unreasoning inspiration to work. Yeats's muse, the Queen, wants a poetry of passion rather than ideas. Yeats told John Sparrow, 'I do not write about ideas; I try to write about my emotions. But my philosophy prevents me from writing much that I might otherwise write about.'[24] Yeats did use ideas, of course, in his poetry, but he was adept at dramatising his thought, giving us the emotional experience of having the ideas. This does not make his ideas the more acceptable or agreeable. It makes them striking, vivid and passionate, when he is at his best.

The Queen's ritual is at the heart of the play. Yeats's magic, though, is the ritual of the play as a whole. *A Full Moon in March* modifies the one-act dance-play to create a pattern not of play within play, but of ritual within ritual. The play opens not with a cloth ceremony, but the rising of the stage curtain to discover two Attendants, the first an elderly woman (soprano) and the second a young man (bass) before an inner curtain. Their function is to be prologue and singers of the play's songs. As prologue, they have a brief dialogue establishing that 'he', perhaps the director or author, has merely told them to improvise, joining in by singing or speaking. They part the inner curtains, singing 'any old thing', which turns out to be a song in couplets (unusual in Yeats's dramatic songs) about the ironies of love, its transforming power which makes louts in love think themselves wise, and sages seem foolish. All men are fools. The refrain is 'Crown of gold or dung of swine' (*V. Plays*, 979). The curtains open, and we behold the Queen and Swineherd together within six lines of dialogue. The refrain is embodied on the stage; the improvisation has become prophecy fulfilled with breathtaking speed.

The couplets of the song are eminently suitable for the coupling of contrasted male/female voices. The use of balance and contrast is extended beyond the couplets to the stanzas themselves which balance fools and wise men. The form of the song, built on contrast and the attraction of opposites, is highly appropriate to the themes of the play, its stagecraft of inner and outer stage, and its structure, which uses the opposition of Queen and Swineherd, anticipated in the refrain of the song, and the contrast between the 'improvised' dialogue and songs of the Attendants and the forward action of the ritual within the ritual. The song's final stanza is a direct command to the Queen and Yeats's own muse: 'Open wide those gleaming eyes, / That can make the loutish wise.' The improvising Attendants have, perhaps unwittingly, brought their song to an end appropriate to the situation they reveal by parting the curtains—a waking Queen whom they ask to make a wise man, perhaps Yeats himself, accept the human condition and 'Thank the Lord, all men are fools' (*V. Plays*, 979).

Yeats has established two levels of action, seeming chance and seeming predestination. The larger ritual of the play continues on this double level. The device emphasises the feeling of a preordained ritual pattern which emerges in the inner play. The Queen quickly decides to permit the Swineherd to sing for her. Later, she reverses her decision and has him beheaded. She thinks she controls her annual ritual, as if she can improvise, pleasing herself. When the Swineherd's head suddenly sings, it is apparent that both of them are figures in a greater mystery neither controls. The Swineherd follows chance, but the Queen exercises will. The two are united by the mystery of the greater pattern in which chance and will seem identical.

The opening of the stage curtains establishes a sense of the lower stage as associated with a real human world where the actors are human beings apart from their ritual function. When the inner curtains open we are presented with a world which is different in two ways. Firstly, it is consciously artificial, existing as the play, rather than the real world of the actors; secondly it is obviously marked off from the rest of the stage area as denoting a higher rank of existence, that of the Queen with her crown of gold and her throne. It is an enclosed area of existence without reference to anything outside it, a magical realm working according to its own laws.

The conjunction of Queen and Swineherd joins this higher realm to the human world, rather as spirit and body are conjoined. In reworking the story of Salome and John the Baptist, Yeats has reversed the symbolism making the dancer spirit, and the victim body. The central stage movement before the Swineherd's execution is the descent of the Queen to the lower stage, where she drops her veil, and his ascent into her upper realm. His looking into the stream suggests the equally solitary bird at the beginning of *Calvary*. He is another of Yeats's subjective men in this respect, and his connection with the roulette wheel later in the play indicates that like the Roman Soldiers of *Calvary* he follows God's chance. But he is also a type of the quester, like the Old Man in *At the Hawk's Well*. He has travelled through a waste land and his loss of memory is a kind of symbolic death. The loss of memory, together with his recovery of it later as he rolls in the dung of swine, seem the symbolic previsaging of his death and resurrection, themselves analogous to the loss and recovery of poetic inspiration by Yeats himself.

The Swineherd is in some way possessed and connected with a divine force, though he is not fully conscious of what it is that possesses him. But his loss and recovery of memory work theatrically in a more obvious way—he 'loses' his memory of his origins in his speech which directly follows the Queen's assertion that she rejects those she abhors—the lowly such as cripples and beggars. He 'remembers' his status as swineherd just at the moment of greatest impact upon the Queen. This has the force of another piece of impudent defiance of the Queen. Interestingly, she seems to warm towards him a little; she permits his song, seemingly by an act of her own free will. But it now appears that events are maybe following some preordained pattern, for the Swineherd reveals that he has heard 'You must be won / At a full moon in March, those beggars say. / That moon has come, but I am here alone' (*V. Plays*, 981–82). Thus a conflict seems to be emerging between the working of free will and predestined action. The Swineherd resembles now some Spring hero or vegetation god, dying and resurrecting in March. The fear she had felt before seeing him ('some terrifying man' she had called him) begins to operate in her for her next speech tells him of her cruelty as she tries to get him to leave. The Queen is here presented as the type of malignant womanhood. Her sadism prepares us for the sacrifice of the Swineherd, and the seasonal imagery links her with those myths of earth goddesses fertilised to revive the vegetation in the spring. The Queen begins to feel less in command of her own will: 'But for a reason that I cannot guess I would not harm you. Go before I change' (*V. Plays*, 982). She warns of her cruelty yet at the same time shows kindness; she tries to exert her will, yet feels as if some unknown force is affecting her feelings.

This ambivalency ends the first 'movement' of the dialogue, which has introduced and placed for us the two characters, setting them in opposition and setting out the bare outlines of the situation. So far the Swineherd has asked questions. The second movement begins with questions instead from the Queen, and his answers to these bring out his sensuality and recklessness, a person similar to that of the poem 'The Wild Old Wicked Man' (*V. Poems*, 634). The Swineherd has an insolent confidence which seems to spring from a recognition that all is foretold and will happen accordingly. The movement ends with more insolence as he snaps his fingers at her kingdom, offering her love only

> A song—the night of love,
> An ignorant forest and the dung of swine.
> (*V. Plays*, 92–3)

He seems recklessly to be throwing away his opportunity in an astonishing volte-face.

The third movement begins with a corresponding volte-face by the Queen as her attitude suddenly changes too. The significance

F

of the moment is marked by her first movement across stage. Yeats directs that she leaves the throne and comes down stage. She has, with his offer of the fallen world of man (its Platonic symbol being the 'ignorant forest' according to Wilson), come down at last from her niche. The stage picture thus emblemises for us the conjunction of spirit and flesh, female and male, mistress and lover, Muse and poet, crown of gold and dung of swine. The conjunction is one not of harmony but conflict. It is as if the two figures are like Yeats's gyres at a moment of violent reversal, for the Queen now begins the third movement of dialogue by revealing that she has led the Swineherd to display his true purpose of insult rather than the poetry of love. And the Swineherd indeed continues in his profanity. The Queen still thinks her own will can end the story in her customary way, yet she feels a power she does not fully understand—on a human level it is the familiar tone of hurt female vanity, and yet a subconscious desire for the desecration and insult she thanks God she has escaped.

Even while her words threaten, she yet holds back from the actual command to execute the Swineherd, giving him a chance to pray. She is insulted, yet fascinated. The Swineherd laughs when he hears that they will bring his severed head after his execution. The laughter, not the reaction of a condemned man, is mad and reckless, elicited by the story he remembers of a woman made pregnant by a drop of blood. This seems one more mad, inconsequential insult, an affront to her delicacy and virginity, yet his madness and laughter, is holy and prophetic. His head will laugh before it sings, and the Queen will conceive of the blood.

The Swineherd is compelled to ruin his chances of fulfilling the Queen's will in the love test. because he is acting out a fate which has ordained a different, more ancient ritual than the marriage of fairy tale, namely the marriage of earth and vegetation through sacrificial death and resurrection. But even as he tells the story of the ritual he will be re-enacting, he does not actually realise fully that it is the story of his own fate. Like a figure in a Greek play, he is a victim of the irony of the god or muse who possesses him. Surprisingly, the Queen seems to know the Swineherd's story—he has mentioned only a blood-drenched woman who conceives from a drop of the blood. It is the Queen who supplies the detail of her holding a severed head in her hands. Yet she cannot have heard the story before, because of her horror and fascination. It is as if she has some extraordinary half-conscious premonition of her own place in the ritual.

In production of the play, the fascination of the Queen with the story becomes very apparent, for she must, at the very time she is listening with disgust and horror, be moving, as if drawn by some power or divinity inside her, towards the Swineherd so that she ends next to him in the inner recess, for the curtains have to be drawn to hide them both. The movement is thus a practical necessity, but at the same time it is suggestive of the way she is now taking on her preordained role in the ancient ritual, just when she thinks she is asserting her own will. The way her will and her angry words are overruled by the superior claims of the ancient ritual to be re-enacted is further emphasised by the final glimpse of her before the curtains close on the tableau. Her back to the audience, she drops her veil so that her victim may see her face before he dies. Her action opposes her words; she both allures and refuses, eternally feminine. The lowering of the veil, symbolic of sexual surrender, clearly anticipates her forsaking of virginity for impregnation by the Swineherd's blood.

At this point then, as we wonder what cold beauty her face displays, the players have enacted on the surface all but the catastrophe of the folk story of a cruel queen's love-test. But simultaneously, despite the will of the players, the ritual is working to a contrasting conclusion in which the prize becomes the dust and mire of human reality and the quester turns out to be the Queen. The contrasting interpretations are bound together in the one set of events.

We are prepared for the sexual violence of the final movement of the play by the strain of sex and blood imagery which has shown itself earlier, culminating in the image of the severed head and its fertile blood. Yeats's imagery obviously makes use of the symbolic association in the human mind between decapitation and castration.[25] This link between head and genitals explains why in the legend the Queen should conceive during her erotic dance with the head. The connection between Yeats's period of poetic barrenness and hopes for a renewal of creativity and the decapitation of the Swineherd becomes clearer. Fertility for the poet is associated with both sexuality and the fertile brain in which his books are conceived. Beheading is thus an intellectual death. After the barren period of death, the renewal of fertility will be expressed by the head that sings again.

The climax now comes swiftly. This movement of the play provides a finale which completes the first three movements, and contrasts with them. Instead of dialogue between the main characters we have only the few brief words of the Attendants necessary for introducing the songs. Instead of speaking, the Queen and Head sing; instead of walking, the Queen dances; instead of a situation we get its culmination in pure ritual; instead of asserting her will the Queen does all as foretold. Love's transforming power is seen working on her as well as on the Swineherd. The Attendants again improvise by singing a song for the reopening of the inner curtain which seems inappropriately to celebrate a different ancient Irish queen from a different story, for she really loves her man and denies ordering his execution. Yet the remarkable sado-masochistic eroticism of the song uncannily links with the first song of the play in its mention of 'clown or king' and with what we have seen of the Queen. The song unwittingly prophesies the climactic miracle of the play by distinguishing the Queen from ordinary lovers:

> O they had their fling,
> But never stood before a stake
> And heard the dead lips sing.
> (*V. Plays*, 986)

Only now do we see the face of this blood-bedabbled Queen. The erotic savagery, the barbarous truth of these lines contrast with the Queen's own song, again rendered by the First Attendant (soprano). This is surprisingly as tender and simple as a lullaby. Its couplets suggest a nursery song: 'Child and darling, hear my song, / Never cry I did you wrong' (*V. Plays*, 987). It is a prelude to, or better still, accompanies the Queen's dance in which she lays the head on the throne, thus making the Swineherd her King. At this moment the Queen seems to be transformed into the type of those worshippers who kill the god while protesting their devotion. She is like the 'staring virgin' who holds Dionysus heart in her hands in *The Resurrection*, and like her, is probably a variant of the cruel old woman in Blake's 'The Mental Traveller' But her song is, at its most directly dramatic level, a simple protestation of love. She has become the wooer, and this first dance completes that wooing. Her song is also an invocation asserting the paradox of her loving cruelty in order to make the head articulate. The head laughs softly and bursts into song (through the bass Attendant). The song of the head, accompanied by the Queen's dance now 'alluring and refusing' as if in some courtship, does not, however, forgive the Queen. The song of the Head is a mysterious variant of the Jack and Jill nursery rhyme. Yeats is not trying here for the same dread of the uncanny he conveyed in the superb ending of *The Resurrection*. The macabre miracle is formalised by the device of the Attendant as singer.

The song of the Head immediately contrasts with the Queen's song in that it is sung by a male bass voice. Moreover it does not seek to deny violence but bluntly accepts it. Where the Queen's song had been personal and referred to her cruelty and love, the Head's song is impersonal, factual and irrefutable. It universalises the murder and describes it by means of the heart image and the refrain 'A Full Moon in March' in such a way that we see it is a ritual murder celebrating the resurrection of a god. The heart is like that of Dionysus or Christ, as the hill is like Calvary or other holy mounds. The winding path up and down is, again, that of the Yeatsian gyre. The song then is a description of the very ritual the Queen is performing. In the play we have noticed that the fairy tale aspect of the situation leads back to the ancient ritual; so in the song, the nursery rhyme turns out to have a deeper meaning. The fact that the resurrection is proclaimed in song clinches the suggestion that the play is not only an interesting dramatisation of ancient ritual and speculation about the relation of spirit and matter fused with a Yeatsian exploration of sexuality, but it also dramatises the failure and renewal of imagination in the drama of the Muse-like Queen and the Swineherd who thinks poetry nonsense and then resurrects to sing a perfect lyric which, in little, embodies the whole play. The lyric is precisely the kind of poetry Yeats valued in his last years.[26]

The Queen performs her dance of orgasm and conception, which appropriately brings to a climax this movement of the play. She completes the ritual part she has to perform by sinking into her 'bridal sleep'. What Yeats's Muse-Queen has conceived is in a sense this new image, the play itself, a product of his renewed creativity. The rather mechanical ritual of writing *The King of the Great Clock Tower* for the sake of forcing himself to sing again in poetry became a wooing of the Muse, enumerating old themes. But his perception of the violence and lust in him and its use as a source of inspiration developed into *A Full Moon in March* with its situation of cruel Queen and rough Swineherd. His new image is sharper, less Irish and less personal. Its aggressive sexuality is distanced by his dramatic strategy which frames the basic situation and then its culminating ritual like two scenes of a play within a play. And here too, the scheme of dramatic contrast is maintained, for the first part is wholly dialogue in dramatic blank verse, while the second has only nine lines of dialogue, the rest being a powerful combination of erotic dancing and two of the best lyrics Yeats wrote.

The final song rises stately and formal out of the silence after the climactic dance. Its question and answer construction suggests the efforts of human intellect to understand the vivid and degrading things of the play, and thereby achieves a sense of immense and hard-won dignity which is very moving: 'My heart is broken, yet must understand' (*V. Plays*, 989). The Queen inspires awe not only through her storm of virgin cruelty, but also because she is now seen to be a spiritual being striving for completion at the fifteenth phase of the moon. The refrain of the song, coming at the end of each questioning stanza, reminds us of the ritual, but has a comforting authority, rather like a response in a Christian service, and supplies the paradoxical answer to the questions:

> What can she lack whose emblem is the moon?
> *Her desecration and the lover's night.*
>   (*V. Plays*, 989)

But the response does not answer the other question, '. . . and what hand / Ran that delicate raddle through their white?' (*V. Plays*, 989). The question itself, like its possible model in Blake' 'Tyger', is better able to suggest a divinity than is a specific answer The descent of the 'holy, haughty feet', the appearance of figure in bloodstained dress with pitchers as described in the third stanza all suggest that while the song is being sung, the resurrection cele brated in the ritual of the severed head must now actually be demonstrated by the appearance of the Queen and Swineherd transfigured. No directions exist for this,[27] though in *The King of the Great Clock Tower* the Queen had come down stage to be framed in the curtains during the song 'O, but I saw a solem night'. But the words of the final song in *A Full Moon in March* clearly demand the physical presence of Queen and Swineherd descending from the inner stage, to consummate the mystical marriage of word made flesh, carrying pitchers symbolising their victory over time: '. . . tight / Therein all time's completed treasure is' (*V. Plays*, 989). The Swineherd, all that fury and blood, and the poet's own experience, out of which the play has been made, have been transformed by the imagination, and gathered up 'Into the artifice of eternity'.[28]

The descent of these emblematic figures during the last song has something of the *deus ex machina* convention about it, insofar as it is a demonstration of the irrational forces which have worked during the play. But unlike the Greek convention it is only implied by the theme and ritual of the play. It is, too, an extension of Yeats's use of the dance in the play. If we glance back at it, we notice that in the previous dance-plays Yeats had used the dance as an expression of an intense moment in the action, with accompanying explanatory comment cut to a minimum. In *A Full Moon in March* the actors are introduced and perform a dialogue which passes into song and dance together, the dance being a series of ritual movements explained by the accompanying songs, spectacle and song each enriching the other, and all performed with little reference to realism, the whole ending in a stately descent from the inner stage. This sounds like a definition of the Renaissance masque. Indeed, the masque, designed as it was for a private, court audience and using poetry, spectacle, song and dance might be considered the nearest dramatic form in our tradition to that of the Japanese Noh. *A Full Moon in March* lacks the splendid lavishness, of course, of the masques of Jonson and Inigo Jones, but its staging is a very successful fusion of elements adapted from both Noh and our own medieval and Elizabethan tradition. The form of the play and its songs, its structure of contrasts and its staging, all serve to frame and hold with the poise of great art the violence and sexuality, so that the audience can remain at a certain remove from what happens on the stage, deliberately distanced. Yeats therefore is not asking us to believe his ritual; he is rather presenting us with an image or series of images so vividly dramatic that we can hold it in our minds as an object of contemplation. The myth and ritual recall to us forces out of our human past, forces out of our own psyches. In a deeply moving way, Yeats appeals to our mind and imagination, but his tight artistic control compels us to feel at the same time. As the play's pattern of contrasts begins to sink into the memory, one can descry the broadest opposition to which all the details have contributed: the contrast between the Dionysiac turbulence of the play's themes and the Apollonian elegance of form which Yeats so carefully wrought. And so completely do these elements fuse and inter-penetrate that the play is a perfect image of that completion the Queen achieves, and the perfect union in art of content and form.

Yeats's ritual magic had worked. He had written one of his best and most beautiful plays. He had also released a spate of new plays, poems and prose in that barbarous tongue which spoke throughout the last five years until his death.

Yeats's last three plays, *The Herne's Egg* (1938), *Purgatory* (1938), and *The Death of Cuchulain* (1939) all differ consider-ably in their dramatic structure and technique. After his extremely skilful and theatrically exciting variation of his dance-play form in *A Full Moon in March*, he had exhausted for the moment its possible uses. His next play could have been a repetition of this stage-worthy formula. Bravely, for a writer of his age and ill-health, Yeats chose to quarry new stone—artistically more satisfy-ing, yet also more demanding and hazardous.

The Herne's Egg forsakes the tight perfection of the dance-play for a more exuberant, episodic and stagey manner. Though first intended as a three-act play to fill an evening, it develops over six short scenes. Its farcical and heroic qualities make it an exercise akin to the earlier *The Green Helmet* and *The Player Queen*, and since it pursues themes not central to this discussion of dramatic imagination we pass to *Purgatory*.

Purgatory reacts against the looser form of *The Herne's Egg*, offering but one intense scene rendered with a bitter, austere sense of tragedy totally different from the extravagant tone of its pre-decessor. In his final play, *The Death of Cuchulain*, Yeats reacted against the brief monologue structure of *Purgatory*, reverting to some of the dance-play conventions and a prologue by a wild old man who seems a fierce mask of the more genial prologue Yeats invented, but never used, for *The King's Threshold*. His last three plays show by their differences in dramatic technique and verse forms that he was by then master enough in his chosen area of drama to use a variety of means to serve his purposes, choosing and inventing devices which seemed appropriate to his purpose in each play. At the same time, there is much that these plays have in common, such as a growing disgust with modern Ireland and politics,[29] and common themes of degradation, defeat and death.

This grimness finds unparalleled intensity in *Purgatory*, where degradation is seen in the spirit and human worlds simultaneously. Desecration and the lover's night for the Lady who married her groom has meant a consequence of degradation for a great house and family which is fixed and repeated in her purgatorial dreaming-back. The ritual death and resurrection of *A Full Moon in March* have become, with savage irony, mere killing in order to finish the family line and so end the degradation. Mythic mystery has become the doom of a house and its line, to make in little a very Greek kind of tragic subject. As in a Greek tragedy the doom of the house implies also the doom of the city or the land, and this political extension of the fable can be counted an important portion of *Purgatory*, though not its only meaning. The death of the hero is always a political event in that the mythology of a society is a reflection of its structure, and its heroes are its index. Yeats, for one, certainly linked dying gods and heroes with political attitudes and their exponents in a quite specific way, as in 'September 1913'. The Attis/Dionysus myth which recurs in *The Resurrection*, and *A Full Moon in March*, and the oblique variations on the theme in the last plays, he had used politically, too, in 'Parnell's Funeral'.

It is in *Purgatory* and the prologue to *The Death of Cuchulain* that we find Yeats's last brief dramatisations of the imagination. *Purgatory* abandons that grimmer revival of heroic farce which Yeats used in *The Herne's Egg* for a concise, bare structure, much of it monologue. It is a drastically reduced variation on the Yeatsian dance-play. The Old Man and his boy are like the travellers who rest at a shrine or haunted place. Ghosts appear to the travellers but do not dance or relate their tragic story; it is their oppressive presence in his thoughts, however, which has made the Old Man into an unhinged killer. The recurring dream of the dead mother in *Purgatory* is one of married love. The ghosts are locked into this dream as surely as the ghosts of *The Dreaming of the Bones* were trapped in a dream of frustration for having let the Normans in. But it is the Old Man's memories and mediumistic imagination which first evoke the vision so that he can interpret his mother's dreaming-back as full of remorse for having married her groom and let the base blood in. The dance—that symbol of unity of being, spiritual completeness, divine possession and perfection of art—is significantly replaced at the climax of the play by the brutal and insane murder of the son. The dignity and splendour of the songs of the dance-plays are torn from the dramatic fabric to leave just a shred of nursery rhyme brilliantly placed straight after the murder to effect the most rapidly and economically achieved moment of true pathos in Yeats's drama:

> *Old Man*: (*He stabs the Boy.*)
> My father and my son on the same jack-knife!
> That finishes—there—there—there—
> (*He stabs again and again. The window grows dark.*)
> 'Hush-a-bye baby, thy father's a knight,
> Thy mother a lady, lovely and bright.'
> No that is something that I read in a book,
> And if I sing it must be to my mother,
> And I lack rhyme.
>
> (*V. Plays*, 1048–9)

The murder of the Boy brings to a crisis and fusion point various aspects of the play's meaning. The murder is a *locus classicus* for demonstrating how Yeats's play can exist on several levels of meaning at once, not all of them immediately obvious, and yet all contributing to a powerful dramatic effect. The murder is a sacrificial killing in the imagination of the Old Man. To the audience it is the brutality of an insane mind. Infanticide and parricide make Cuchulain and Oedipus, Celtic and Greek influences on Yeats's dramaturgy, fuse in the Old Man. On the political level the death of the sixteen-year-old suggests Yeats's disgust with the sixteen-year-old Irish Free State. Returning to the Old Man's mind, the murder demonstrates how the imagination may work with passions, in this case hatred and contempt, to produce catastrophic action. Firmly fixed in his imagination is the theory of the dreaming-back and the notion that its chain of images may be broken and the soul released from its self-imagined purgatory by the intervention of those who suffer the consequences of its actions, or by the intervention of God. His belief in the former is so intense and compelling that he has murdered his father because of it, and he now murders his son in front of us.

Had he remembered his own exposition of the need for God's intervention he might not have acted in this way. The fact that the Old Man imparts to us information about the ghosts and yet is surprised to find that the murder has not stopped his mother's torment points out to us the supremely important aspect of the killing—it purports to be a rational, if paradoxical, act of mercy towards the dead mother; by making it inconsistent with what the Old Man tells us about the soul in purgatory, Yeats has made it obvious that the murder is profoundly irrational and, indeed, savage. In moments of stress, passions, more often than not, over-power the reason. The Old Man's inconsistency is very natural. Male rivalry is central to his crimes. His violence is an effort to destroy his sexual rivals—the father who had given the mother so much sexual pleasure that she had transgressed class boundaries for him; and the son, now sixteen, pubescent, ready to run away from him, ready even to kill him and ready now to enjoy the sexual experience which is all before him, while the Old Man cannot but jealously realise that his own is over, and that it was in any case highly unsavoury, unsatisfactory and degrading to him. He is tormented by the fact that his own sexual life has repeated the mother's 'crime' of weakening the stock by mating with an inferior. He bitterly describes his son as 'A bastard that a pedlar got / Upon a tinker's daughter in a ditch' (*V. Plays*, 1044). The words of the lullaby he sings brokenly over his dead son he can apply only to his mother, for she alone is the aristocrat among them.

The diseased imagination of the Old Man can summon only momentary compassion for the victims of his obsession, his father and son, killed with his old knife. The Old Man's imagination in life leads to actions which make him far more dangerous than the dreaming ghosts he and his son see in the gutted house. But his fervent prayer with its anguished curtain line, 'Appease / The misery of the living and the remorse of the dead' (*V. Plays*, 1049) cannot hide a further implication of the central doctrine of the persistence of imagination beyond death. The dreaming-back which awaits the Old Man himself when he dies will be far more terrible than that of his dead mother. The play opened with the Old Man trying to recreate in memory and imagination the house he knew as a boy. It ends with our realisation that his imagination will be an instrument of torment to him in life and in death. The action of the play has established the scenario for his own dreaming-back. Moreover, it is not merely a snobbish imagination; it is rather one that has been on the losing side in a protracted class warfare, a political imagination schooled in Latin, old and new learning, and descended from members of a ruling-class who had fought at 'Aughrim and the Boyne', but now inhabiting a murderous vagrant. Yeats's portrait of this imagination uses with great economy and power the resources of the dramatic imagination he had developed over a life-time of playwriting.

It is because the Old Man dominates everything else in the play by his horrific vitality and fanatic regret for the past that this miniature tragedy succeeds, its economy and concentration making it the shortest and maybe the greatest one-act tragedy of our time.

Every feature of the play contributes to the dramatic rendering of the agonised mind of the Old Man. The symbolic set itself, with its ruined house and bare tree, emblematic of the lost culture and ruined family line, seems an externalisation of the Old Man's obsessive thoughts, preventing the theme becoming in any way abstract. We have to bear in mind, too, that just as the killing had a wider and deeper significance than its political and specifically Irish meaning, so the lost culture and the decay of aristocracy is not a parochial theme—it is one which applied not only to Yeats's Ireland but to Europe, and to the twentieth-century world in general. The ruined house is all that is left of the proud setting of classical drama; the bare tree a rueful parody of the luxuriant pine tree of the Noh; Yeats's two main dramatic models are part of that ancient, aristocratic tradition that the filthy modern tide was sweeping away. To accept the Old Man's command to study the set is to realise its suggestiveness as well as its starkness. We do not find such simplicity of stage-setting that is so richly suggestive again until the première of Beckett's *Waiting for Godot*.

Since the events, the themes, preoccupations and even the set of the play all contribute to our picture of the Old Man, and are expressions of his mind, it is in him that the greater part of the dramatic interest lies. In the Old Man, Yeats has created an acting part of great scope despite its brevity. It demands intensity and mobility of feeling. It is a virtuoso role, full of fine speeches packed with opportunities for the actor to portray the psychopathic switching of his moods from tenderness and love towards the dead mother to his sickening verbal, mental and eventual physical brutality towards his son. The good director or the good actor has ample material in *Purgatory* for an interpretation which would reveal the full ambivalence of Yeats's attitude to the Old Man; because he is the dominant character and it is his consciousness which is made most immediate to us, we tend to sympathise with him, but we are not encouraged to accept or identify with his point of view. Yeats has made him also into a vile creature. He is both hero and villain. His love of the past is a degraded kind of love. His learning is only a half-learning.[30] He wants to be wise, but fails to be so; attempting to help his mother he kills father and then son; he has the gift of vision, but is also sordidly materialistic, fighting over the money with the Boy; he is sensitive, but he is callous, rough and unfastidious. The killing of the Boy perfectly illustrates and grows out of his double nature; the crime is understandable but is by no means presented as justifiable. The Old Man's expression of love for his mother is shown to be a particularly brutal murder, and one which turns out to hold an agonising irony. Instead of finishing 'all that consequence', his action does more and less than that: it adds a further crime to the chain of suffering which his mother's ghost must contemplate in its dreaming-back and ensures a lengthier suffering for his own soul both in life and its purgatorial dream that awaits on the other side of death.

There is an irony, too, in that the Old Man's attempt to recall the lighter past of his youth, 'the jokes and stories' and the humour of a drunken gamekeeper, leads in fact to his encounter with the tragic past and the very different drunkenness of the groom, his father. At the end of the play, thinking that his crazy sacrifice of his son has solved the problem of his mother's suffering, he returns to his thoughts of jokes:

> I'll to a distant place, and there
> Tell my old jokes among new men.
> (*V. Plays*, 1049)

This shrugging off of the murder as he wipes clean his old knife shocks us by its insane callousness and indifference. He has forgotten the horror of the action which has, as it were, interrupted his jocular train of thought.

Even the straightforward expository speeches in the play give plenty of opportunity for the Old Man's unhinged moodiness to flare like an unstable chemical. His anger, bitterness and frustration at his father's neglect of his education can mount and then suddenly switch to a mood of mellow reminiscence of the woman who taught him to read and of the curate who taught him his Latin, and he becomes almost jocular with his 'books by the ton'. But when the Boy asks about his own education, the Old Man's anger and scorn unleash a stunningly brutal mental blow, the violence of which anticipates the viciousness of the killing itself:

> *Boy*: What education have you given me?
> *Old Man*: I gave the education that befits
>   A bastard that a pedlar got
>   Upon a tinker's daughter in a ditch.
>   (*V. Plays*, 1044)

With the first sound of hoof-beats, the vision of the dead begins, and this makes up the core of the play which follows the exposition. Now more than ever, it seems the Old Man is mad—his speeches take on a new frenzy, excitement and urgency. He becomes like a spectator at some melodrama who involves himself so much in the situation that he cries out to the heroine thinking to alter the predestined pattern of the plot: 'Do not let him touch you! It is not true that drunken men cannot beget' (*V. Plays*, 1046). His crazy distraction reaches a peak as he ponders his conception on the wedding night, letting his own imagination dwell upon it; he first pushes the Boy off to get the book from their pack, and then suddenly rushes and pulls him back as the lad tries to get away. Thus the intensity of vision alternates with excursions into the 'real' world of the theatrical present on the stage.

His monologue which surrounds the killing and continues to the end of the play is a masterly piece of dramatic verse, a splendid vehicle for the actor, and brings to its culmination our sense of the Old Man's doubleness and volatile, lunatic temperament; but Yeats also achieves intense pathos and horror as we watch the Old Man constructing on earth the Purgatory he will inhabit when his turn comes to die. Even his prayer can bring no spiritual equilibrium, for his mind is still insanely focused upon only the dead mother and himself. The speech gives a brilliant, compressed study of obsessive madness, and Yeats was well pleased with the performance of Michael Dolan in the Abbey production of August 1938, staged by Anne Yeats.[31]

Yeats's last version of the wild old man as a stage persona is the Old Man who speaks the prologue to *The Death of Cuchulain*. It was this play together with 'Under Ben Bulben' that Yeats was revising on his death-bed the day before he sank into the final coma. Critics often note that his last poems fittingly complete his life and work. The fact that Yeats was revising both his poem and his last play on his death-bed suggests that he thought of the play, too, as a fitting farewell to life and art. Moreover, he linked the play to the last poems very obviously by writing the poem 'Cuchulain Comforted' as 'a kind of sequel' to the play which he considered 'strange and the most moving I have written for some years'.[32] Thus plays, poems and life were linked into a kind of unity, a symmetry which must have been pleasing and imaginatively necessary to this most conscious artificer.

The Old Man's prologue serves to conjure on a bare stage the few brief scenes that end the Cuchulain cycle of plays in a form recalling through its mixed conventions both the heroic Abbey plays and the dance-plays. Yet it contrasts the darkening contemporary world, about to plunge into the brutal turmoil of World War II, with a bitterly ironic vision of the heroic. The Old Man's imagination, then, does not give us the mythology of Standish O'Grady and Lady Gregory, whose account of the death of Cuchulain is very different from Yeats's dramatisation. For example, in Lady Gregory's account Niamh not Eithne Inguba is Cuchulain's mistress at the time of his death. By bringing in Eithne Inguba, whose beauty and tenderness we remember from *The Only Jealousy of Emer*, Yeats can quickly establish the pathos of lovers quarrelling at such a moment, and parted on bitter terms by the Morrigu, the crow-headed war goddess. The brutality of the magic which cancels their love is thereby emphasised the more. Lady Gregory's version does not show a Cuchulain bereft of love going out to meet his death. Yeats's hero is more human, his death more bitter and desolate. Anyone who knows the legends will know at once that Cuchulain was killed by Lugaid, a great warrior. Yeats denies him his death, using instead the loathsome Blind Man from *On Baile's Strand*.

Yeats once more deliberately stresses the bitterness and degradation of his theme by introducing baseness, squalor and a slow, fumbling horror onto the stage; we cannot forget that in *On Baile's Strand* this Blind Beggar embodied low cunning and a mean-souled materialism which in the presence of tragedy could think craftily of filling the belly. The fact that Aoife's encounter with Cuchulain does not occur in the legendary account of his death at the pillar-stone serves to suggest to us again that Yeats is not concerned to remind us of the legend in accurate detail but to dramatise it so as to present a powerful image relevant to his age. Aoife enters all set to take revenge for the death of her son, but this is brushed aside by the entry of the Blind Man, and heroic fitness is sent off-stage by the low and the ugly. Yeats's dramatic imagination, full of images of degradation, still maintained its sense of decorum, preserving the coarseness of his new vision even in the theatrical use of the musicians who end the play. The magical and hieratic quality they have in *On Baile's Strand* and in the dance-plays is suddenly abandoned in the last play, for they appear in rags, as street musicians, as if poetry has been brought down and crippled, like Baudelaire's albatross. And yet, out of the gutter comes a vision, coarsened maybe, but a heroic vision. It is a powerful emotional effect which is wholly of the theatre; for the bitter irony of the play is embodied in the changed appearance of these choric personages, creating what we might term an effect of 'costume irony'. Yeats, then, gives us the heroic age conjured and sifted through the dramatic imagination of the Old Man in two scenes, a dance by Emer and a harlot's song. The bitter distortion of the myth makes us realise how far the heroic age is from the world of 1938.

Yeats's scene for his last play is completely bare. He denies himself and his audience the fantastic stage set, such as the strange architecture of *The Player Queen*; nor does he allow the austere, Japanese beauty of a single emblem such as hawk, mountain top or Great Herne; nor even the sparse and wholly symbolic set, such as that of *Purgatory*. This nakedness, though, is functional. It emphasises the death of an era of myth and heroism, and together with the use of darkness to punctuate the scenes throughout the play, it suggests that what we see is mythological dream hovering above a present time in which, at the end of a gyre, chaos is come again.

The desolation and darkness of the scene are also appropriate in the hinted stage management of the crow-headed war goddess, the Morrigu, who presides over the enactment of Cuchulain's universally significant death. It is, too, a calculated piece of anti-theatre, used years before that term became fashionable, which stresses the Old Man's isolation and his aspect as an old mummer, just as the ragged Musicians at the end are out of fashion, social rejects. Just as his theme and personae oppose the age, so his use of the stage opposes the theatre of the fashionable and opulent set. Interest is thus focused not on the gaudy environment of the actor, but on the personae, their movements, their words, and the musical effects of the play. After the prologue, before anyone enters, after the Old Man has been consumed by the darkness, our attention is directed for a full half minute to 'a bare stage'. We are not allowed to admire a set and be drawn into its world. We start from theatrical scratch, as it were, an area and a silence to be filled by players.

The Old Man's prologue introduces this bitter vision in a wholly appropriate tone of scorn and belligerent rancour. The dramatic imagination embodied in the Old Man is fighting a vigorous action in a war of ideas, attitudes and stagecraft. It must have seemed to the dying Yeats a doomed action.

The Old Man's prologue cannot be lifted out of its context and censured for its tone. That tone is a vivid element in the total dramatic design which is tempered and referred back to in the epilogue. A harangue is in any case a lively way of starting any play; this particular harangue is a most appropriate start to a play which shows the death of heroism, Cuchulain being representative of an age and its spirit. The Old Man embodies the mythological dramaturgy Yeats developed. He is a personification, and it is greatly to Yeats's credit that he is not a dull, lifeless figure, but a vivid, intensely theatrical dramatisation of an 'out-dated' mode of thought completely at odds with routine orthodoxies of a scientific, mechanical, but hardly democratic age. He is swiftly, unerringly established by the accumulation of vivid detail, from the scrap of newspaper where he jotted his guiding principles to his spitting at the pretty little Degas dancers. Such detail gives him not only an alignment with a certain approach to art, but also makes him something too of a portrait of the artist as an Old Man, another manifestation of the wild, wicked old man persona which had already appeared in Yeats's poems. It was the dancing of the Parisian music halls, Loie Fuller and her ex-pupil, Isadora Duncan, which had in Yeats's youth attacked a moribund Classical Ballet and no doubt influenced Diaghilev's Company in their brilliant regeneration of serious ballet. Yeats had rightly seen the costumes and settings of Loie Fuller and her Chinese (*sic*) dancers and of the Diaghilev Company as part of a vital new approach in the theatre.[33] The Old Man's preference for abstract parallelograms instead of carved wooden heads also testifies to his avant-gardism, one which turns back to the primitive and mythological and away from doctrines of democracy and progress. His alleged 'snobbery' is in fact something far more critical, scornful and dangerous than mere snobbery, which is always weak-minded, incomplete thought and feeling about its object. When the Old Man asserts that he can bank upon no more than a hundred people in an audience capable of knowing both Irish legend and Yeats's own plays he is being absolutely realistic. Moreover, scorn for the 'people who are educating themselves out of the Book Societies and the like, sciolists all, pickpockets and opinionated bitches' (*V. Plays*, 1052) is a full-blooded attack more than snobbery, and it is a perfectly legitimate attack for a dramatist and poet to make, though it would be unfair and inconsistent if it came from a political optimist or an educator.

The poet can make this sort of onslaught upon the reader because the writing of great or even good poetry requires qualities of mind which have had the leisure to work and gain the special kind of cultivation needed to reveal genius or talent. Yeats passionately believed that his poetry, achieved by disciplined toil, could be appreciated best by two kinds of mind—the one fortunate enough to have leisure and cultivation, and the Irish folk mind, unspoiled by ill-digested pseudo-learning, superficialities and potted facts all too often the content of so-called 'education'. Indeed, modern educationists now stress the need for teachers to recognise that there is a great gulf between the educational chances of children from homes where cultivation and learning is inherited and those which lack such a tradition. The educator must be able to adjust his own taste and artistic standards to the needs of his pupils at their particular levels in the continuous strategy of shepherding, leading and shocking the pupils into a situation where they discover, learn and mature. But the poet must always write at his own artistic level and out of his own taste and preoccupations, knowing that his present audience will be small, his financial gain therefore most probably very small, and that should his poetry survive him, it might find a larger audience only after his death.

Had Yeats made his Old Man come onto the stage and remind us that superficial or little learning was no substitute for a poetic education, or even that it was a dangerous thing, no eyebrows or hackles would be raised. But the dramatist has a special obligation to surprise and shock and insult as well as to flatter and soothe an audience. His scorn is in the great Irish tradition of those 'Fili' whose words could kill. The dramatist's onslaught upon his audience is very varied; Yeats's Old Man gives a very good performance in the art of eliciting the reaction and involvement of the audience by arousing anger and feelings of self-defence. The Old Man's prologue is a brief example of just one way of involving an audience, a means recently flogged to death by informal, 'underground' theatre groups interested in disturbing the political and social complacency of audiences, but which operate with less sophistication and self-irony than Yeats's Old Man, who has instructed the musicians to interrupt him by playing a few bars should he become too unmannerly. The Old Man's bitter and scornful harangue, by involving us, achieves very quickly the feeling that whatever is to follow, though it comes from the world of ancient myth, is directly important to us and to the world we inhabit. We are forced to ponder whether our age is as vile as the Old Man assumes it is.

When we have witnessed the two scenes which follow, we realise that Yeats has drastically selected from the body of legend as retold in Lady Gregory and refashioned his sources to show two major values of the heroic age (love and heroic death) cruelly denied by the malign Morrigu. But just before his squalid death Cuchulain reasserts or glimpses his own heroic spirit, and in the third scene, the Morrigu arranges for Emer to express her great sorrow and great fidelity in her dance. The epilogue switches us back to the vile modern age; but the harlot is also a timeless figure who reminds us that in the continuum of history the spirit of courage and heroic death can resurge. The prologue, it seems, reveals what kind of dramatic imagination is at work in the whole design of the play.

Another function of the speech then, is that it defines the theatrical idiom in which the play will work. It tells us, 'There is a singer, a piper, and a drummer. / I have picked them up here and there about / the streets, and I will teach them, if I live, the music of the beggar-man, Homer's music' (*V. Plays*, 1052). Their music is that of the folk imagination, appropriate to the ancient legendary material which is Ireland's equivalent of Homer. The speech tells us, too, that there must be stylised severed heads, and a dance by Emer. In a play of this brevity, her appearance is in any case sufficiently prepared by the amount of the prologue devoted to her and to her dance of love and loathing, by her letter and by the discussion of her seeming and real messages in the first scene. She is swiftly established as the person most able to protect Cuchulain. We recall her role in *The Only Jealousy of Emer*, but Yeats now does not let Emer appear. Her very absence becomes an ironic counterpoint to the moment when Emer explains to Eithne in *The Only Jealousy of Emer* that only they may watch over Cuchulain, for they have loved him best. Brutally Yeats brings on the vengeful Aoife to be near Cuchulain before his death. When Emer is finally allowed to appear, the Morrigu casually reveals that it is by her arrangement that Emer will dance with love for Cuchulain and grief at his loss—a perfectly appropriate coda to the action.

Finally, the Old Man's speech has an air of improvisation and informality combined with a meta-theatrical element which makes us aware from the beginning that the play is a contrivance, a conscious welding together of legend, theme, character and theatrical technique to produce a form (variant upon the dance-play) capable of combining the manner and concerns of the earlier Cuchulain plays with the death, resurrection and desecration motifs found in the later plays. The way in which the Old Man takes the audience into his confidence about the arrangements for the play seems to be a development of the manner of the two Attendants in *A Full Moon in March* who discuss what the director has told them to do. In *The Death of Cuchulain*, Yeats has brought this director onto the stage as the Old Man. In another respect, however, he is a finally successful version of the prologue figure who had been planned for earlier plays— *The King's Threshold* for instance—but never used. He hints simultaneously at being Chorus, director, the writer himself, and a sort of presiding deity in control of the events, rather as the Morrigu is within the action itself. In short, he is Yeats' dramatic imagination itself facing death.

Indeed, the typescript of the play (filed as MS. 8773 and endorsed Corrected January 22nd, 1939: National Library of Ireland) has the direction for the Morrigu's first entry as it is printed in *Collected Plays*, but the earlier MS. 8772 (1) directs that the Old Man wears a mask very like that of the Old Man of *At the Hawk's Well*, and for the first entry of the Morrigu, it will be that the 'Producer enters in crow's head.' That Yeats had obviously thought of the bitter Old Man and the Morrigu as connected[34] points to the fact that he saw his play as, in one aspect, showing the way in which the destiny of Cuchulain is manipulated by forces above him, hovering, elusive and triumphant. One is reminded of the hints of such forces as the birds which dominate the skies of *The Shadowy Waters*, the magic in *On Baile's Strand*, the mysterious Herne which swoops outside Tara. The Old Man is in this respect a mature development of the Black Jester, a figure who crystallised this theme of supernatural fate, but which Yeats did not allow into his published plays. As Ellmann noted in *The Identity of Yeats*, when the first stage performance of *The Shadowy Waters* made Yeats more concerned to clarify his dense symbolism for a theatre audience, he wrote a prologue for the play to be delivered by an old juggler called the Black Jester, who is an aspect of the dramatist himself.[35]

A lesser aspect of the concern of the prologue with consciousness of the play as a piece of theatre (rather than a story which compels our sympathetic self-identification) is the Old Man's hint that he hopes to cause controversy—besides giving us 'fighting talk' and spitting, the Old Man invokes the name of the great French tragic actor, Talma (1763–1826), whose performance in Joseph Chenier's antimonarchical and revolutionary play, *Charles IX*, caused riots in the theatre. The Old Man is clearly offering a challenge to the Abbey rowdies, remembering with a certain relish, as well as bitterness and contempt, the history of rioting at the Abbey—one of the signs that it was bravely tackling its job as an educating force in the community, a calculated provoker of ideas as well as outraged feelings. He aligns himself with Talma's revolutionary romanticism, but stands at the opposite end of an era, raging against a new dispensation.

A final aspect of the self-consciousness of the prologue is its assertion that the audience 'must know the old epics and Mr Yeats' plays about them' (*V. Plays*, 1051–2). And that brings us face to face with Yeats's dramatic imagination working on his mythic material. The play and prologue reveal an imagination holding the heroic and the degraded in its gaze, interpreting by contrasts and savage irony, finding expression through the basic elements of Yeatsian theatre: monologue, dialogue, mask, myth, dance and song. The irony and pattern of contrasts which lead to the end of the play, so theatrical in its idiom of dance and song, do not rest there. Yeats pushes the spirit up, out of the gutter again, and he does it through music. When the beggars play, it is with pipe and drum, the kind of music we have heard the prologue associate with Homer and his heroic age, become as beggars. Among the outcasts, underground, awaiting the reversal of an age, are the values we have lost.

7

The Secret Working Mind

ONE of the most delightful aspects of Yeats's imagination is his
sense of the telling gesture. Milton has it in the vivid detail of
'Laughter holding both his sides' in 'L'Allegro' but Yeats's use of
it usually springs from the context of a specific human incident or
situation. He compels us to feel the physical presence of those
friends or enemies he evokes. The clash of a kindly and a passion-
ate voice in 'The Folly of Being Comforted' works towards the
poignancy of vivid, familiar gesture. The counterpoint of attitudes
and voices finds its appropriate form in the couplet, while the
break in the sixth line marks the switch from the friend's solici-
tations to the swelling passion of the heart's voice. But when the
poet's own voice returns in the final couplet, Yeats abandons the
fervour of the heart's rhetoric for the simple, head-shaking re-
petition, and the solid image of the beloved's gesture:

> O heart! O heart! if she'd but turn her head,
> You'd know the folly of being comforted.
> <div align="right">(<i>V. Poems</i>, 200)</div>

That turn of the head would bring tenderness and desire flooding
back; the couplet reveals its final power: it has the force of a
Shakespearean scene-closer or a curtain line, delivered, as it were,
over the shoulder, on the pause, before the player makes his exit.
And it is the voice of the heart which provokes the poet's imagina-
tive response. The imagination is a cerebral phenomenon, but it
is the emotive heart which makes it leap and follow like the butter-
fly the 'crooked road of intuition' (*V. Poems*, 827).

Yeats intimately traces his imaginative process in its relation
to his heart very clearly in 'Among School Children' where, as
the children gaze at the poet 'in momentary wonder,' he suddenly
takes us inside himself behind the smiling exterior. His eye flicks
from one child to another, but the thought of Maud as a child

mixes with his perception of the real children, and a new image out of imagination bursts into his consciousness and feeling: 'And thereupon my heart is driven wild: / She stands before me as a living child.' The image is as immediate and vivid as an apparition, and it releases 'Her present image' (*V. Poems*, 444), as it also unleashes that rich blend of thought, memory, sentiment and humour that follows, and the final questioning wonder of the adult mind which complements the 'momentary wonder' of the children, and which completes the poem.

In the series of poems 'Meditations in Time of Civil War' Yeats asserts that 'only an aching heart / Conceives a changeless work of art' (*V. Poems*, 421). Yet at the same time he warns us that the heart cannot always be trusted, because it is susceptible to false images, delusions which can inspire the nightmare of civil violence: 'We had fed the heart on fantasies, / The heart's grown brutal from the fare' (*V.* Poems, 425). This self-questioning and the setting of one attitude against a contrasting one is typical of the perplexed honesty of his imagination, exploring contradictory even incompatible truths. The two kinds of house evoked in this sequence of poems symbolise two contrasting eras in the history of imagination.

The courtly imagination he suddenly confronts with the harsh struggle and violence within his own fanatic heart, symbolised by the bloody history of his tower of Ballylee, its thorns and its 'acre of stony ground, / Where the symbolic rose can break in flower' (*V. Poems*, 419). This setting, the interior of the tower and its furniture are shadows of Yeats's personal imagination, belonging in the history of imagination to late Romanticism, evolving its own features and its own products through the specifics of the real place: the flowering rose takes us back to his early poetry, the thorns to the barren landscape of *At the Hawk's Well*; the winding stair is his gyre made stone; the poet labouring over his books and manuscripts, like '*Il Penseroso's* platonist', is the poetic imagination made flesh, and is in turn both a symbol and a fragment of God's creative process, '. . . shadowing forth / How the daemonic rage / Imagined everything' (*V. Poems*, 419). Even the 'benighted travellers' who see his study window lit recall the Robartes and Aherne of 'The Phases of the Moon'. The poet's table carries not food but necessities for the feast of imagination. Sato's sword beside pen and paper suggest the poet's eternal, imagining soul and his art. The sword reminds us of the careful craftsmen in the long tradition of Japanese art, handing on their skills from father to son. Its curved shape is like a moon, but a changeless moon, just as the revelation of man's soul through great art might seem changeless amid the flux of history. This progeny of art Yeats sets against the mouse-like descendants of a haughtier age in the country house culture. The sword and its scrap of some lady's embroidered dress signify also the twin themes of war and love, thus anticipating the lines in 'A Dialogue of Self and Soul' where these themes occupy, too, 'the imagination of a man / Long past his prime' (*V. Poems*, 477). And the tower itself, of course, recalls his poem 'The Tower' in which he declared it his symbol, uttered the manifesto of his great middle poems, and described his imagination as growing in power within a decaying body.

Then a third house appears in the sequence: the stare's or starling's nest. The use of the Irish 'stare' which holds the other meaning, too, of gaze, and the proximity of the nest to the tower's window, suggest that the nest is connected with seeing or perception. The loosening wall of the tower is analogous to war-torn Ireland and to the poet's decaying body, the soul's prison in the flesh: 'We are closed in, and the key is turned / On our uncertainty' (*V. Poems*, 425). The sickening violence outside is not glorified by Yeats. Always the dramatist, he rather confronts us with it, accepting it as part of our unfortunate experience which has to be faced before imagination can come back to this now empty nest. Come back it does, for the poet's mind is crammed with dramatic imaginings of some long-dead age whose violence shadows the vicious present of the Irish troubles. The cries of a vengeful mob, the bestial hand-to-hand fighting of troopers and the staring Yeats, like a bystander eager to join the fray, build into a sketch for a battle scene out of some tragic history play. Curtain up on the next scene, a spectacular contrast to the turmoil: languorous intricacies of courtly elegance appear in the images, the slow rhythm and suspenseful inversion of

Their legs long, delicate and slender, aquamarine their eyes,
Magical unicorns bear ladies on their backs.
The ladies close their musing eyes.

(*V. Poems*, 426)

Yeats, with acute visual sensitivity, masterfully employs Moreau's painting *Ladies and Unicorns*[1] to dramatise through startling contrast the courtly elegance of the cultivated, subjective heart and the hard, objective turmoil raging beneath the tower; the sweetness of bees set against 'brazen hawks' and 'indifferent multitude'. The vision is extinguished as suddenly and mysteriously as it came. But this dramatisation in the mind's eye of a reversal of the gyres does not end in a catharsis of pity and fear, 'Nothing but a grip of claw, and the eye's complacency, / The innumerable clanging wings have put out the moon' (*V. Poems*, 427). The poet forsakes the impulse to be a man of violent action, realising inside his tower (not of ivory but weather-beaten stone) that it is the life of the imagination which has been his continuity and, Wordsworth-like, the nurture of his artistic being:

> The abstract joy,
> The half-read wisdom of daemonic images,
> Suffice the ageing man as once the growing boy.
> (*V. Poems*, 427)

The last lines of the poem again refer us to the early Yeats. The poems which make up the sequence 'Meditations in Time of Civil War' not only link one to another (in a chain of contrasts) but refer outwards beyond themselves to Yeats's life and his other poems. The sequence is a paradigm of his method of linking individual poems within a volume, and of patterning a volume as in *Last Poems*, so that poems sing in harmony and counterpoint to each other, reverberating with mutual and growing significance. That is also how a good dramatist uses scenes.

In the wisdom of 'daemonic images', however, we meet again the transcendental side to Yeats's notion of imagination. The ghostly panoply, as much as specific human gesture, makes his ideas and symbols vivid to us. The precise memories of Coole Park render the Ascendancy culture with poignant immediacy. No less immediate, no less poignant, no less vivid is the ruined abode of that ascendancy imagination which, invisible to all but the mind's eye, dominates *Purgatory*.

For Yeats, as we have seen, the imagination receives its data from both the mortal and the immortal worlds. Thus the dreams and the voices of spirits may be received and dramatised in the imagination of the living poet. Yeats made effective use of the refrain in many of his poems, and nowhere does he use it more effectively than when it becomes a voice from beyond the grave, by turns nudging, mocking, and dominant, its harmonious questions making human wishes discordant, increasingly out of tune, nearer to vanity:

> All his happier dreams came true—
> A small old house, wife, daughter, son,
> Grounds where plum and cabbage grew,
> Poets and Wits about him drew;
> *'What then?' sang Plato's ghost. 'What then?'*
> (*V. Poems*, 577)

The supernatural voices are usually aphoristic, like the one which speaks through the medium's mouth in 'Fragments'. These voices are, of course, Yeats speaking for at least a part of himself, usually his intuitive self, as when he lists things which excite his spleen, ventriloquising through that splendid compound of Renaissance and Celtic past, 'the man in the golden breastplate / Under the old stone Cross' (*V. Poems*, 598). From one point of view, visions, voices, the entire fabric of reality are spun in the Berkeleyan mind, the imagination drawing its fuel from the passions and instincts: 'Whatever flames upon the night / Man's own resinous heart has fed' (*V. Poems*, 438). However ephemeral these creations, they are everything we know and they are ours:

> Death and life were not
> Till man made up the whole,
> Made lock stock and barrel
> Out of his bitter soul . . .
> (*V. Poems*, 415)

The soul endures, imagining, inventing and bitter in a way which hints of colossal, even universal violence through the metaphor Yeats uses here for the whole of life—a gun. Nothing is more powerful or more dangerous, therefore, than the soul imagining. As his 'The Spirit Medium' put it, 'An old ghost's thoughts are lightning, / To follow is to die;' (*V. Poems*, 600). But art is demanding, too, for, like the medium, the artist must open his imagination to other souls and imaginations, dead or alive. Yeats's poetry regularly exhibits this mediumship, as did a number of his plays. He will receive an image from a past life, or conjure ghosts, as in 'All Souls' Night', drumming up a fit audience for *A Vision*, the dead friends and fellow students of occult matters, Horton, Florence Farr Emery and MacGregor Mathers. He draws on sympathetic spirits for strength and confidence, making the poem a manifesto, like 'The Rose'² or 'The Tower', indicating the direction his imagination and writing will now take, and making it, too, an incantation to renew inspiration. 'All Souls' Night' embraces the imagination's power to evoke and also its passive receptivity 'when thoughts rise up unbid / On generous things that he did'—as if MacGregor's ghost itself is influencing Yeats's thoughts so that he might forgive and feel compassion for that troublesome man, 'half a lunatic, half knave' (*V. Poems*, 473).

The rush of confidence Yeats felt at having constructed in *A Vision* his startling geometry of mind from his reading, his spiritual experiences and his wife's mediumship, gave aphoristic and oracular force to his new poetry, a poetry based upon a system which enabled him to imagine heaven, hell and all that lies between:

> Nothing can stay my glance
> Until that glance run in the world's despite
> To where the damned have howled away their hearts,
> And where the blessed dance.
>
> (*V. Poems*, 474)

Yeats's aphoristic talent is not that urbane, witty polish we find in Dryden or Pope. Yeats's imagination, demanding histrionics in no pejorative sense, pegged aphorism to a different kind of voice, that of the medium, the sage, the oracle, as well as the passionate heart. This kind of aphorism is not the result of analysis of manners, but rather the result of the sharp focus of imagination into embodied insight, that thinking in the marrow-bone, where heart and mind achieve unity.

The focusing power of the imagination is capable of concentrating enormous energy, enough to create the world as we see it in life, and our own purgatory in death. And the vision we achieve is by no means always under our control. In 'Her Vision in the Wood', for instance, the woman's vision of what seems to be the ancient myth of Adonis, or the death of Diarmuid witnessed by Grania, has come involuntarily, though not unbidden, out of *Spiritus Mundi*; its unforeseen content is yet so vivid as to make her fall and shriek when she recognises the dying Adonis or Diarmuid as her lover. The vision, full of meaning for her, and conjured when 'Too old for a man's love I stood in rage / Imagining men' (*V. Poems*, 536) seems the result of both her efforts at imagining and her frenzied self-mutilation. Imagination in her, as in Yeats, is triggered by intense emotion. As she stares like some maenad at the blood running down her fingers, the vision assaults her senses. Colour changes, torchlight shines out 'And deafening music shook the leaves'. Yet the vision, a procession of women with a dying man, seems propelled by its own energy, as if it were instinct with a life of its own. As Yeats's persona recalls it, the vision is all sensation, expressing no thought or intellectual meaning:

> It seemed a Quattrocento painter's throng,
> A thoughtless image of Mantegna's thought—
> Why should they think that are for ever young?
> (*V. Poems*, 537)

Yet it is full of significance for the seer, communicating with a physical impact which is faster and more direct than thought, and which embodies but does not expound ideas. It is a different order of experience from the rational. The metaphor from Mantegna's painting links the experience to Yeat's aim of producing art which, though the product of thought, seemed in itself spontaneous, and as inexplicable as nursery rhyme. We recall the song of the head in *A Full Moon in March*. But in its careful artistry and deliberate, sombre contrast to the 'fair attitude' of Keats's 'Ode on a Grecian Urn', we recall Yeats's position as a 'last' Romantic.[3] 'Her Vision in the Wood' is a tragic variation on Keats's poem, sharing its view of art as able to 'tease us out of thought'. But it is also a dramatic variation. Yeats's poem is characteristically the monologue of the woman, not the poet. The vision is dramatised, presented to us directly, and the comment comes from the woman, too, with all her hysteria, her shock and that mixture of love and hatred which makes her sing her 'malediction with the rest' (*V. Poems*, 537). Yeats, presenting the situation like a dramatist, and at the same time having the advantage of Keats's great ode before him in the tradition, does not need to underline and make the implications of the vision explicit. His poem can take on the aspect of some revelation scene from an ancient play, reaching its climax in the collapse of the heroine 'in grief's contagion caught' (*V. Poems*, 537). We experience the sensations of vision: first, the sense of perception, feeling, instinct and thought held together in the mystery of a mental phenomenon vivid to the senses and felt along the pulse; second, the exhaustion following the expense of imaginative energy.

Yeats's position, then, is that imagination thrives on the beliefs of the folk, the beliefs of poets, works of art, wild speculation, the heart in conflict, the mind in conflict, the heart and mind in conflict with each other, 'the heart's victim and its torturer' (*V. Poems*, 537), the turmoil and suffering of history and politics, when embodied in some great personality, and symbols and spirits which invade and dramatise themselves through the human medium of body and mind. The imagination is malleable when made passive by trance. Recounting the story of an Irish faery doctor whose wife 'got the touch' from the supernatural Sidhe so that looking at a pitchfork she saw it as a broom, Yeats in his Notes to 'The Host of the Air' comments: 'She was, the truth is, in a magical sleep, to which people have given a new name lately, that makes imagination so passive that it can be moulded by any voice in any world into any shape' (*V. Poems*, 804). Imagination is energy which can be released by one's own will or manipulated by others in the human and spirit world. Its images, self-begotten or involuntary, because of its great focusing or concentrating power, can project themselves outside us to be perceived by our senses. In his 'A Dialogue of Self and Soul' Yeats asserts that the soul, by concentrating imagination on spirit, the 'ancestral night', 'That quarter[4] where all thought is done' (*V. Poems*, 477), may liberate itself from 'the crime of death and birth'. The cost of this would be great, for it entails that 'imagination scorn the earth'. Merely thinking of the soul at phase one of the cycle of being, described in the fifth stanza of the poem, makes the poet dumb: 'my tongue's a stone' (*V. Poems*, 478). Imagination would be at inarticulate peace. And so Yeats suddenly unleashes the magnificent second part of the poem, giving the Self the last word in the debate, four stanzas in which imagination, far from scorning common bird or petal, embraces life in its impurity and squalor, thereby achieving the articulate energy of poetry.

Yeats the visionary and the magician pursued his visions for the sake of repeating the experiences. Yet invocation was not merely an exercise and a sensation, but a discipline, affording over a life-time of study experience of the working of imagination. We have seen how Yeats could renew his imaginative life in periods of barrenness by disciplined invocation of past experiences and friends, as in 'All Souls' Night' or 'The Municipal Gallery Re-Visited'. In 'A Dialogue of Self and Soul' he reaches that point in the inner life which Coleridge reached when his mariner blessed every foul and slimy thing that lives. Yeats, in the second section of the poem, tells over his 'toxic' experiences, accepting all, and thereby turning his tongue and its word from stone back into flesh. The imagination can accommodate all experience, if only it can accomplish self-forgiveness, for some the hardest of all for-giveness of sins, as it contemplates the daily ruin of the heart.

Beatific vision, for Yeats as much as Coleridge, is a healing flow of imaginative energy. In his Notes to 'The Second Coming' Yeats insisted upon the speculative 'geometry' of the double cone, asserting that 'The mind, whether expressed in history or in the individual life, has a precise movement, which can be quickened or slackened but cannot be fundamentally altered, and this move-ment can be expressed by a mathematical form' (*V. Poems*, 823). These ideas he presents as coming from the (imaginary) desert tribe of Judwalis, a name, he tells us, which means 'makers of measures' or 'of diagrams' (*V. Poems*, 825). Through the Judwalis, he explains how the beatific vision works. It is clearly for him nothing less than a description of his own imagination at an in-tense moment of creativity:

> A supreme religious act of their faith is to fix the attention on the mathematical form of this movement [the mathematical movement of the living mind in its double cone] until the whole past and future of humanity, or of an individual man, shall be present to the intellect as if it were accomplished in a single moment. The intensity of the Beatific Vision when it comes depends upon the intensity of this realisation. It is possible in this way, seeing that death is itself marked upon the mathe-matical figure, which passes beyond it, to follow the soul into the highest heaven and the deepest hell. (*V. Poems*, 824)

This is the state of mind behind 'Leda and the Swan', where individual godhead and the history of civilisation fuse in that in-tense dramatisation of myth which bursts the sonnet asunder like a hatching egg. It is also the state of mind which issued in those imaginative portraits of poets and friends which move into the phantasmagoria of Yeats's personal mythology, a mythology he has contrived to make public and international.

The images which fill the dreaming imagination in our sleep are not dredged up from memory, but are part of that invasion of the mind from outside itself. In his Notes to 'An Image from a Past Life' Yeats elaborates this startling doctrine and describes the process by which we see images from a state preceding our own birth, or from the *Spiritus Mundi* 'that is to say, from a general storehouse of images which have ceased to be a property of any personality or spirit' (*V. Poems*, 822). Again the ideas are fictionalised, expounded indirectly to Yeats's readers through a supposed letter from Robartes to Aherne, describing various tenets of the Judwalis. This enables Yeats to feed us convictions not as thoughtout generalisations of the rational mind, but as 'aperçus' embodied in the symbolic personages who appear in different parts of his work, early and late. The device also permits a good measure of self-irony to be externalised. By dramatising his convictions Yeats could render both the ideas themselves and the shocks they delivered to his sceptical intellect. The bare idea simplifies mental process; the idea, embodied in a fiction and dramatised, renders, or at least signifies, the teasing complexity of mental processes not wholly available to scientific description and explanation.

Whatever comes into the mind, from whatever source, the imagination, if working properly, orders, arranges, patterns and so interprets; thought becomes sentences spoken by a voice within the head; perceptions become some kind of sensation, whether it be in the body's or in the mind's eye.[5] It is the writer's task to embody these images and their emotional life in language. This requires discipline. When in 'Supernatural Songs' Yeats imagines his ascetic hermit reading his book by the light shed from the intercourse of purified spirits in 'Ribh at the Tomb of Baile and Aillinn,' Ribh tells us that his visionary power is the result of discipline, 'these eyes, / By water, herb and solitary prayer / Made aquiline, are open to that light' (*V. Poems*, 555). The writer builds his soul through the long, hard discipline of that singing school of the soul encountered in 'Sailing to Byzantium' whose repertoire is nothing less than the history of the imagination embodied in the great imaginative works of mankind, 'Monuments of unageing intellect' (*V. Poems*, 407). This we might call the Apollonian disciplining of sensibility through form, tradition and the constant labour necessary to make words obey the writer's call. Yeats's careful and persistent revision is ample proof of his efforts to put his imagination through singing school. At the same time, the effort is lifeless without the Dionysiac energy he conjures in his opposite kind of old man, not the ascetic Ribh but the wild old man who will plunge blindly back into life's fecund ditch; who will lie down in the tatters of his murky heart; who, though wise as in 'A Prayer for Old Age' will 'seem / For the song's sake a fool' (*V. Poems*, 553). Yeats's discipline is also, therefore, the discipline of pursuing his mask. At its best Yeats's imagination, always dramatic, embodies the energy of vision in strong formal patterns. His aim is to bring vision down into the human realm rather than to allow the bifurcation which results in the evaporation of the spiritual part of man on the one hand, and the withering of the heart on the other. The greatest art is a celebration of the marriage between shaping intellect and blood-sodden breast which occurs in the unified imagination:

> Michael Angelo left a proof
> On the Sistine Chapel roof,
> Where but half-awakened Adam
> Can disturb globe-trotting Madam
> Till her bowels are in heat,
> Proof that there's a purpose set
> Before the secret working mind:
> Profane perfection of mankind.
>   (*V. Poems*, 639)

We are at the beginning only of a scientific enquiry, if such be possible, into a mental experience Yeats spent his life-time exploring through study, experiment, fictional and critical prose, his poetry and his plays. That god-given mental experience, part body, part spirit, we call imagination. It works in all of us. It worked in Yeats to the point of genius, a genius that was essentially dramatic. The imagination can, as we have seen, work involuntarily; it can be a matrix for alien thoughts, whatever their source; it can produce a chain of self-begotten images. The writer's 'secret working mind' orders, through the long and subtle discipline of art, the intricacies of language and experience. The justly famous 'Coole

G

Park and Ballylee 1931' superbly dramatises the secret working mind, the feeling heart and the discipline of tradition, life and art Yeats found so necessary for his own work. And it was only through this discipline of powerful precedents that the imagination of Yeats, feeding on his own heart, could compose both man's image and his cry. For Yeats that image was always dramatic, the cry always histrionic.

Notes

Chapter One
(pp. 3–12)

1. In 'Swedenborg, Mediums, Desolate Places', *A Vision* and elsewhere Yeats expounded or used the theory that after death the soul 'dreams back' over its life by means of imagination, memory and guiding spirits.

2. Here Yeats followed Berkeley's *Commonplace Book*. See his brief comment on this book in *E*, p. 320.

Chapter Two
(pp. 13–33)

1. The fullest account of Yeats's activities in this organisation is in George Mills Harper, *Yeats's Golden Dawn* (London: Macmillan & Co., 1974). See also, George Mills Harper, ed., *Yeats and the Occult* (Toronto: Macmillan Co., 1975).

2. S. T. Coleridge, *Biographia Literaria*, ed. J. Shawcross (1907; reprint: Oxford University Press, 1969) 1:95.

3. Coleridge, 1:95.

4. See William O'Donnell, ed., *Literatim Transcription of the Manuscripts of William Butler Yeats's 'The Speckled Bird'* (New York: Delmar, Scholars' Facsimiles & Reprints, 1976). The same editor has previously published *The Speckled Bird* (Dublin: Cuala, 1974) and *The Speckled Bird* (with variant versions) (Toronto: McClelland and Stewart, 1976).

5. Maud Gonne, who dominated Yeats's emotional life for so long, repeatedly refused to become his wife. See Joseph Hone, *W. B. Yeats 1865–1939* (London: Macmillan, 1965).

6. This suggests a parallel with Shaw's career, just as the basic duality of Yeats's mind suggests a parallel with the contrariety of Shaw. An excellent recent discussion is J. L. Wisenthal, *Marriage of Contraries, Bernard Shaw's Middle Plays* (Cambridge: Harvard Univ. Press, 1974).

7. See Archibald MacLeish, 'Public Speech and Private Speech in Poetry', *Yale Review* 27, Pt 2 (Spring 1938), 536–47.
8. For a study of Yeats's and Eliot's poetic see C. K. Stead, *The New Poetic: Yeats to Eliot* (1964; reprint London: Hutchinson, 1975).
9. For full discussion of this aspect of Yeats see Alex Zwerdling, *Yeats and the Heroic Ideal* (New York: New York University Press, 1965). The theory of the daemon and Yeats's daemonic politics have been given careful and lucid discussion by Fahmy Farag in 'The Poet as the Nation's Daimon', *The Canadian Journal of Irish Studies* 2, no. 2 (December 1976), 32–46.

Chapter Three
(pp. 34–50)
1. W. B. Yeats, ed., *The Oxford Book of Modern Verse 1892–1935* (1936; reprint London: Oxford University Press, 1966), xiii.
2. Cf. A. Norman Jeffares, *A Commentary on the Collected Poems of W. B. Yeats* (London: Macmillan & Co., 1968), 497.

Chapter Four
(pp. 51–66)
1. Sean O'Casey in a conversation reported by David Krause in 'Towards the End', reprinted in E. H. Mikhail and John O'Riordan, eds., *The Sting and the Twinkle* (London: Macmillan & Co., 1974), 162.
2. Lady Gregory, *Our Irish Theatre* (London: Putnams, 1913), 6.
3. See Frank O'Connor, 'A Classic One-Act Play', *The Radio Times*, 5–11 January 1947.
4. In his essay, 'Poetry and Drama' (the first Theodore Spencer Memorial Lecture delivered at Harvard and published by Harvard University Press and Faber & Faber, 1951). See also James Hall and Martin Steinmann, eds., *The Permanence of Yeats* (New York: Collier Books, 1961), 296–307 for Eliot's lecture at the Abbey Theatre, June 1940.
5. See Curtis Bradford, *Yeats at Work* (Carbondale: Southern Illinois University Press, 1965); S. B. Bushrui, *Yeats's Verse Plays: the Revisions 1900–1910* (London: Oxford University Press, 1965); David R. Clark, *W. B. Yeats and the Theatre of Desolate Reality* (Dublin: Dolmen Press, 1965); John Rees Moore, *Masks of Love and Death* (Ithaca: Cornell University Press, 1971); Leonard E. Nathan, *The Tragic Drama of William Butler Yeats: Figures in a Dance* (New York: Columbia University Press, 1965); Michael J. Sidnell, George P. Mayhew and David R. Clark, *Druid Craft: The Writing of 'The Shadowy Waters'* (Amherst: University of Mas-

sachusetts Press, 1971); Helen Vendler, *Yeats's Vision and the Later Plays* (Cambridge: Harvard University Press, 1963); F. A. C. Wilson, *Yeats's Iconography* (London: Gollancz, 1960).

6. This and subsequent words widely used to describe or discuss the main features in the structure of plays are here italicised in order to draw the reader's attention to the way in which Yeats's play follows a well-tried, orthodox pattern.

7. Readers unfamiliar with this term can find a lively discussion of the structure and technique of the one-act play in Percival Wilde, *The Craftsmanship of the One-Act Play* (New York: Crown Publishers, 1951).

8. Frank Fay's Abbey promptbook of the play is in the National Library of Ireland as MS. 10950 (3).

9. A letter to Lady Gregory (11 June 1917) establishes that the play was at that time near completion. See *L*, 626.

10. Further discussion of this motif can be found in P. L. Marcus, 'Yeats and the Image of the Singing Head', *Eire-Ireland* 9, no. 4 (Winter 1974): 86–93. See also Andrew Parkin, 'Yeats's Orphic Voice', *The Canadian Journal of Irish Studies* 2, no. 1 (May 1976): 44–50.

11. The love and loathing in Yeats's song recalls Blake's 'Jerusalem' with its 'bound in the bonds / Of Spiritual Hate, from which springs Sexual Love as iron chains.' See Geoffrey Keynes, ed., *The Writings of William Blake* (London: Nonesuch Press, 1925), 3 : 246.

12. See Robert Hogan and Michael J. O'Neill, eds., *Joseph Holloway's Abbey Theatre: A Selection from his Unpublished Journal 'Impressions of a Dublin Playgoer'* (Carbondale: Southern Illinois University Press, 1967), 58.

Chapter Five
(pp. 67–115)

1. Yeats's use of Shakespeare is well discussed by Rupin W. Desai in *Yeats's Shakespeare* (Evanston: Northwestern University Press, 1971). My remarks, though, are not based on this book, nor have I tried to condense its elegant argument, since it is not strictly relevant to my discussion here.

2. The revision of Yeats's plays has been discussed in Curtis Bradford, *Yeats at Work* (Carbondale: Southern Illinois University Press, 1965); S. B. Bushrui, *Yeats's Verse Plays: The Revisions 1900–1910* (London: Oxford University Press, 1965); D. E. S. Maxwell and S. B. Bushrui (eds.), *W. B. Yeats: Centenary Essays* (Ibadan: Ibadan University Press, 1965). See also the Manuscripts of W. B.

Yeats series under the general editorship of David R. Clark, of which the first is Michael J. Sidnell, George P. Mayhew and David R. Clark (eds.), *Druid Craft: The Writing of 'The Shadowy Waters'* (Amherst: University of Massachusetts Press, 1971).

3. Their letter attacking Yeats's play appeared in the *Freeman's Journal*, 10 May 1899. For an amusing account of the incident and partial reprinting of the letter see R. Ellmann, *James Joyce* (London: Oxford University Press, 1966), 68–9, 765.

4. Lady Gregory, *Our Irish Theatre—A Chapter of Autobiography* (London: Putnams, 1913), 3.

5. It was also a family tradition that 'a sea-bird is the omen that announces the death or danger of a Pollexfen' (*A*, 10). In *The Shadowy Waters* the birds are ambivalent, either guides to eternity or decoys leading towards death at sea.

6. Pamela Colman ('Pixie') Smith in a letter to Albert Bigelow Paine, 19 December 1901 (Huntingdon Library), tells of Yeats's secret society The Brotherhood of the Three Kings. It was evidently so secret that all other trace of it seems to be as yet unknown. Ann Saddlemyer pointed the letter out to me at the exhibition of Smith's work arranged by Joan Coldwell and Ann Saddlemyer in McMaster University Art Gallery, February 1977.

   For Yeats's occult interests see Virginia Moore, *The Unicorn: William Butler Yeats's Search for Reality* (New York: Macmillan Co., 1954), George Mills Harper, *Yeats's Golden Dawn* (London: Macmillan & Co., 1974) and his collection *Yeats and the Occult* (Toronto: Macmillan of Canada, 1975). This last volume makes it impossible for critics to ignore the extent and seriousness of Yeats's study of occult matters.

7. I.e., perfect beauty born of the blossoming of cross into rose—the union of spirit and nature, masculine and feminine, and maybe Christian and pagan.

8. *'John Sherman' and 'Dhoya'* (London: Fisher Unwin, 1891), 189.

9. Holloway reports that Yeats told him in October 1905, 'he was gaining knowledge each day in dramatic work and could make an old work all right in a few weeks whereas a wholly new one might take him a year to write. Later on he might gain such knowledge that, when once done, his dramatic work might be considered complete' (Holloway, 61).

10. Thomas F. Parkinson, *W. B. Yeats, Self-Critic; a Study of his Early Verse* (Berkeley: University of California Press, 1951), 50; S. B. Bushrui, *Yeats's Verse Plays: The Revisions 1900–1910* (London: Oxford University Press, 1965), 16.

11. This could be a reference not only to the obvious symbolic aspects

of the play, but also to the deeper secret of its ritual-based form. Yeats was inventing secret rituals coevally with the play. A description of some of these can be found in Virginia Moore's *The Unicorn* (New York: Macmillan Co., 1954). Moreover, *MS.* 13568 (1) and (2) in the National Library of Ireland, which consists of 'Notes for a Celtic Order' by Yeats and Miss Horniman, describes rituals rather like scenes for plays, involving such things as the Voyage of Life, a ship with a look-out man and helmsman, a wayfarer who is following 'the four birds which Aengus made of his kisses, in the desolation of the world'. From an examination of this *MS.* it seems clear that Yeats was groping towards a suitable dramatic form for his ideas, whether he realised it or not, when he invented these rituals for his mystical Celtic Order.

12. In 1887 Hargrave Jennings published a two-volume history and description of the Rosicrucians which has this to say about the harp: 'The Woman of the Harp of the seven strings, or the seven vocables, vowels or aspirations, or intelligent breathings, or musical notes, or music-producing planets (in their progress) is purely an astrological sigma—although a grand one—adopted into heraldry. . .' In heraldry this woman is '. . . represented as a dragon with extended forky pinions, a piscine or semi-fish-like or basilisk extremity. . . . There is a wonderful refluent, or interfluent, unaccountable connection, in the old mythology, between the 'Woman', the 'Dragon' or the 'Snake' and the 'Sea': . . .' (*The Rosicrucians— The Rites and Mysteries* (London: Nimmo, 1887), 2: 116).

In 1911 the second of the prefatory poems for the play tells how Edain wove seven strings from sleeping Aengus's hair with loving hands. In the acting versions of the play Dectora makes explicit the connection between the harp and the sea when she tells Forgael: 'You have a Druid craft of wicked music, / Wrung from the cold women of the sea—' (*V. Plays*, 328).

13. S. B. Bushrui, *Yeats's Verse Plays: The Revisions 1900–1910* (London: Oxford University Press, 1965), 11.

14. W. B. Yeats, *Plays for an Irish Theatre* (London: Bullen, 1911), 143.

15. Cf. Yeats's story 'The Twisting of the Rope' which shows Hanrahan charming Oona with his talk. He dances with her and sings of cheating death in the land of the Ever-living. It seems as if Oona is ready to follow him there. But the crafty peasant mother gets Hanrahan to help her twist hay into a rope until he passes out of their cottage with it. The mother slams the door, and the poet is left to wander to the sea shore, mist and shadow gathering about him. A Faery voice mocks his weakness. The rope seems, like

Dectora's, to become 'a great water-worm'. He gets free of it but 'grey shapes were flying here and there around him' (cf. Forgael's visions) and they say to him that he who refuses the call of the daughters of the Sidhe will find no comfort in the love of mortal women—only death awaits him: 'let him die, let him die, let him die' (*M*, 232–3). The story works out the theme of Yeats's play from the point of view of a weaker hero not strong enough to choose Forgael's course of action.

16. R. Ellmann, *The Identity of Yeats* (London: Faber, 1964), 84.
17. His notes to the 1906 edition of *The Shadowy Waters* show that Yeats would stress the ritualistic, impersonal aspects of the play in production by using stylisation of movement and speech: 'The play will, I hope, be acted as on its first production, with a quiet gravity and a kind of rhythmic movement, and a very scrupulous cherishing of the music of the verse. The "O, O, O" of the lamentation will be sung as Miss Farr sings the "Ochones" in her recitation of "The Lament of Emer". . . .' The use of symbolism was also partly a means of achieving impersonal and 'non-human' effects—'If the harp cannot suggest some power that no actor could represent by sheer acting, for the more acting the more human life, the enchanting of so many people by it will seem impossible.' (*V. Plays*, 342).
18. Yeats based his broad scheme upon *Seancan the Bard* (1895), a play written by his friend Ellis who had been alerted to the legend by Yeats. Yeats's play considerably improves on its predecessor, being stylistically superior and making the leprosy theme into a substantial dramatic element: it is linked to the ideas of beauty and ugliness and their relation to the influence of poetry, and given substance and intensity by the introduction of cripples into the play. Yeats also added the Mayor, Chamberlain, Monk and Soldier to enliven the basic situation, and by avoiding Ellis's mistake of including nine songs, he maintained a clear line of action and considerable dramatic tension. For a full discussion of the reworking, see Bushrui, *Yeats's Verse Plays: The Revisions 1900–1910*.
19. Mr Padraic Colum, who played a cripple in the first performance at the Molesworth Hall on 7 October 1903, recalls how Yeats was not pleased with the King's speech of greeting as far as its immediate intelligibility to the audience was concerned:

Yeats was discomfited. I knew that the speech couldn't be made clearer no matter how the actor tried. I went to Yeats who was standing ruefully aside and said to him, 'The speech is frankly a public oration. What the audience will know is that the King is making a speech; it does not have to be intelligible line by line.' His head went up and his face cleared. Running across to Fay he said, 'Colum says that the speech is frankly an oration.' It was then given as an oration without any attempt to make it parti- cularly intelligible.

(F. MacManus, ed., *The Yeats We Knew* (Cork: Mercier Press, 1965), 20). Leaving aside for a moment the question of whether in fact the speech *is* unintelligible to any theatre audience, or to the audience of 1903, here is Yeats learning how to write his play practically, rather than in the modern theatre workshop way. So far as the production of the play is concerned our first sight and impression of Guaire is to be in terms of the King as public figure, authoritative and oratorical.

20. Yeats briefly explained this circumstance in the notes to *Seven Poems and a Fragment* (1922) and *Plays in Prose and Verse* (1922). See *V. Plays*, 316.

21. The comic possibilities of the debate about art, society and politics have been recently brilliantly exploited by Tom Stoppard in *Travesties* which, coincidentally, has the old man as prologue device, extending the role to form the framework of the entire play.

22. Cf. *V. Plays*, 315. Even in the 'happy' version of the play, Yeats sensibly envisaged Seanchan as nevertheless estranged forever from the Court.

23. This device is an exciting and unusual piece of theatre. It has been used recently of course in 'Absurdist' plays. An interesting attempt to 'orchestrate' voices frequently within a play for farcical effect is George Mully's, *The Master of Two Servants* (in *Traverse Plays*, Penguin, 1966).

24. The 1952 version of the text cuts all directions suggesting simul- taneous speech, despite the fact that these are included in the 1937 edition which was the last edition to be issued during Yeats's life- time, and instead prefaces the series of speeches by: 'The five following speeches should be spoken in a rhythmical chant, or should rise into song' (*V. Plays*, 280). This follows the 1934 edition of *The Collected Plays of W. B. Yeats*. The less detailed direction is more a summary than a revision toning down the experiment in choral speech found in earlier texts and restored in the 1937 edition.

25. It is tempting to see here a reference to bigoted churchmen who attacked *The Countess Cathleen.*

26. For the druidical aspect of early Irish poets it is necessary to dis- tinguish between 'Bards'—writers of verse and sometimes musicians

and reciters—and 'Fili', who were not only poets but scholars, guardians of tradition, prophets, seers and wielders of supernatural power. The words 'Fili' and 'Drui' are sometimes synonymous in early Irish manuscripts. But according to Eleanor Knott and Gerard Murphy in *Early Irish Literature* (London: Routledge, 1966): 'The distinction between "bard" and "fili" in the earlier period is still an obscure subject and has not been fully investigated' (p. 21). Yeats side-stepped historical accuracy by dropping Ellis's 'bard' and calling Seanchan 'Chief Poet'. What is clear, however, is that Seanchan was a 'court poet', which implies not sycophancy but a privileged noble of hereditary 'nemed grade' whose main function was the composition of eulogy and satire (*ibid.*, p. 62). This satire was magically potent: 'The wound from satire or lampoon was not only sore and rankling to the over-sensitive pride of an Irish nobleman, but, according to popular belief, it might even prove mortal' (*ibid.*, p. 78). Knott and Murphy go on to quote the story of Caiér, King of Connacht who was unjustly satirised by his poet nephew Néde and received three blisters on his face and later died in exile and shame, for Néde had taken the throne (*ibid.*, pp 79–80).

27. The changing moon is connected in Yeats's mind even at this early stage with the changing of a social order.

28. Cf. 'Adam's Curse' (*V. Poems*, 204).

29. The fullest treatment of this group is in Reg Skene, *The Cuchulain Cycle of W. B. Yeats* (London: Macmillan & Co., 1974).

30. The play follows the same legend as Lady Gregory's superb version of the killing of Conlaoch by his father, Cuchulain, in *Cuchulain of Muirthemne* (London: John Murray, 1919). In dramatising Irish heroic legend, Yeats was to a great extent following the prescriptions of Standish O'Grady, author of the *History of Ireland* (1878), who tried to reconstruct imaginatively the life of the Irish of the past. He is clearly writing with a specific aim—the beginning of a popularisation of Irish national legend as part of an attempt at finding a national identity. He is also writing for particular players—the parts of Cuchulain and the Fool were most suitable for the respective talents of Frank Fay (celebrated for his remarkable speaking of dramatic verse) and of W. G. Fay, his brother, that comic actor of great distinction to whom the play is dedicated.

31. Yeats's 'At Stratford-on-Avon' partly explains the oppositions of character in his play, the contrast beween Fool and Blind Man parallel to that between Cuchulain and Conchubar: 'To pose character against character was an element in Shakespeare's art, and scarcely a play is lacking in characters that are the complement of one another, and so, having made the vessel of porcelain,

Richard II, he had to make the vessel of clay, Henry V' (*E&I*, 108).

The invention of the Fool and the Blind Man as representatives of the hardness and squalor of life, complicating the main heroic action with something partly choric in effect, a copy in little of the sub-plots and multifariousness of life encountered in Elizabethan drama, must owe something to the peasant life observed by Yeats in Ireland, something perhaps to the ideas of Lady Gregory, and much to the dramatic practice of Shakespeare himself.

32. Craig, in fact, produced some designs for *The Hour Glass* and *On Baile's Strand*, and Yeats used some of them to illustrate *Plays for an Irish Theatre* (1911). In 1909–10 Yeats showed a good grasp of the way Craig's latest invention, the set of screens, could be used, with the result that Craig gave Yeats a model stage and set of screens to experiment with, and the Abbey became the first theatre to use Craig's idea. But after the London visits Craig made in 1914 and 1915, there was little contact between the two, or actual collaboration. Yeats, though, had thought of joining Craig's school at the Arena Goldoni, but had never done so. However, he had been stimulated by Craig's work and ideas which made a lasting impact and revealed some of the great possibilities of a theatre of beauty. See Edward Craig, *Gordon Craig* (London: Gollancz, 1968). For a good discussion of Yeats and Craig see the essays by Karen Dorn and James W. Flannery in Robert O'Driscoll and Lorna Reynolds (eds.) *Yeats and the Theatre* (Toronto: Macmillan of Canada, 1975).

33. See Gilbert Murray, 'Hamlet and Orestes' in S. E. Hyman (ed.) *The Critical Performance* (New York: Vintage Books, 1956), 23.

34. National Library of Ireland MS. 13568 (1) and (2).

35. Cf. Shakespeare, *Henry IV*, Part 1, Act II, Sc. IV.

36. Masefield tells us 'One of the main interests of his young manhood was chess.' See J. Masefield, *Some Memories of W. B. Yeats*, (New York: Macmillan Co., 1940), 1.

37. In a letter to Alan Wade (see *L*, 674).

38. See *V. Plays*, 761.

39. W. Becker suggests this. For a lively and cogent analysis of the play see his article, 'The Mask Mocked' in *Sewanee Review*, 61 (Winter 1953): 82–108.

40. Cf. *AV*, 116.

41. Holloway, 206.

Chapter Six
(pp. 116–170)

1. In 1908 Joseph Holloway was still recording Yeats's enthusiasm for the theatre: 'Yeats took a delight in the Abbey. Henderson had

told him he was wasting his time there rehearsing, etc., instead of writing deathless lyrics, but his heart was in the place. He loved it. It had become a part of himself. He was happy in it' (p. 109). By 1910 Holloway was observing Yeats's gloom at the success of the satirists and realists at the Abbey (p. 135). The moment for enthusiastic receptions of verse-plays was finished, it seemed. Moreover, the coming of World War I almost meant the collapse of the Abbey.

2. A. Norman Jeffares in Chapter Seven of his *W. B. Yeats, Man and Poet* (1949; revised ed. London: Routledge and Kegan Paul, 1962) has an excellent discussion of this difficult period in Yeats's creative and personal life from 1910 to 1916. Yeats was still loyal to and on occasion working for the Abbey, though on the whole he disliked its new realistic phase; at the same time he still felt deeply the loss of Maud Gonne and the death of Synge; he examined the depths of his own being in his diaries, elaborating his theory of the mask or antiself; he became disgusted with the Irish philistinism which surfaced in the affair of Hugh Lane's pictures; his sexual life was highly frustrating as he renewed his old love for Maud Gonne MacBride, was rejected, and then tried to marry her daughter, Iseult; ill health emphasised the fact that he was nearing his fifties. Probably under Pound's influence, he wrote with a harsher, more outspoken tone and deliberately turned away from the past.

3. *The Well of Immortality* (1917) listed in Wade's bibliography was not authorised by Yeats.

4. The best account of the distinctions between the Noh and Yeats's dance-plays is Miss Hiro Ishibashi's *Yeats and the Noh: Types of Japanese Beauty and their Reflection in Yeats's Plays* (Dublin: Dolmen, 1965), being No. VI in the series, Yeats Centenary Papers. The most recent book about the influence of Noh, Pound and Fenollosa on Yeats the dramatist is Richard Taylor's *The Drama of W. B. Yeats: Irish Myth and the Japanese Noh* (New Haven and London: Yale University Press, 1976). It contains some good discussion but undervalues Yeats's earlier drama and ignores for no good reason Ishibashi's book.

5. Yeats must have been delighted to find that Noh dramatised much folk belief and legend connected with locale, just as he had already discovered 'that Greek literature was founded on a folk belief differing but little from that of Ireland' (*V. Plays*, 573).

6. Even the temporary 'mock-up' stage used by the Noh players at the Aldwych for the World Theatre Season, 1967, was considered sacred by the players and their back-stage people.

7. This similarity of structure is not surprising, since such a pro-

gression from beginning to end is the obvious human way of think-
ing about structure. Moreover, like the western one-acter, Noh is
'classical' in its economy and control: 'Le nô est en effet un art
essentiellement classique, et le classicisme de Zeami, auteur
dramatique, se définit par les mêmes critères que le classicisme d'un
Eschyle ou d'un Racine: économie des moyens, équilibre, précision
verbale et technique en vue d'un effet exactement calculé.' See
*Zeami: La Tradition Secrète du Nô-Traduction et Commentaires
de René Sieffert* (Paris: Gallimard, 1960), 9.

8. Cf. the discussion of *The Dreaming of the Bones* in Chapter
   Four.
9. I refer to David Grene's translation in D. Grene and R. Lattimore
   (eds.), *Greek Tragedies* (Chicago: University of Chicago Press,
   1960), 1 : 74.
10. Peter Ure's *Yeats the Playwright* (London: Routledge and Kegan
    Paul, 1963), Chapter 6, discusses *Calvary* and *The Resurrection* as
    plays of ideas.
11. MS. 8276 (3) in the National Library of Ireland.
12. T. R. Henn, in a most eloquent and suggestive passage, discussed
    Mantegna's picture 'The Agony in the Garden' as a probable source
    of the heron and rabbit images of *Calvary*. See *The Lonely Tower*
    (London: Methuen, 1965), 204–5, 285.
13. The dumbfounded dream of the Heron suggests a parallel with
    Christ's dreaming-back and also the state of the soul at phase 15
    where 'all effort has ceased, all thought has become image' in *AV*,
    p. 136.
14. This practice is repeated for the three Marys. The device is
    developed further in *The Cat and the Moon* of course, where the
    Musician suddenly becomes the saint and actually has a dialogue
    with the beggars. How much gesture, mime and expression must
    accompany the Musician's words is something which can be
    decided only by the tact of the director and cast in a given
    production.
15. See Helen H. Vendler, *Yeats's 'Vision' and the Later Plays* (Cam-
    bridge: Harvard University Press, 1963).
16. One wonders whether Yeats's 'God of dice' is in some sense a
    conscious rebuttal of Einstein's position that God does not play dice
    with the universe.
17. See Wilson, *Yeats's Iconography*, 195–8.
18. Samuel Beckett's *Play* uses a purgatorial dreaming-back. For con-
    nections between Yeats and Beckett see Ruby Cohn, 'The Plays of
    Yeats Through Beckett Coloured Glasses', *Threshold* 19 (Autumn
    1965), 41–7; Katherine J. Worth, 'Yeats and the French Drama',

Modern Drama 8, no. 4 (February 1966), 382–91; Andrew Parkin, 'Similarities in the Plays of Yeats and Beckett', *Ariel* 1, no. 3 (July 1970), 49–58.

19. For a fuller discussion of this aspect see H. Popkin, 'Yeats as Dramatist', *Tulane Drama Review* 3, no. 3 (March 1959), 73–82.

20. There had also been, of course, the Oedipus 'translations', excellent and powerful in themselves, but not strictly relevant to the discussion of the dramatic imagination of Yeats.

21. See Robinson's essay on Yeats in Stephen Gwynne (ed.) *Scattering Branches* (London: Macmillan & Co., 1940), 112–13. Some of Robinson's annotation, presumably part of his preparation for the play's Abbey Production in 1930, may be seen in MS. 8768 (4) in the National Library, Dublin.

22. See his *Yeats the Playwright* (London: Routledge and Kegan Paul, 1963), 97–103.

23. See Shelley, 'Hellas', the concluding chorus.

24. Quoted in Jeffares, *W. B. Yeats, Man and Poet*, 268.

25. See Sigmund Freud, *The Interpretation of Dreams*, tr. and ed. James Strachey (London: Allen and Unwin, 1954), 357.

26. It embodies rather than tries to know or explain the truth of the myths it relies upon. Just before he died Yeats wrote to Lady Elizabeth Pelham: 'When I try to put all into a phrase I say, "Man can embody truth but he cannot know it." I must embody it in the completion of my life. The abstract is not life and everywhere draws out its contradictions. You can refute Hegel but not the Saint or the Song of Sixpence' (*L*, 922).

27. Cf. F. A. C. Wilson, *W. B. Yeats and Tradition* (1958; reprint London: Gollancz, 1961), 91. Whether they descend from the inner room to stand framed by the stage curtains as they are closed, or are brought on in some other way, or do not appear at all is left to the discretion of the director. Yeats evidently forgot to clarify the matter, and it remains something of a puzzle which can be treated in different ways in production.

28. 'Sailing to Byzantium', from which I quote, seems highly relevant as an insight complementary to that of the song here; in that poem the emblematic sages are invoked like muses to descend from holy fire and transfigure the poet and his experience into art.

29. For excellent discussion of the political and historical implication of *Purgatory* see Donald Torchiana, *W. B. Yeats and Georgian Ireland* (Evanston: Northwestern University Press, 1966).

30. See Ure, *Yeats the Playwright*, 109–11.

31. See his letter to Lady Dorothy Wellesley, 15 August 1938, in *DWL*, p. 184.

32. From a letter to Edith Shackleton Heald on 1 January 1939, in *L*, p. 922.
33. Cf. Yeats's letter to Bullen in *L*, p. 579. Significantly, Dame Ninette de Valois, who worked with Yeats in Dublin, had gained experience in the Diaghilev Company. See also Frank Kermode's very interesting essay 'Poet and Dancer Before Diaghilev' for a helpful discussion of the mystique of the dancer among poets of the Nineties and her contribution to their aesthetics in *Puzzles and Epiphanies* (London: Routledge and Kegan Paul, 1963), 1–28.
34. This doubling is also, of course, a suitable economy, for one actor will suffice for the two parts, and that of the Servant, for at his entry MS. 8772 (1) has 'Producer enters as attendant in grey now. The MS. referred to is in the National Library of Ireland. Another possibility is for the Old Man to double with the Blind Man.
35. See R. Ellmann, *The Identity of Yeats* (1954; reprint London: Faber, 1964), 313–14. Ellmann quotes the speech from an unpublished MS. Ann Saddlemyer's already cited thesis has a full discussion of the significance of this figure.

Chapter Seven
(pp. 171–182)
1. See T. R. Henn, *The Lonely Tower*, 255.
2. It is delicately linked to that manifesto of a poetry of Eire and the ancient ways, 'To the Rose upon the Rood of Time', by the image of the bouquet of the muscatel and the perfume of the rose. The poet in the earlier poem needed a distance between himself and the rose, just as no living palate can 'drink from the whole wine' (*V. Poems*, 474). The rose may be seen as Muse of the esoteric imagination which yet does not desert common human experience.
3. Full discussion of connections between Yeats and Keats may be found in James Land Jones, *Adam's Dream: Mythic Consciousness in Keats and Yeats* (Athens: University of Georgia Press, 1975).
4. I.e., that part of the phases of the moon (phase one, in fact).
5. Sight is here used as one example of the way each of the five senses can produce sensations in the imagination.

Select Bibliography

1. WORKS BY YEATS

Allt, P. and Alspach, R. K., eds., *The Variorum Edition of the Poems of W. B. Yeats*, London: Macmillan & Co. 1957; New York: Macmillan Co. 1957.

Alspach, R. K., ed., *The Variorum Edition of the Plays of W. B. Yeats*, London: Macmillan & Co. 1966; New York: Macmillan Co. 1966.

Bax, C., ed., *Florence Farr, Bernard Shaw, W. B. Yeats, Letters*, Dublin: Cuala Press 1941; London: Home & Van Thal 1946; New York: Dodd, Mead 1942.

Bridge, U., ed., *W. B. Yeats and T. Sturge Moore: Their Correspondence*, London: Routledge & Kegan Paul 1953; New York: Oxford University Press 1953.

Donoghue, Denis, transcriber and ed., *Memoirs of W. B. Yeats*, London: Macmillan & Co. 1972; New York: Macmillan Co. 1973.

Eglinton, John; Yeats, W. B.; Larminie, W. and A. E., *Literary Ideals in Ireland*, London: Fisher Unwin 1899.

Ellis, John Edwin and Yeats, W. B., *The Works of William Blake, Poetic, Symbolic, and Critical*, 2 vols., London: Quaritch 1893.

Frayne, John P., ed., *Uncollected Prose of W. B. Yeats* I, London: Macmillan & Co. 1970; New York: Columbia University Press 1970.

Frayne, John P. and Johnson, Colton, eds., *Uncollected Prose of W. B. Yeats* II, London: Macmillan & Co. 1975.

McHugh, Roger, ed., *Ah, Sweet Dancer* (a correspondence between W. B. Yeats and Margot Ruddock), London: Macmillan & Co. 1970; New York: Macmillan Co. 1970.

O'Donnell, William H., ed., *Literatim Transcription of the Manuscripts of William Butler Yeats's 'The Speckled Bird'*, New York: Delmar Scholars' Facsimiles & Reprints, 1976.

O'Donnell, William H., ed., *The Speckled Bird*, Dublin: Cuala Press 1974.

O'Donnell, William H., ed., *The Speckled Bird with Variant Versions*, Toronto: McCelland & Stewart 1976.

Pearce, D. R., ed., *The Senate Speeches of W. B. Yeats*, London: Faber & Faber 1961; Bloomington: Indiana University Press 1960.

Pound, E. and Fenollosa, E., *The Classic Noh Theatre of Japan*, Introduction by W. B. Yeats, New York: New Directions Paperback 1959; 1st ed. Knopf 1917.

Reynolds, Horace, ed., *Letters to the New Island*, Cambridge: Harvard University Press 1934.

Wade, Allan, ed., *The Letters of W. B. Yeats*, London: Rupert Hart-Davis 1954; New York: Macmillan Co. 1955.

Wellesley, Dorothy, *Letters on Poetry from W. B. Yeats to Dorothy Wellesley*, London: Oxford University Press 1940; New York: Oxford University Press 1940.

Yeats, J. B., *Letters to his Son W. B. Yeats and Others, 1869–1922*, ed. Joseph Hone, London: Faber & Faber 1944; New York: Dutton & Co. 1946.

Yeats, William Butler, *Autobiographies*, London: Macmillan & Co. 1956/*Autobiography*, New York: Macmillan Co. 1953.

Yeats, William Butler, *Collected Plays*, London: Macmillan & Co. 1953; New York: Macmillan Co. 1953.

Yeats, William Butler, *Collected Poems*, London: Macmillan & Co. 1952; New York: Macmillan Co. 1956.

Yeats, William Butler, *Essays and Introductions*, London: Macmillan & Co. 1961; New York: Macmillan Co. 1961.

Yeats, William Butler, *Explorations*, London: Macmillan & Co. 1962; New York: Macmillan Co. 1962.

Yeats, William Butler, *Four Plays for Dancers*, London: Macmillan & Co. 1921; New York: Macmillan Co. 1921.

Yeats, William Butler, *Mythologies*, London: Macmillan & Co. 1959; New York: Macmillan Co. 1959.

Yeats, William Butler, *Plays and Controversies*, London: Macmillan & Co. 1923; New York: Macmillan Co. 1924.

Yeats, William Butler, *Plays for an Irish Theatre*, London: Bullen 1911.

Yeats, William Butler, *Plays in Prose and Verse*, London: Macmillan & Co. 1922; New York: Macmillan Co. 1924.

Yeats, William Butler, 'The Shadowy Waters', in *North American Review* CLXX.

Yeats, William Butler, *A Vision*, revised ed., London: Macmillan & Co. 1962; New York: Macmillan Co. 1961.

Yeats, William Butler, *Wheels and Butterflies*, London: Macmillan & Co. 1934.

Yeats, William Butler, [Ganconagh], *'John Sherman' and 'Dhoya'*, London: Fisher Unwin, 1891; New York: Cassell 1891. Edited by J. Finnernan, Detroit: Wayne State University Press 1969.

Yeats, William Butler, ed., *The Oxford Book of Modern Verse, 1892–1935*, London: Oxford University Press 1966.

Yeats, William Butler with Moore, G., 'Diarmuid and Grania', in W. Becker, ed., *Dublin Magazine* XXVI, no. 2 (April–June 1951); Chicago: De Paul University Press 1974.

2. SECONDARY SOURCES

Albright, Daniel, *The Myth Against Myth: A Study of Yeats's Imagination in Old Age*, London: Oxford University Press 1972; New York: Oxford University Press 1972.

Arieti, Silvano, *Creativity: The Magic Synthesis*, New York: Basic Books 1976.

Bablet, D., *Edward Gordon Craig*, London: Heinemann 1966; France 1962; New York: Theatre Arts Books 1966.

Bloom, Harold, *Yeats*, London: Oxford University Press 1970; New York: Oxford University Press 1970.

Boyd, E. A., *Ireland's Literary Renaissance*, Dublin and London: Maunsel 1916; New York: John Lane 1916.

Boyd, E. A., *The Contemporary Drama of Ireland*, London: T. Fisher Unwin 1918; Boston: Little, Brown & Co. 1917.

Bradford, Curtis, *Yeats's 'Last Poems' Again*, Yeats Centenary Papers No. VIII, Dublin: Dolmen Press 1966.

Bradford, Curtis, *Yeats at Work*, Carbondale: Southern Illinois University Press 1965.

Bushrui, S. B., *Yeats Verse Plays: The Revisions 1900–1910*, Oxford: Clarendon Press 1965; New York: Clarendon Press 1965.

Clark, D. R., *W. B. Yeats and the Theatre of Desolate Reality*, Dublin: Dolmen Press 1965; Chester Springs, Pa.: Dufour Editions 1965.

Collingwood, R. G., *The Principles of Art*, Oxford: Clarendon Press 1938.

Craig, Edward, *Gordon Craig*, London: Gollancz 1968; New York: Knopf 1968.

Craig, Edward Gordon, *On the Art of the Theatre*, London: Heinemann 1911; Chicago: Browne's Bookstore 1911.

Desai, Rupin W., *Yeats's Shakespeare*, Evanston: Northwestern University Press 1971.

Donoghue, D., *The Third Voice: Modern British and American Verse Drama*, Princeton: Princeton University Press 1959.

Donoghue, D., *Yeats*, London: Fontana (Modern Masters Series) 1971; New York: Viking 1971.

Donoghue, D., ed., *The Integrity of Yeats*, Cork: Mercier Press 1964; Folcroft, Pa.: Folcroft Library 1971.

Donoghue, D. and Mulryne, J. R., eds., *An Honoured Guest: new essays on W. B. Yeats*, London: Arnold 1965; New York: St Martin's Press 1966.

Ellis-Fermor, U., *The Irish Dramatic Movement*, London: Methuen 1964.

Ellmann, R., *Yeats, the Man and the Masks*, London: Faber & Faber 1961; 1st ed. London: Macmillan & Co. 1949; New York: Macmillan Co. 1948.

Ellmann, R., *The Identity of Yeats*, London: Faber & Faber 1964, 1st ed. London: Macmillan & Co. 1954; New York: Oxford University Press 1954.

Ellmann, R., *Yeats and Joyce*, Yeats Centenary Papers No. XI. Dublin: Dolmen Press 1967.

Engelberg, E., *The Vast Design: Patterns in W. B. Yeats's Aesthetic*, Toronto: University of Toronto Press 1964.

Finneran, Richard J., ed., *Anglo-Irish Literature. A Review of Research*, New York: M.L.A. 1976.

Flannery, James W., *W. B. Yeats and the Idea of a Theatre: The Early Abbey Theatre in Theory and Practice*, Toronto: Macmillan of Canada 1976.

Genet, Jacqueline, *William Butler Yeats: Les fondements et l'évolution de la création poétique*, Villeneuve-d'Ascq: Publications de l'Université de Lille 1976.

Gibbon, M., *The Masterpiece and the Man: Yeats as I knew him*, London: Hart-Davis 1959; New York: Macmillan Co. 1959.

Gregory, Lady A., *Cuchulain of Muirthemne*, London: Murray 1902.

Gregory, Lady A., *Gods and Fighting Men*, London: Murray 1904; Toronto: Macmillan of Canada 1976.

Gregory, Lady A., *Journals 1916–1930*, ed. Lennox Robinson, London: Putnam 1946; New York: Macmillan Co. 1947.

Gregory, Lady A., *Our Irish Theatre—A Chapter of Autobiography*, London and New York: Putnam 1913.

Gregory, Lady A., *Seventy Years, 1852–1922*, ed. Colin Smythe, Gerrard's Cross: Colin Smythe 1973.

Gwynn, S., ed., *Scattering Branches. Tributes to the Memory of W. B. Yeats*, London: Macmillan & Co. 1940; New York: Macmillan Co. 1940.

Gwynn, S., *Irish Literature and Drama*, London and New York: Nelson 1936.

Hall, J. and Steinmann, M., eds., *The Permanence of Yeats*, New York: Collier Books, 1961; 1st ed. New York: Macmillan Co. 1950.

Harper, George Mills, *The Mingling of Heaven and Earth: Yeats's Theory of Theatre*, Dublin: Dolmen Press 1975; Atlantic Highlands, N.J.: distrib. Humanities Press 1975.

Harper, George Mills, *Yeats's Golden Dawn*, London: Macmillan & Co. 1974; New York: Barnes and Noble 1974.

Harper, George Mills, ed., *Yeats and the Occult*, Toronto: Macmillan of Canada (Yeats Studies Series) 1975.

Henn, T. R., *The Lonely Tower*, London: Methuen 1965; New York: Barnes and Noble 1965.

Hogan, R. and O'Neill, M. J., eds., *Joseph Holloway's Abbey Theatre: A Selection from his unpublished Journal 'Impressions of a Dublin Playgoer'*, Carbondale: Southern Illinois University Press 1967.

Hone, J. M., *W. B. Yeats 1865–1939*, London: Macmillan & Co. 1965; New York: St Martin's Press 1962.

Hough, G., *The Last Romantics*, London: Methuen 1961; New York: Barnes and Noble 1961.

Howarth, Herbert, *The Irish Writers (1880–1940)*, London: Rockliff 1958; New York: Hill and Ware 1959.

Ishibashi, Hiro, 'W. B. Yeats and the Noh', M.A. Thesis, Keio University 1956; revised and published as *Yeats and the Noh: Types of Japanese Beauty and their reflection in Yeats's plays*, ed. Anthony Kerrigan, Yeats Centenary Papers No. VI., Dublin: Dolmen Press 1965.

Jacquot, J., ed., *Les Théâtres d'Asie*, Paris: Editions du centre National de la Recherche Scientifique 1961.

Jeffares, A. N., *A Commentary on the Collected Poems of W. B. Yeats*, London: Macmillan & Co. 1968; Stanford: Stanford University Press 1968.

Jeffares, A. N., *W. B. Yeats, Man and Poet*, London: Routledge & Kegan Paul 1949, 1962; New Haven: Yale University Press 1949; New York: Barnes and Noble 1966.

Jeffares, A. N. and Cross, K., eds., *In Excited Reverie*, London: Macmillan & Co. 1965; New York: St Martin's Press 1965.

Jeffares, A. N. and Knowland, A. S., *A Commentary on the Collected Plays of W. B. Yeats*, Stanford: Stanford University Press 1975.

Kermode, F., *The Romantic Image*, London: Routledge & Kegan Paul 1957, 1966; New York: Macmillan 1957.

Kermode, F., *Puzzles and Epiphanies*, London: Routledge & Kegan Paul 1962; New York: Chilmark Press 1962.

Macneice, L., *The Poetry of W. B. Yeats*, London: Faber & Faber 1967; 1st ed. London and New York: Oxford University Press 1941.

Malins, E., *A Preface to Yeats*, London: Longman 1974.

Maxwell, D. E. S. and Bushrui, S., eds., *Centenary Essays*, Ibadan: Ibadan University Press 1965.

Melchiori, G., *The Whole Mystery of Art*, London: Routledge & Kegan Paul 1960; New York: Macmillan Co. 1961.

Miller, Liam, *The Noble Drama of W. B. Yeats*, Dublin: Dolmen Press 1977.

Miner, Earl, *The Japanese Tradition in British and American Literature*, Princeton: Princeton University Press 1958.

Moore, J. Rees, *Masks of Love and Death: Yeats as Dramatist*, Ithaca: Cornell University Press 1971.

Moore, Virginia, *The Unicorn: William Butler Yeats' Search for Reality*, New York: Macmillan Co. 1954.

Nathan, L., *Figures in a Dance: The Tragic Drama of W. B. Yeats*, New York: Columbia University Press 1965.

O'Connor, F., *The Backward Look, A Survey of Irish Literature*, London: Macmillan & Co. 1967; title of American ed. *A Short History of Irish Literature*, New York: Putnams 1967.

O'Driscoll, R. and Reynolds, Lorna, *Yeats and the Theatre*, Toronto: Macmillan of Canada, 1975.

O'Grady, Standish J., *History of Ireland*, 2 vols., Dublin: E. Ponsonby 1878–80.

Oshima, Shotaro, *W. B. Yeats and Japan*, Tokyo: Hokuseido Press 1965.

Parkinson, T., *W. B. Yeats, Self-Critic*, Berkeley and Los Angeles: University of California Press 1951.

Parkinson, T., *W. B. Yeats: the Later Poetry*, Berkeley and Los Angeles: University of California Press 1964.

Peacock, R., *The Poet in the Theatre*, London: Routledge & Kegan Paul 1946; New York: Harcourt Brace 1946.

Price, A., *Synge and Anglo-Irish Drama*, London: Methuen 1961.

Raine, Kathleen, *Yeats, the Tarot and the Golden Dawn*, Dublin: Dolmen Press 1972.

Rajan, B., *W. B. Yeats: a critical introduction*, London: Hutchinson 1965.

Ronsley, J., *Yeats's 'Autobiography': Life as Symbolic Pattern*, London: Oxford University Press 1968; Cambridge, Mass.: Harvard University Press 1968.

Sieffert, R., *Zeami: La Tradition Secrète du Nô—Traduction et Commentaires*, Paris: Gallimard 1960.

Skelton, R. and Clark, D. R., eds., *Irish Renaissance*, Dublin: Dolmen Press 1965.

Skelton, R. and Saddlemyer, A., eds., *The World of W. B. Yeats: Essays in Perspective*, Dublin: Dolmen Press 1965; Seattle: University of Washington Press 1965.

Skene, R., *The Cuchulain Plays of W. B. Yeats: A Study*, London: Macmillan & Co. 1974; New York: Columbia University Press 1974.

Stallworthy, Jon, *Between the Lines: Yeats's Poetry in the Making*, Oxford: Clarendon Press 1963.

Stallworthy, Jon, *Vision and Revision in Yeats's Last Poems*, Oxford: Clarendon Press 1969.

Stallworthy, Jon, ed., *Yeats: Last Poems*, London: Macmillan & Co. 1968; Nashville: Aurora Publishers 1970.

Stock, A. G., *W. B. Yeats, his Poetry and Thought*, Cambridge: Cambridge University Press 1964.

Taylor, R., *The Drama of W. B. Yeats: Irish Myth and the Japanese No*, New Haven: Yale University Press 1976.

Torchiana, D. T., *W. B. Yeats and Georgian Ireland*, Evanston: Northwestern University Press 1966.

Tuohy, Frank, *Yeats*, London: Macmillan & Co. 1976; New York: Macmillan Co. 1976.

Unterecker, J., *A Reader's Guide to W. B. Yeats*, London: Thames & Hudson 1959; New York: Noonday Press 1959.

Ure, P., *Yeats the Playwright*, London: Routledge & Kegan Paul 1963; New York: Barnes and Noble 1963.

Ure, P., *Yeats*, Edinburgh and London: Oliver & Boyd 1963; New York: Barnes and Noble 1965.

Ussher, A., *Three Great Irishmen: Shaw, Yeats, Joyce*, New York: Devin-Adair 1953; Mentor 1957.

Vendler, H. H., *Yeats's 'Vision' and the Later Plays*, Cambridge: Harvard University Press 1963.

Warnock, Mary, *Imagination*, London: Faber & Faber 1976; Berkeley: University of California Press 1976.

Whitaker, T. R., *Swan and Shadow: Yeats's Dialogue with History*, Chapel Hill: University of North Carolina Press 1964.

Wilson, E., *Axel's Castle*, London and New York: Scribner's 1931.

Wilson, F. A. C., *W. B. Yeats and Tradition*, London: Gollancz 1958, reprint 1961; New York: Macmillan Co. 1958.

Wilson, F. A. C., *Yeats's Iconography*, London: Gollancz 1960; New York: Macmillan Co. 1960.

Zwerdling, Alex, *Yeats and the Heroic Ideal*, London: Peter Owen 1966; New York: New York University Press 1965.

3. BIBLIOGRAPHIES

Cross, K. G. W. and Dunlop, R. T., *A Bibliography of Yeats Criticism, 1887–1965*, London: Macmillan & Co. 1971; New York: Macmillan Co. 1971.

Jochum, K. P. S., *W. B. Yeats: A Classified Bibliography of Criticism*, Chicago: University of Illinois Press 1977.

Kersnowski, Frank L.; Spinks, C. W., and Loomis, Laird, *A Biblio-*

graphy of Modern Irish and Anglo-Irish Literature, San Antonio: Trinity University Press 1976.

Mikhail, E. H., *A Bibliography of Modern Irish Drama, 1899–1970,* Introduction by William A. Armstrong, London: Macmillan & Co. 1972; Seattle: University of Washington Press 1972.

Stoll, John E., *The Great Deluge: A Yeats Bibliography,* Troy, N.Y.: Whitson 1971.

Wade, Allan, *A Bibliography of the Writing of W. B. Yeats,* London: Hart-Davis, 1951; revised ed. 1958; 3rd ed. 1968.

Index

Abbey Theatre, 40-1, 51, 58
aestheticism, 26
Aherne, Owen, 44, 45-7, 114, 172, 180
Anima Mundi (Great Mind or Spirit), 8, 9, 19, 78, 90, 176, 180
anti-self, 12, 22, 28, 78, 112
Axël, 75-6, 83

Balzac, Honoré de, 11
Beckett, Samuel, 31; *Not I*, 31; *Play*, 193n; *Waiting for Godot*, 160
Behmen, Jacob, 14
Bernhardt, Sarah, 30
Bhagwan Shri Hamsa 12; 'Story of a Pilgrimage to Lake Manas and of initiation on Mount Kailas in Tibet', 12
Bishop (*see also* Crazy Jane), 5, 44
Blake, William, 6, 11, 12, 18, 27, 64; 'Jerusalem', 185n; 'Mental Traveller',152; 'Tyger', 125, 154
Blind Man, 5, 64, 96-104 passim, 136, 163-4, 190n, 195n
Browning, Robert, 35
Burke, Edmund, 3
Byzantium, 47-8

Campbell, Mrs Patrick, 108, 112
Canaletto, Antonio, 27
character, theory of, 28
Chatterji, Mohini, 13
Chaucer, Geoffrey, 29
Christ's Ministry (Chester Cycle), 134-5
Coleridge, S.T., 3, 13, 14, 18, 179; 'Ancient Mariner', 75; *Biographia Literaria*, 14
Commedia dell' Arte, 35
Conchubar, 5, 96-112 passim
Corneille, Pierre, 36
Craig, Gordon, 68, 74, 97, 191n

Crazy Jane, 5, 44, 45
Criterion, 12
Cuchulain, 5, 27, 42-3, 55, 58, 63-6, 96-104 passim, 120-6 passim, 128, 130, 158, 163-5

Dante Alighieri, 26, 62; *Convito*, 26
Davidson, John, 34
Diaghilev Ballet, 166, 195n
Donne, John, 27, 34, 44
Dowson, Ernest, 34, 113
dreaming-back, 4, 47, 129-36 passim, 140-1, 158-9, 161, 183n, 193n
Dulac, Edmund, 36

Eithne Inguba, 42, 63, 123-6, 130, 163
Eliot, T.S., 9, 10, 26, 27, 52, 53, 184n; dissociation of sensibility, 26; objective correlative, 9, 10, 26; 'Tradition and the Individual Talent', 10
Emer, 30, 42, 64, 66, 123-6, 130, 164, 167, 168

Farr, Florence (Mrs Emery), 36, 56, 78, 176
Fay, Frank, 20, 30, 85
Fay, William, 20, 85
Ferguson, Sir Samuel, 26
Fili, 38, 93, 167, 190n
folk-lore, 2, 5-7, 14, 16, 18-20, 100, 105
Frencken, Frans (the younger), 27
Freud, Sigmund, 7

Goethe, Johann Wolfgang von, 26
Golden Dawn, Order of, 13, 75, 183n
Gonne, Maude, 16, 30, 71-2, 75, 94, 98, 101, 171-2, 183n, 192n
Gregory, Lady Augusta, 22, 51-2, 61, 73, 90, 117, 145, 163, 167;